**Mannerling:
An Honorable Betrayal
By
W.W. Anderton**

An Honorable Betrayal

ISBN 978-0-6151-6101-3

©2007
All rights reserved

Published by Hiram Publishing

TABLE OF RANKS

United States	German Army/Navy/SS	British
General of the Army Fleet Admiral	Generalfeldmarschall Grossadmiral Reichsfuhrer	Field Marshal Admiral of the Fleet Marshal of the Air Force
General Admiral	Generaloberst Generaladmiral Oberstgruppenfuhrer	General Admiral Chief Air Marshal
Lieutenant General Vice Admiral	General Obergruppenfuhrer Admiral	Lieutenant General Vice Admiral Air Marshal
Major General Rear Admiral	Generalleutnant Vizeadmiral Gruppenfuhrer	Major General Rear Admiral Air Vice Marshal
Brigadier General Commodore	Generalmajor Konteradmiral Brigadefuhrer/Oberfuhrer	Brigadier Commodore Air Commodore
Colonel Captain	Oberst Kapitan zur See Standartenfuhrer	Colonel Captain Group Captain
Lieutenant Colonel Commander	Oberstleutnant Fregattenkapitan Obersturmbannfuhrer	Lieutenant Colonel Commander Wing Commander
Major Lieutenant Commander	Major Korvettankapitan Sturmbannfuhrer	Major Lieutenant Commander Squadron Leader
Captain Lieutenant	Hauptmann Kapitanleutnant Hauptsturmfuhrer	Captain Lieutenant Flight Lieutenant
First Lieutenant Lieutenant J. G.	Oberleutnant Oberleutnant zur See Obersturmfuhrer	First Lieutenant Sub-lieutenant Flying Officer
Second Lieutenant Ensign	Leutnant Leutnant zur See Untersturmfuhrer	Second Lieutenant Commission WO Pilot Officer

An Honorable Betrayal

Prologue
September 28, 1946

Ottawa, Canada
National Defense Ministry

Brigadier Mannerling lit a cigarette and slowly rubbed his eyes trying to get the words on the paper to refocus. After almost six months in this position, he realized the true aftermath of war for a soldier was boredom, mind numbing boredom. The Brigadier had spent the last weeks of the war in Europe struggling to survive in the crumbling Nazi empire. He then spent the next six months in hospital in northern Scotland recovering from wounds received during that time.

During his stay in hospital, his world changed. Prime Minister Churchill thanked for winning the war against Germany was voted out of office being replaced by the Labour party. The next change in his world was more personal. Lord Hallesy, on his only visit to the hospital, informed him that the Labour government would abolish the Special Operations Executive as quickly as possible and cut the budgets of MI5 and MI6. The left leaning Labour Party had been uneasy about the intelligence community during and would most likely treat it as pariah in the post-war world.

Lord Hallesy explained that his department would be transferred back to MI6, but at a size smaller than pre-war. This meant the powers-that-be in MI6 would hardly welcome back their bastard rivals with open arms. MI6 and the SOE had been at loggerheads for most of the war because of the sharp differences in operational policy. Hallesy and Admiral Lord Crosland would be tolerated because of their long association with them. The Brigadier and the others would not be welcomed back.

It was then that Mannerling learned that Lord Hallesy and the Admiral had pulled strings and he would be transferred back to the Canadian Army at his present rank. However pleasant that was it was tempered by the fact that the position Ottawa was offering was contingent on the Brigadier returning home. Lord Hallesy made very clear that going back home was the Brigadier's only real option if he wanted the opportunity of returning. Brigadier Mannerling could retire on half-pay and wither on the vine.

"Sir Edward." The familiar voice said. "Are you busy?"

"No, Nyby." The Brigadier said lighting a cigarette. "What is it?"

"There is a man outside from London sir." Nyby said.

"Did he give you a name Lieutenant?" The Brigadier asked.

"He said his name was Tremayne." Nyby said. "He does not have an appointment."

"Let him in Nyby." The Brigadier said bluntly. "I do not want to be disturbed by anyone Lieutenant."

"You have an appointment with the War Memorial sub-committee at 2:00 PM sir." Nyby said nervously.

"Cancel it." The Brigadier said. "Have the tea-lady bring in a pot." Mannerling moved to the windows and looked down at Parliament Hill to await his visitor.

"This is not a social call Colonel." The Brigadier said picking up his teacup after offering Colonel Tremayne a seat.

"No." Tremayne said formally. "They have found him Brigadier Mannerling."

"Who have they found?" Mannerling asked sharply.

"They have found Major Colquhoun." Tremayne answered dryly lighting his pipe.

"Are they certain this time?" Mannerling asked harshly.

"This has been confirmed." The Colonel said. "The Americans took fingerprints."

"Where have they found him?" Mannerling asked.

"He was found in the American hospital, which was once the former German military hospital, in the village of Jaegerfeld sir." Tremayne said.

"The hospital was searched when the war ended Colonel." Mannerling snapped.

"I know that sir." Tremayne said. "At the time there were over 1,000 casualties at the hospital when that search was made."

"How did they find him?" Mannerling asked. "I've written over 100 letters about him."

Tremayne relit his pipe and took a long puff on his pipe. "*Albatross* told us."

"So that bastard is still alive." Mannerling said. "He made it out of Germany?"

"No, he is in the Soviet Zone of Occupation." Tremayne said. "They are holding him as a war criminal."

"London is doing what?" Mannerling asked.

"London, as usual, is doing nothing." Tremayne said dully. "London Control doesn't want his real identity revealed to the NKVD."

"How the hell did he tell you then?" Mannerling asked.

"He slipped a note to a Canadian war crimes investigator who was with a group questioning him." Tremayne said.

"That is odd behavior for the Russians." Mannerling said.

"General Mikhailov arranged the interview." Tremayne said. "We told the Russians that we want *Albatross* for the murder of twelve POWs during the Battle of the Bulge."

"Who else has been told?" Mannerling asked lighting a cigarette in an agitated manner seeing that nothing had changed.

"I really don't know sir." Tremayne said.

"What condition is he in?" Mannerling asked.

"They haven't said sir." Tremayne said. "I have RAF transport waiting Edward."

"I have duties here." Mannerling hissed.

"Lord Hallesy has cleared your absence with the Ministry." Tremayne said.

"This will take more than a few days." Mannerling said.

"You will be on indefinite leave." Tremayne said. "I have car waiting."

[2]

Washington D.C.
OSS Headquarters

Brigadier General Henry C. Crawford sat in his nearly vacant office drinking a cup of coffee staring at the calendar.

"Is this the wake?" Colonel Nollan asked.

"Yes." Crawford said turning in his chair. "Pull up a seat."

"Are you going back to the NYPD?" Nollan asked sitting down taking the coffee pot and pouring himself a cup.

"Looks like it." Crawford said. "This is a mistake."

"I agree Henry it is most likely a mistake." Nollan said grimly. "There is too much pressure to get back to normal."

"J. Edgar must be dancing a jig." Crawford said. "I doubt the boys at the Pentagon are shedding any tears Bill."

"You can bet the farm on that Henry." Nollan said.

"What brings the Adjutant General's office here?" Crawford asked. "You office commandos are not night owls."

"Major Colquhoun has been found." Nollan said in a low voice.

"I'll be damned." Crawford hissed his face turning dark. "Where in hell did they find him?"

"Germany." Nollan answered. "A place called Jaegerfeld."

"Is he alive or dead?" Crawford asked.

"Alive." Nollan said. "Apparently he has been there since the Adlerberghof mission."

"How the hell did we miss him?" Crawford snorted. "That place was searched."

"You know what Germany was like after the war Henry." Nollan said. "People frightened that the Russians would swallow the whole damn country; one goddamn big mess."

"This was an accident?" Crawford asked.

"Some German General being held in the Soviet Zone palmed a note to a Canauck officer interviewing him." Nollan said.

"He is very good to do that in the Soviet Zone?" Crawford quipped.

"Mikhailov arranged the meeting with the war crime boys." Nollan said. "You worked with him during the war."

"He was the GRU liaison officer with Austen-Halton's group for three years." Crawford said. "This kraut general has a name?"

"They called him von Tanz." Nollan answered.

"Why tell me Bill?" Crawford asked.

Nollan stood up and went to the window. "Call it unfinished business Henry. Colquhoun was your man."

"You're opening a goddamn can of worms." Crawford said. "Pick him up and bring him in quietly."

"We need to talk to him first." Nollan said. "The brass thinks you are the one to do it."

"The hell I am." Crawford said bluntly. "Get his room mate Taggert."

"Taggert was killed on Okinawa." Nollan said frankly. "Sorry Henry, that leaves you."

Crawford lit his cigar. "Does the Senator know this?"

"We can't keep it away from him forever." Nollan said.

"Why destroy his illusion?" Crawford said. "A dead hero is a better icon."

"The Senator has always held out hope that his son was alive." Nollan said. "It's his brother we have to worry about. The old man is in the twilight of his life, but Brother John is a raising politician."

"Who else knows?" Crawford asked.

"Air Marshal Lord Hallesy as far as we know" Nollan said.

"That means Mannerling knows." Crawford said grimly.

"Completes the circle I'm afraid." Nollan said.

"Do I have a choice?" Crawford asked sourly

"By the end of the month you'll be out of a job." Nollan said. "Your travel orders are being cut as we speak. You'll have a reunion of sorts in Twickem-Hallesy."

"Reunions are for friends Nollan." Crawford said bluntly. "Has the senator been told?"

"I doubt it." Nollan said. "The brother knows, but the senator is too ill to be told. They will wait until the major gets home before they do that."

"I think I'll retire to that farm in upper State New York or that shanty in Gloucester Massachusetts." Crawford said. "I'm getting too old for this crap."

[3]

Twickem-Hallesy
Austen-Halton Manor

"When are they coming Peter?" Viscount Crosland asked pouring a drink.

"Tomorrow at the earliest Nyland." Austen-Halton, now Lord Hallesy, replied adjusting his crippled arm and lighting his trademark cigar. "Officially we'll be visiting the British Army of the Rhine."

"There is no need for you to be involved Peter." Crosland said. "This was an American operation after all."

"We used them Nyland." Austen-Halton said.

"They allowed themselves to be used." Crosland said firmly. "It was just fortunate that our motives interwove with each other. The mission was to protect *Albatross* at all costs."

"Yes." Austen-Halton said.

"It was the Americans who were wrong about him all along." Crosland said pausing to light his pipe. "How did you learn about him?"

"Colonel Gerhardt." Austen-Halton answered. "Hard man to kill it seems."

"Sudden, isn't it?" Crosland hissed.

"It's an SOS from *Albatross*." Austen-Halton said wryly. "We finally found him too."

"Good news all over the place." Crosland said blandly. "How thrilling this is going to be."

"The Russians are liable to shoot *Albatross* on general principles." Austen-Halton said. "We better formulate a plan to get him out of the Soviet Zone before they do."

"That will have to wait until you return from Germany." Crosland said.

[4]
September 30, 1946

Occupied Germany
Jaegerfeld, American Zone

The olive drab Ford staff automobile sped quickly down road heading for the former German military hospital outside the town of Jaegerfeld. The escort motorcycles had their sirens blaring clearing the road of traffic. The German civilians hardly paid any attention to the Americans, simply because they were always rushing somewhere. The American military on the road stopped and saluted because of the stars on the bumper pennant.

Inside the staff car were three Allied officers. Sitting in the back were Air Marshal Viscount Hallesy (Peter Austen-Halton) KCB, OBE, DSO, DFC and Brigadier General Henry C. Crawford. Sitting in front was Brigadier Sir Edward T. Mannerling, KCB, DSO, and MC. They sat in stony silence ignoring the scenery and each other despite the fact that they had worked closely together during the war. This journey to Jaegerfeld was going to be a sobering experience for each man for different reasons and they did not need small talk to gloss over their feelings.

Waiting for them at the bottom of the front entrance stone steps was the Chief Administrator of the hospital, Colonel Robbins of the Medical Corps. General Headquarters had informed the colonel that his visitors were coming, but not why. The brass usually visited the medical facilities at Stuttgart (a near by golf course was the incentive) rather than Jaegerfeld.

Robbins escorted them to his office after they showed little or no interest in making the pro forma inspection of the hospital. They quietly settled into office.

"Headquarters didn't go into detail gentlemen on why you are here." Robbins said as he sat down behind his desk. "This is off the beaten path, so to speak."

"I'm sorry for the lack of details Colonel." Crawford said flatly. "You still have German military personnel here correct?"

"Yes." Robbins said. "Sad cases I'm afraid."

"You have a Luftwaffe officer here?" Mannerling asked.

"Several." Robbins said. "Which one in particular Brigadier?"

"Hauptmann Rudolf Bekker." Mannerling said. "Train wreck in December of 1942."

"Yes." Robbins said surprised that the Brigadier would know about Bekker. "He is an extremely sad case, gentlemen."

"Is he well?" Lord Hallesy asked lightly a long black cigar with his good arm.

"Medically he has recovered from his wounds quite some time ago." Robbins said in a flat voice. "He should have been discharged months ago, but the German medical records indicate that the German medical personnel kept him here because he never recovered psychologically." Robbins paused. "My staff has come to the same conclusion." Robbins looked at each man before he spoke. "Why such an interest in a severely injured German pilot with mental problems gentlemen, is he perhaps a wanted war criminal?"

"We have many reasons Colonel." Crawford said.

"He is unfit to stand the trial." Robbins said. "Is that the reason you are here?"

"That is hardly our intention Colonel." Mannerling said in a soft voice. "The fact is that Bekker is not a German officer."

"His records say German." Robbins said in a puzzled voice. "He speaks German, when he does speak. The records show that he has been here since December 1942."

"What do the German records say about him?" Lord Hallesy asked.

"They had orders from a General named von Tanz to keep him here." Robbins said. "My German predecessors were afraid of this von Tanz."

"They had reason to be." Mannerling said. "Von Tanz is on the list of wanted war criminals."

"Who is Bekker then?" Robbins asked. "If he isn't a German officer Brigadier Mannerling, who is he?"

"An OSS officer by the name of Colquhoun, he has been listed as missing-in-action." Crawford replied.

Robbins expression was a complete blank and lighting his cigarette was by force of habit. "The war has been over here since May 1945." Robbins tone hardened. "How the hell did he get here?"

"We, in a manner of speaking, brought him here." Mannerling said coldly.

"Why in hell did it take you so long to get here?" Robbins hissed.

"That is none of your business." Crawford said bluntly.

"Pretty shitty treatment if you ask me." Robbins grunted. "Do you have ice water for blood?"

"No one has asked you." Crawford snapped.

"Damn, how could you leave him here for so long?" Robbins rasped sourly.

"We had no intention of leaving him behind." Mannerling said curtly. "Fortunes of war kept me from getting him."

"Bekker…Colquhoun had been wounded prior to the train crash that brought him here." Robbins said. "He was badly burned- reconstructive surgery was not a German Army medical skill during the war."

"May we see him?" Lord Hallesy asked somberly.

"Of course, I will get my translator." Robbins said.

"I speak German." Mannerling said.

"Dr. Cohen, my Chief of Psychiatry, should be with you." Robbins said. "Dr. Cohen needs to know the circumstances on how he got here."

"We betrayed him." Lord Hallesy said dryly with no remorse in his voice.

"I see, this explains a lot." Robbins said. "What are your intention's gentlemen?"

"Bring him home." Mannerling said. "He deserves that much."

"He'll still need treatment." Robbins said.

"He will get that." Crawford said.

"He may never recover." Robbins said grimly. "He most likely will have to be in an institution for the rest of his life."

"He'll receive the best care in the world Colonel." Crawford said. "Colquhoun will never be alone again."

"I'll have an orderly to bring you to Dr. Cohen's office immediately." Robbins said.

"Thank you, Colonel." Mannerling said.

Dr. Cohen removed his glasses and rubbed his eyes after reading the classified dossier his visitors gave him.

"You people were on our side?" Cohen hissed.

"You may skip the editorial commentary Captain." Crawford said. "Does the dossier help?"

"Colquhoun is suffering a form of battle fatigue." Cohen said. "Did he know you deliberately did this to him?"

"At the end he most likely knew." Mannerling said. "We tried to get him out, but were unable to."

"The Major was very lucky to have a guardian angel on the German side." Cohen said flatly.

"Will he respond to us Doctor?" Lord Hallesy asked.

"He might." Cohen said. "We have known him only as Bekker. I tried to have Headquarters check on his Luftwaffe record, but they found nothing. We have only spoken German to him."

"Will this cause anymore harmful damage to him Doctor?" Mannerling asked.

"With this new information we are obligated to try." Cohen said. "Colquhoun will never leave a civilian facility even if you should re-establish his true identity to himself."

"It would be good for his family to have him come back home." Mannerling said.

"He might never come home so to speak." Cohen said.

"There is always hope." Crawford said.

An Honorable Betrayal

Chapter One
November 1, 1942
13:00 hrs

Bern, Switzerland
Gasthof Europa

Hermann Karl Jung angrily glanced at his watch swearing to himself because his lunch guest, Dr. Viktor Karl Skasch, was late as always. Jung always believed that Skasch deliberately did this to annoy him. Skasch knew Jung disliked meeting him in public places in the daytime, but Skasch insisted that their meetings be in public places with people around them.

Jung preferred the nighttime at the Embassy's chalet. Hermann knew the Swiss Federal Security Police watched him and Allied agents every time they left official residences. By having the meetings at the chalet, he would be comfortable and secure. Griem, the Embassy's security chief, had the chalet checked every day and the Swiss Federal Security Police guarded it for them. Skasch should have known that Jung, being a diplomat, would bring the shadows. Skasch seemed to enjoy thumbing his nose at the shadows.

Hermann was more worried about the Swiss regular police than Allied agents were. Some in the police believed Skasch was a criminal, a master criminal. They suspected him of running a very lucrative black-market from Basel. Interpol, before the war, issued a report that he was behind the largest non-Mafia cartel in Central Europe.

The police throughout the continent always put a watch on him whenever he left Switzerland. The French Republic bluntly told him if they caught him in France again, he would be transported to French Guyana without trial. Spain, the Republic, and now Franco told him they would just shoot him out of hand if they caught him. Prosecutors in ten countries had tried for twenty years to send him to prison or the gallows, but they could never find enough evidence or live witnesses to accomplish.

Jung had met Skasch a few years before the war at a party given by the Italian Ambassador at his summer home on Lake Geneva. Jung's counterpart from the OVRA introduced them. Jung kept on meeting him at parties within the diplomatic circles in Switzerland.

Skasch's family had belonged to the petty nobility of the morbid Dual Monarchy. Skasch's father was a court physician in Vienna and Budapest before the First War. Viktor Karl Skasch was an honor graduate of Prague University and a legitimate professor of Medieval History. He had avoided military service during First War by becoming a Swiss citizen on July 30, 1914. During the war, he made a small fortune by forging citizenship documents for everyone.

At their first meeting Skasch seemed to know that Jung was a Sturmbannfuhrer in the Sicherheitsdienst not the trade envoy his papers said he was. During the course of the evening, Skasch made over 50,000 Swiss francs selling papers. Skasch offered to sell Jung classified Romanian documents. Jung berated him since he was an Austrian by birth and a citizen of the Reich since the Anschluss. Skasch told him he was always an executive first, patriot second. Jung bought the documents and sent them to his superior in Berlin, Gruppenfuhrer Krieger. He told Hermann to keep in contact with Skasch.

The ramrod straight figure of Skasch entered the restaurant of the Gasthof followed by his constant shadow, a detective from the Bern police. Skasch was below average height, but the way he carried himself he looked taller. He was over fifty but the jet-black hair made him appear younger. Skasch had deep-set cold blue eyes that cut right through you if he was angry. Skasch went directly to Jung's table in the far corner of the restaurant.

"Hermann, you've lost weight." Skasch said politely as he sat down. "I'm glad you waited." Skasch quickly switched to English without pausing. "Detective Clauswitz can't understand the language."

"How do you know that?" Hermann hissed.

"I make it my business to know." Skasch said wisp fully. "If you must carry a weapon my friend, wear looser clothing or use a smaller pistol."

"I have immunity." Hermann grunted. "Berlin wants to know if there are any other bidders."

"I'm giving you an exclusive Hermann." Skasch said flatly lighting a Turkish cigarette.

"Really, is that because you like me so much Herr Skasch?" Jung hissed.

"Your people pay in gold." Skasch said. "This transaction will make us both rich."

"Damn you." Jung hissed. Hermann had been skimming a few hundred Reich marks a month from the expense money Krieger's wife, The Countess, had been sending him secretly. Skasch was always expensive and to buy from him Krieger had to supplement the meager money Berlin sent with his wife's money. Quietly Jung had been converting the Reich marks into Swiss francs or government bonds using a banking house in Geneva run by Jews.

Stealing the money was bad but could be over looked. However, converting the Reich marks was illegal and punishable by death. Even the Abwehr had to go through an elaborate procedure to take money out of Germany. Berlin would hardly be interested in the reasons why Hermann converted the money only that he did.

"Are we doing business Hermann?" Skasch asked. "Or am I wasting my time?"

"We don't want this to be an auction." Jung said bluntly. "You deal only with us."

"I said you had an exclusive." Skasch said pouring a cup of coffee. "However, this has a time limit Hermann." Skasch looked at Jung. "72 hours, then I take the highest bid."

"You have the documents?" Jung asked. "Krieger doesn't pay on speculation."

"You mean the Countess doesn't. " Skasch said coldly. "It is her money after all."

"Do you have them?" Jung asked bluntly.

"I can get them within seven days after my bank confirms the payment." Skasch said. "For this all the money has to be paid upfront."

"You can cross an ocean in that amount of time." Jung said.

"I want half the money now Hermann." Skasch said. "You have 48 hours."

"What about the exchange Herr Doctor?" Jung asked. "Will it be the usual place?"

"No." Skasch lit another Turkish cigarette. "Not this time Hermann."

"Then where?" Jung asked.

"The exchange will be at an old ski resort near the border." Skasch said. "They call it Adlerberghof."

"Tell me why the hell there?" Hermann sputtered.

"It will be for my safety." Skasch said. "You could put a bullet in me and get the documents out in a diplomatic pouch."

"We could do that in Adlerberghof." Jung said coldly.

"I'll be with friends." Skasch said with a half-smile. "There will be no deal unless Krieger is there in person."

Skasch watched the blood drain from Jung's face at this suggestion. It took a few minutes for Jung to regain his composure. Jung lit a cigarette shaking his head.

"Impossible." Jung hissed. "He rarely leaves Berlin now. Himmler wants him, needs him. Stahlwald is not that far from Berlin."

"Make it possible." Skasch said firmly. "At the moment the Allies have no idea that they have been compromised. The Americans believe their courier skidded off the road accidentally and everything was destroyed in the fire."

"He likes playing Sejanus." Jung rasped.

"Tell the Countess that with what I have it will make her husband very important." Skasch said. "The RSHA needs a new master since the Czechs killed the 'Hangman' in Prague last May. She will be investing in her husband's future."

"How long will this be on the table?" Jung asked. "How much are we talking about?"

"Ten days." Skasch said. "No Reich marks $100,000 American dollars."

"That will be extremely hard." Jung said. "We'll want everything."

"The Countess can squeeze her Jews harder." Skasch said. "Or have Eidernau rob a few more graves."

"I relay your offer." Jung said. "Once I do Krieger will consider this a done deal."

"You have my sacred oath." Skasch said.

"The General has a long memory and an unforgiving nature." Jung warned.

"I know." Skasch said. "You pay for lunch and send a coffee over to Clauswitz with a sandwich."

[3]
16:00 hrs

Bern
Gasthof Chernault

The Englishman put down the *London Times* as Skasch entered the room and lit a cigarette. Skasch then sat down.

"Do you have my money Captain?" Skasch asked sitting down.

"Your job is not finished." The Englishman said dryly.

"Jung will tell Krieger." Skasch said. "That is what you contracted for Captain."

"No, not exactly what I contracted for." The Englishman said. "The bait has to be taken Viktor, and then you'll be paid."

"Switzerland is becoming a little too warm for me." Skasch hissed. "It is becoming unhealthy."

"We are keeping the Russians at bay." The Englishman said. "We have convinced them that you didn't mean to cheat them."

"My police contacts say that Ryeski is in Geneva." Skasch said. "That hardly fills me with confidence in your ability to keep me alive."

"Major Igor Ryeski?" The Englishman asked and Skasch nodded. "One of their best shooters I am impressed."

"All I want is my money and my account cleared with them so I can leave for South America without looking over my shoulder every minute." Skasch said. "Blackmail is not very British Captain."

"That's only a fairy tale about fair play." The Captain said. "Do what you are told and you will be basking in the sun in Rio?"

"I don't trust the Communist." Skasch hissed. "They never keep their word."

"This time they will." The Englishman said. "We have something they want and the price of obtaining it is letting you live."

[4]
18:00 hrs

Bern
British Embassy

"Did he play his part well Thomas?" Major Sidney Greene asked pouring the captain a tall whiskey.

"He is an excellent actor." Captain Thomas Withgate said drolly. "He has a backup career when he decides to stop being a master criminal."

"Multitalented." Greene mused as he handed Withgate the drink. "His file is fascinating to read Thomas, puts Graham Greene to shame."

"He makes my skin crawl." Withgate said hollowly. "He just oozes corruption sir."

"What about our large German friend?" Greene asked.

"Jung took the bait." Withgate said. "He is a typical German civil servant."

"He understood the conditions?" Greene inquired.

"He agreed to everything." Withgate said.

"I'll inform London Control." Greene said. "You have completed your job Thomas."

"I didn't do much sir." Withgate said. "All he really deserves is a bullet."

"Real cloak & dagger is incredibly boring." Greene said. "It is all the little pieces that make the whole picture."

"Sir Peter was a little vague why we are dealing with that rodent in the first place." Withgate said sourly. "Our Red friends are not too enthused about the necessity of keeping him alive."

"The SOE doesn't deal with political things." Greene said with a half-smile.

"That might change." Withgate said. "I'll see you in the morning sir."

Greene lit his pipe as he waited for Withgate to leave the room. He turned his attention to Nevins his chief assistant. "Did Gunnarsohn pass on the information about Ryeski?"

"Skasch knows he is here." Nevins said. "What in hell did he do to piss them off?"

"Haven't the foggiest idea." Greene said wryly. "Austen-Halton thinks it has to do with the Spanish Civil War. Skasch sold weapons and medical supplies to both sides at inflated prices. The Russians believe he cheated them out of £10,000 pounds in hard to come by gold rubles."

"They are paranoid to begin with." Nevins said. "Ryeski was not sent here for his health." Nevins paused. "We never intended to carry out our part of the deal."

"They are very patient." Greene said. "They will wait for the word."

"Control does have a sadistic streak." Nevins said flatly. "This is all surreal at times."

"They have all read Kafka." Greene said blandly. "I think it is mandatory."

"Skasch doesn't strike me as stupid sir." Nevins said as he inserted his cigarette into the ivory cigarette holder. "He has to smell a double cross."

"His only option is to run." Greene said dourly. "I doubt that he would make it out of the country once he starts."

"Ryeski is that good sir?" Nevins asked blandly.

"Yes." Greene said dully with no emotions.

An Honorable Betrayal

Chapter Two
November 12, 1942
11:00 HRS

London
U.S. Army GHQ

    Lieutenant Colonel George Custer Taggart removed his reading glasses and looked up at the officer standing in front of his desk. Captain Jefferson Davis Colquhoun was in his late twenties; in fact, Taggart was the same age as Colquhoun. The Captain was the product of the Southern military tradition and West Point '38. Taggart had known Colquhoun since childhood and had been his roommate at the Point for four years.
    "Sit down Jeff." Taggart said lighting a cigarette. "Have you finally taken leave of what sense you still had?"
    "I had my reasons George." Colquhoun said dully.
    "Turning down Crawford was stupid." Taggart said firmly. "Or do you harbor a secret desire to be the oldest captain in the United States Army? Your record in this man's army looks like used toilet paper."
    "I would hardly say that George." Colquhoun said crisply. "That ersatz general was short on details."
    "A simple yes would have taken your career out of the shit house." Taggart said tersely.
    "Then what my dear Colonel, rot the rest of the war?" Colquhoun asked sarcastically with a thick Southern accent.
    "You're not a coward Jeff." Taggart said. "Men have to be taught how to kill, some need more time."
    "I need information to make rational decisions George." Colquhoun said firmly.
    "Christssake Jeff." Taggart snarled. "You've been in the Army long enough to know not to screw with a Brigadier General, reserve or not. If you weren't Senator Colquhoun's son, you would have been court-martialed and sent to Leavenworth. "
    "Old Crowbait is a damn retread looking for lost glory." Colquhoun said harshly. "I'm not going to have men die to make him look good."
    "You are on one helluva of a shit list son." Taggart said bluntly. "Old Crowbait is giving you a second chance. Damnit, Jeff you should have been a bird colonel by now with your damn connections. He is giving you a chance for redemption Jeff or would have preferred to have been a prisoner-of-war for the duration?"
    "I don't need redemption George." Colquhoun said flatly. "The Senator is pulling strings all over Washington trying to get me into the Pentagon George." Colquhoun said. "I know if I didn't have the connections I would be a private shoveling shit in Leavenworth."
    "The gods have smiled on you again Jeff." Taggart said. "We have been ordered to go to Twickem-Hallesy to have you reconsider your rash decision."
    "Why?" Colquhoun asked.
    "You made an impression on him despite your record." Taggart said. "This time no will not do."
    "I made an impression on old Crowbait?" Colquhoun quipped. "The British must have told him about Dieppe."

"You impressed someone perhaps that Limey with the crippled arm." Taggart said. "Where we are going, this Twickem-Hallesy he has a manor house there."

"I'm not going George." Colquhoun said.

"I'm not going to have my career go into the crapper because you want to be stubborn." Taggart said bluntly. "This is not a request but an order

"You'll end this war as a General." Colquhoun said. "You will be rising to the level of your father and grandfathers in much quicker time."

"So could you, but not if you play stupid." Taggart said. "You elected to go to the Point and choose the Army as a career."

"Come on what choice was really available to me Georgie?" Colquhoun lamented. "I preferred Harvard to the Point, but the family needed a hero."

"The fact is Jeff is that you made a deal with the Army." Taggart said. "The Army expects you to keep it."

"I owed the Army four years." Colquhoun said flatly. "Only four years. How in hell was I supposed to know that a damn world war would break out and I'm stuck for the duration?"

"The Army and your father think otherwise." Taggart rasped bluntly.

"What are they going to do court-martial me?" Colquhoun hissed.

"The Senator wants a hero." Taggart said bluntly. "A court-martial wouldn't get you any votes and he wants you to be President, however the Army could put you someplace cold and dark and even the Senator could manage to avoid a court-martial the people of your state would know that you were spilling your guts to the Krauts while good men died around you."

"The raid was appallingly stupid to begin with." Colquhoun said. "They died for nothing on those stinking beaches."

"The Army buried this because they couldn't have a member of their elite Ranger unit being court-martial for cowardice." Taggart said bluntly. "Believe me Jeff some hot shot in the Judge Advocate office would have had you charged with treason along with cowardice."

"It wasn't cowardice." Colquhoun said. "I just saw that being a hero would have gained me nothing. Remember I didn't dance out of that building."

"Just your bad luck you ran into a true believer in the Nazi cause." Taggart said. "Then that British officer showed up during your recital and ruined everything. He gave you back to us along with a witness to your gutlessness."

"An American court-martial board would believe a Kraut sergeant?" Colquhoun hissed.

"Not one with the Iron Cross, but a British officer they would." Taggart said. "Just be glad that the West Point protection society dislikes scandal more than your father."

"Thus the famous Harry-Bob Colquhoun deal." Colquhoun growled. "What is it?"

"The Senator will make some noise and your bony ass is shipped off to Dutch Harbor for a few months your records being lost." Taggart rasped. "If you screw up this with Crawford you'll be a second lieutenant with me in the state militia of North Dakota until hell freezes over."

"Damn, I didn't mean to drag you into this George." Colquhoun said.

"You've never done anything easy Jeff." Taggart said. "Just make certain you get highest price."

"What about redemption?" Taggart hissed.

"That will be included in the price." Colquhoun said.

"It damn well better be ole son." Taggart said bluntly. "Don't be a damn fool in doing this my friend. Try to be smart for once in your life Jefferson."

"When do we leave?" Colquhoun asked.

"We shall leave this afternoon Captain at 13:00 hours." Taggart said. "You will have a Class A uniform, shiny shoes and not smell like a brewery."

[2]
13:00 hrs

Berlin
Reich Security Main Office

Gruppenfuhrer Helmuth Fredrich Krieger entered the private office of the most feared man in Germany the Reichsfuhrer of the SS, Heinrich Himmler. It was hard to make the connection that the bespeckled Himmler ran the largest terror organization in the world.

"Sorry to bring you back here Helmuth." Himmler said politely as he polished his nez-prez glasses. "I have received more information."

"Elsa understands sir." Krieger said. "Her father was a Prussian state councilor."

"Wives are necessary." Himmler said motioning Krieger to sit down. "I need your insight about the North African landings."

"The French are not to be trusted." Krieger said. "Petain should have sacked Darlan a long time ago."

"The landings took us by surprise." Himmler said sternly. "Also Admiral Darlan going over to the Allies was another. However, we are moving into the Free zone and occupying all of France."

"The Abwehr was caught napping." Krieger hissed. "They should have known about this sir. Moving a fleet that large is not sailing in the Albert Canal Reichsfuhrer."

"The same may be said of the SD Helmuth." Himmler said bluntly. "Our stupidity has given the Admiral another lifeline to cling to. This could have destroyed Carnaris' creditability in the eyes of the Fuhrer."

"We'll have to do something about that sir." Krieger said. "We have to be independent of the Abwehr in these matters sir."

Himmler smiled opening a file folder on his desk. "Exactly, what I have envisioned Helmuth. We should have our own network overseas."

"Carnaris will scream to the Fuehrer about the 1935 agreement." Krieger said coldly.

"It is a matter of interpretation." Himmler said. "Lawyers can justify everything. We have the best lawyers in Germany in this building."

"OKW will not be pleased either." Krieger said. "The Wehrmacht doesn't like amateurs messing with military intelligence."

"They can be handled." Himmler said firmly. "Keital has no guts and will do what the Fuhrer tells him to do. Carnaris, however, has a backbone and will be the main obstacle."

"Obstacles can be overcome." Krieger said. "Carnaris is an old man."

"Starting a civil war will not help." Himmler said. "We have to accomplish this without the Silver Fox knowing what we are doing."

"By using unorthodox methods I assume." Krieger said. "The Abwehr is too bogged down with tradition to try anything new. The Velno Bridge would never have occurred to them sir."

"Quite." Himmler said. "That's why I'm authorizing you to start your plan immediately Obergruppenfuhrer."

"I'm honored sir." Krieger said. "I will do my best sir."

"That I had no questions about." Himmler said firmly handing him the folder. "This is ultra secret Helmuth and under no circumstances is the Abwehr to know. I want to implement your plan immediately."

"You mean the entire plan sir?" Krieger asked somberly.

"Yes." Himmler said grimly. "This *Albatross* has to be destroyed. You are authorized to do anything necessary to find and destroy him."

"I must thank you sir for your confidence in me for this assignment." Krieger said.

"You will officially be appointed the SS Chief for Southern France," Himmler said in a plain voice. "That will explain your absence from Berlin."

"Naturally, I would take leave before I start my new assignment sir." Krieger said.

"That would not be out of the ordinary." Himmler said. "It is time you step from out of his shadow."

[3]
15:00 hrs

Twickem-Hallesy
Austen-Halton Manor

Brigadier General Henry Clay Crawford was a stern looking man in his mid-fifties. Before entering the Army this time, Crawford had been a New York City police superintendent. During the last war, Crawford spent his time fighting the war from behind a desk as Lieutenant in G-2. Crawford wanted to be at the front-line because he spoke street German. He had learned how by being with the NYPD's famous Flying Squad.

After the war, Crawford stayed in the New York National Guard rising to the rank of major before the attack on Pearl Harbor. On December 8, Crawford's commission reactivated and assigned again to intelligence, but in February 1942, Crawford moved to the OSS. Late April 1942 Crawford's new assignment was to work with the British Special Operation Executive.

With him was Crawford's British counterpart Air Vice- Marshal Sir Peter Austen-Halton, KCB, DSO, DFC, MC. Sir Peter was a demure looking man in his early sixties who looked like an English squire. Austen-Halton had flown with the Royal Flying Corps until shot down in 1917. The crash left him with a crippled left arm and a slight limp. Austen-Halton had been with MI6 for twenty years. The manor house they were using belonged to Halton's family.

"The Operation is called Roundup." Crawford said flatly. "This is top secret and all the usual precautions are in place gentlemen."

"Sounds American for a change; will we be leading this?" Colquhoun quipped.

"Glad that we could accommodate your sense of language, Captain, we worked hard at that." Sir Peter said drolly. "This time the name is appropriate Captain. The sole objective to his operation is to escort a VIP in Germany to safety."

"I must ask, why me sir?" Colquhoun rasped.

"You speak German and have experience in winter survival." Crawford said. "They are talents required for this particular mission."

"Virginia does have mountains sir." Colquhoun rasped. "There are plenty of captains in the Army, why pick me sir?"

"Your commanding general recommended you." Crawford said sternly. "He called General Donovan personally."

"Lord Mountbatten, of Combined Operations, was also impressed." Sir Peter said. "Not easy to do captain. He knows you were at Dieppe in August."

Colquhoun remained silent. The General was an old friend of his father and had undoubtedly pulled strings and cashed in markers to keep his record clean.

"I'm impressed sir." Colquhoun said. "Then I shall not disappoint them."

"You'll want to discuss details gentlemen." Taggart said. "So I will leave."

"Please, stay Colonel Taggart." Crawford said. "You have become part of this."

"Relax Colonel." Sir Peter said relighting his cigar. "We are always short of staff here."

"I'm in no rush sir." Taggart said. "It should be interesting."

"Who is this VIP sir?" Colquhoun inquired lighting a cigarette.

"His name is Helmuth Christian Krieger." Sir Peter said dully. "He holds the rank of Gruppenfuhrer in the SS and the *Sicherheitsdienst*, SD"

"You are telling me that he is a damn Nazi?" Colquhoun hissed. "Not just a Nazi, a member of the damn SS?"

"Krieger is a very bright boy Captain." Crawford said firmly. "Unlike his friends he knows the war is lost and being bright he wants to survive the war."

"What are we now?" Colquhoun quipped. "The Salvation Army or out of a clear blue sky we suddenly like Nazis?"

"He has something very important to trade for his life." Sir Peter said drolly.

"What could he possibly have?" Colquhoun asked tartly.

"The bastard has a list of Nazi agents in England along English collaborators." Crawford said bluntly.

"Anybody can say he has a list." Taggart interjected.

"We have seen a sample of it." Crawford said. "Sir Peter's people have verified it."

"Where did you find this creature?" Colquhoun asked. "What kind of rock was he under?"

"Unfortunately many of our finest families have German relatives." Sir Peter said dourly as he relit his cigar. "They, despite the war, have kept in contact with their relatives. Krieger persuaded one of them to contact us."

"How long ago was that?" Colquhoun asked.

"That is not pertinent to this matter Captain." Crawford said.

"I think it is sir." Colquhoun said firmly. "I get a little nervous when English lords exchange love letters with their Nazi relatives and a SS officer uses them to contact you."

"I see no problems with the question Henry." Sir Peter said. "Six months ago Captain. We had our man in Switzerland confirmed the meeting."

"How have you been communicating?" Colquhoun asked.

"Krieger is not a fool." Sir Peter said. "He is using a middleman to handle the negotiations between us."

"I'll be given the dossiers on them?" Colquhoun asked.

"Everything will be in your room Captain." Sir Peter said.

"When and where will this happen?" Colquhoun asked.

"He'll be in a small village near the Swiss border named Adlerberghof sometime in December." Crawford said. "The village is remote. We'll have the exact time before you leave."

"How near the Swiss border is that?" Colquhoun asked.

"I would say about 40 kilometers. The terrain is heavily forested and mountainous." Sir Peter said. "You can ski cross country?"

"Yes." Colquhoun said. "I was training for the 1940 Winter Games before the war broke out. I'll assume there are no roads to use?"

"Roads have checkpoints and border guards on both sides of the line." Sir Peter said. "The Swiss border guards have orders to shoot to kill just like their German counterparts."

"I could bluff our way through." Colquhoun said.

"You might be able to, but the cargo is not an actor." Crawford said.

"I'm not doing this alone, am I?" Colquhoun said brusquely.

"We have assembled a team, six others have been selected." Crawford said. "Sir Peter's private air force will deliver you near Adlerberghof by parachute drop." Crawford paused looking at Colquhoun's eyes. "You'll be wearing German Army uniforms."

"That is a little dangerous sir." Colquhoun said warily.

"If the Germans capture you Captain you'll be shot as a commando/ saboteur." Crawford said. "Shooting you as a spy would be redundant even for them."

"My Major Greene will be waiting for you at the border to take Krieger and his party off your hands." Sir Peter said. "The whole operation should take less than 72 hours."

"Party sir, I thought he was solo?" Colquhoun asked.

"Krieger might have someone with him." Crawford said. "We are not certain yet."

"What about the German military?" Taggart asked.

"There is a Jaeger training battalion stationed 35 kilometer north of the village in Jaegerfeld." Sir Peter said. "No Waffen SS in the area."

"What about training?" Colquhoun asked. "The team needs time to get aquatinted with each other."

"We can give you two weeks." Sir Peter said. "We have a training base in Scotland that we use on regularly."

"What will be the composition of the team sir?" Colquhoun asked.

"It will be a mixed team." Crawford said. "The team will consist of three British SOE agents and four Americans from OSS. You'll be given the temporary rank of Major."

"May I ask why the upgrade sir?" Colquhoun asked flatly.

"Krieger is a snob I am afraid." Sir Peter said. "Major is the highest rank we can use without causing too much attention. Krieger is a snob no doubt and would be insulted if only a captain came for him."

"Am I part of the team sir?" Taggart asked.

"Colonel Taggart, you will act as our liaison with Major Colquhoun." Sir Peter said.

"I'll inform London of your transfer Colonel." Crawford said.

"I'll inform Colonel Tremayne that you'll both be staying with us." Sir Peter said. "Rooms at the Red Dragon will be readied for you. Colonel Tremayne will drive you to the village."

Austen-Halton swirled the drink in his hand. "Why involve Taggart?"

"Taggart is well aware of Colquhoun's background." Crawford said. "They were classmates at West Point."

"Will he be told the whole story?" Sir Peter asked. "I understand the risks in using Colquhoun for this mission."

"The Senator is pragmatic Sir Peter." Crawford said as he relit his cigar. "He would rather have a dead hero as a son than a condemned coward."

"I see you are no longer novices in the body politic." Austen-Halton said slyly.

"Politics back home is a blood sport." Crawford grunted.

[4]
18:00 hrs

Red Boar Pub

The Red Dragon Pub was located in the center of the village of Twickem-Hallesy. The pub had been built in 1670 as an inn on the post road going to Gloucester. The rest of the quaint English village grew up around the pub. The Finley family had owned the pub since 1766. The pub was the closest thing to a restaurant and Gasthof in the village. The third and fourth floors were added in the 1920s to accommodate the growing number of visitors to the manor house.

The two American Army officers were in one of the private booths at the rear of the pub. Taggart pushed the pint of ale in front of Colquhoun. "Let's not do something stupid Jeff."

"They are goddamn insane George." Colquhoun said bluntly.

"Insane or not Jeff you are committed to this." Taggart said firmly. "You can not back out now."

"Why can't I?" Colquhoun hissed. "This little venture is a one-way ticket to suicide. Papa Colquhoun didn't raise any idiots."

"Stop being a jerk Jeff." Taggart hissed. "Crawford might not kill you, but that Limey RAF officer would have your throat slit with out a second thought."

"You're talking murder George." Colquhoun quipped.

"It is survival my friend." Taggart said. "You are a security risk now and the Limeys know how to keep you quiet forever. Like it or not Jeff you are going."

"Damn." Colquhoun said grimly his mind's eye drifting back to Dieppe.

The General had told the assembly of Rangers that they were going with the Canadians and British primarily as observers of the raid on the French seacoast. The Army high command thought it would be an excellent opportunity to give their men some experience. The raid at Dieppe was to last six to eight hours then the force would leave. The Rangers would be scattered throughout the Royal Marine commandos.

Colquhoun tried to get the assignment to stay aboard the escort vessels to observe the raid from deck side however, someone else with more influence got that job. Colquhoun found himself attached to the Royal Marine commando comprised of Polish soldiers. Colquhoun wanted the French commando, but that was over staffed with Americans. Colquhoun was attached with a young British officer who could speak Polish and enough of the Poles understood German the language that Colquhoun spoke.

After their commando hit the beach and moved into the town Colquhoun and the British officer some how got separated from their unit. While dodging through the alleyways they stumbled across a German patrol. The British officer decided to fight and the Germans killed him for his efforts. Colquhoun dropped his weapon and raised his hands. The German sergeant walked up to him and backhanded him before bringing him to his officer.

The German officer was about his age and Colquhoun saw the NSDAP pin on the officer's tunic pocket.

"You speak English?" Colquhoun asked.

"No." The German answered. "What about German?"

"Yes." Colquhoun replied.

"Are you with the goddamn Poles?" The Lieutenant asked. Colquhoun started to give the Geneva Convention answer when the Lieutenant smashed his fist into his gut doubling him over.

"What the hell are you doing?" Colquhoun snarled.

"Sergeant Meyer, bring him to that café across the street." The Lieutenant ordered.

They moved him into the kitchen of the deserted café. The other soldier with them found some rope and tied Colquhoun's arms behind his back. Sergeant Meyer went to the stove and started to cook something.

"What do you want Herr Leutnant?" Colquhoun asked.

"I want information." The Lieutenant said. "How many men are here?"

"How the hell do I know?" Colquhoun said.

"Wrong answer American." The German said smashing Colquhoun across the face.

"Okay, you made your point." Colquhoun said. "What's in it for me?"

"Life." The German said plainly.

"I need more than that." Colquhoun rasped.

"I would say most likely a prisoner-of-war camp for officers." The German said contemptuously in English. "Why be a soldier you gutless wonder?"

"You can be a soldier for 40 years, even become a general without ever having anyone shoot at you." Colquhoun said.

"You see what the Americans send Feldwebel?" The Lieutenant hissed. "Just human garbage, this is the best they have?"

Before Colquhoun could answer the Lieutenant burst open and a tall British officer stepped in pointing a Sten at them.

"What the hell is this?" The German lieutenant snarled.

"Raise your hands Herr Leutnant." Mannerling said motioning with his Sten-gun. "Cut the Yank loose and you'll live to make general."

"Drop your weapon major." The Lieutenant said. "You are loosing this battle."

"Okay, untied him lieutenant." Mannerling said bluntly. "Do it now!"

"Honecker shoot this pig." The Lieutenant said in German. Mannerling swung the Sten over and pulled the trigger. Honecker hit the wall and slowly slid down leaving a path of blood on the wall. Mannerling swung the Sten back and killed the lieutenant.

"You understand German." The Sergeant said his hands still pointed upwards.

"Yes." Mannerling answered. "Untie the Yank."

"The lieutenant was right about one thing Herr Major." The Sergeant said moving towards the American.

"What's that?" Mannerling asked.

"You're loosing." The Sergeant said.

"Pick him up and carry him." Mannerling ordered.

"Where are we going Herr Major?" The Sergeant asked.

"We head for the beach Herr Feldwebel." Mannerling said. "What did the Lieutenant do to him?"

"He did nothing really tough." The Sergeant said. "A few slaps and he started to talk."

"Head for the beach and don't try anything stupid." Mannerling snapped.

"Not me." The Sergeant said. "My ambition is to make civilian."

"Who the hell are you?" Colquhoun rasped.

"Shut-up you cowardly bastard." The British Officer growled.

"You're not British." Colquhoun hissed.

"Get going you sonofabitch or I'll shoot you myself." The officer said.

"Jeff." Taggart said breaking him out his daze. "You do this mission and you'll get a ticket home."

"What in a pine box George?" Colquhoun rasped.

"Christssakes Jeff." Taggart muttered. "Go by the book on this and you'll end up in Switzerland a hero. This majority you have could turn into an eagle with little effort."

"While your eagle turns into a star George, am I right." Colquhoun said firmly.

"I'll need all the rank I can get Jeff." Taggart said sternly after draining his beer mug. "I don't have a rich and powerful family behind me. When this war ends I don't want to be a thirty-five year lieutenant."

"Then make certain I get out alive." Colquhoun said.

[5]
19:00 hrs

London
Soviet Embassy

Major General Yuri Vladovich Pushkin was officially listed as the third secretary to the Trade Section of the Embassy. The Foreign Office politely acknowledged this and knowing he was the NKVD security chief at the embassy. Pushkin was one of the few 'Spaniards' who escaped the gulag or the firing squad after the Spanish Civil War ended in 1939. Stalin thought the Russian 'volunteers' had absorbed too many Western ideas while fighting Franco. Beria had him transferred to the Soviet Far East to watch the Japanese because Beria didn't waste talent. Pushkin was transferred back in late 1941 after the German Army had been stopped at the gates of Moscow. Beria had Pushkin transferred to their Embassy in London to watch their new Allies and the GRU assigned to their military mission.

Pushkin's counterpart from the GRU, Soviet military intelligence, was Major General Semyon Vassily Sergeyev, who was officially part of the Soviet military mission to SHAEF in London. Sergeyev had been in the Army since he lied about his age during the Russo-Japanese War in 1905. By the outbreak of the First World War, he was a Sergeant Major and the holder of two George Crosses for bravery. Sergeyev by earlier 1917 was a Lieutenant station outside of Saint Petersburg. During the Revolution Lieutenant Sergeyev joined the rebels and served in the Red Army during the civil war, a White Russian artillery shell ended his frontline career and he became an intelligence officer.

"What sort of deal did you make with the British about Skasch?" Pushkin asked sourly as he lit an American cigarette with an American Zippo lighter.

"I'm surprised Nardinov hasn't told you." Sergeyev grunted pouring the vodka into a large glass.

"Moscow says you requested Major Ryeski." Pushkin said blandly.

"I needed someone Skasch actually fears." Sergeyev said. "They tangled in Spain in 1937, but Sasha did not have orders to kill him."

"You're using him like a red flag." Pushkin said. "What the hell are our friends up to?"

"They plan to kill a German officer." Sergeyev said. "They ask for our help, which surprised the hell out of me. The Swiss security police know who Ryeski is."

"I think we better send someone to find out, don't you think Comrade Sergeyev?" Pushkin asked harshly.

Sergeyev smiled. "What's wrong Comrade Pushkin?"

"I find your lack of concern alarming." Pushkin snapped. "You commit a man under our control to help the British without contacting me."

"If you stayed in your office instead of night clubbing Yuri you would find out things." Sergeyev said. "Moscow made the arrangements not me."

"Did your Western friends bother to tell you the name of the goddamn German officer?" Pushkin hissed.

"Actually he is an SS officer, a close personal friend of the late Heydrich." Sergeyev said.

"I need a name Comrade." Pushkin growled.

"His name is Krieger." Sergeyev answered. "Helmuth Krieger."

"Who do you have watching Austen-Halton and the American Crawford?" Pushkin asked anxiously.

"Mikhailov, I have him acting as liaison officer." Sergeyev answered. "Good man for the job."

Pushkin's face turned ashen for a few seconds on hearing about Mikhailov. "Have you gone mad?"

"No." Sergeyev snapped. "What's wrong with him? He speaks fluent English."

"Does Moscow know this?" Pushkin asked somberly.

"Moscow sent the orders." Sergeyev said dryly. "They sent along instructions Comrade Pushkin."

"Instructions, what sort of instructions?" Pushkin asked.

"They concern a deep mole." Sergeyev said. "Moscow wants him protected."

"How in hell do we do that?" Pushkin asked sharply sensing trouble. "What is Mikhailov's connection?"

"Marshal Beria will explain that at 23:00 hrs." Sergeyev said handing him the vodka bottle.

An Honorable Betrayal

Chapter Three
November 12, 1942
18:00 hrs

Germany
Stahlwald

    As Krieger's automobile headed for his wife's estate at Stahlwald just outside of the city of Potsdam, Kaiser Wilhelm I gave this Prussian estate to her grandfather after the Franco-Prussian War of 1870 for military service rendered. His wife's father was one of Kaiser Wilhelm I's advisors and created a count of the Empire in 1910 by Wilhelm II, Krieger leaned back in the seat to relish the moment.

    Reinhart Heydrich had been dead for almost six months and Himmler had not named a permanent replacement. An administrative officer was handling the day-to-day running of the Reich Security Main Office (RSHA). Himmler seemed to vacillate on his choice to become head of the RSHA and SD. He needed someone who could run the department efficiently, but had no desire to become Reichsfuhrer. This was going to be a test and if he succeeded, he would become Chief of the RSHA and Himmler's heir apparent.

    Krieger lit a cigar knowing what Himmler meant by coming out of the shadows. Heydrich was the closest thing Himmler had for a friend. Heydrich, the tall blond blue-eyed ex-naval officer, was the complete opposite of the mild-mannered ex-chicken farmer. There was no other person in the SS that Himmler trusted as thoroughly as Heydrich and feared.

    Helmuth first met Heydrich in Berlin in 1931. A mutual friend amazed by the striking physical resemblance they had brought them together for each to see the amazing resemblance. Heydrich, amused by this, offered Helmuth a position in the SS corresponding to his Army rank of Captain. Krieger politely refuses, but they part as friends with a letter from Heydrich giving him a commission in the SS whenever he wanted it. Helmuth's wife however, seeing the political and career advantages urges him to join the Nazi party secretly. As a serving officer in the Reichwehr, he was prohibited from belonging to any political party.

    At his wife, urging Helmuth resigned from the Army in 1933 and formally joined the SS as an Obersturmbannfuhrer and one of Heydrich's aides-de-camp. Helmuth remained in the background becoming Heydrich's sounding board. Krieger made it a policy of never being photographed with Heydrich. Helmuth preferred the background but was always with Heydrich at every meeting standing in the shadows. The only time he was not with him was in Prague when the Czech resistance assassinated Heydrich. Krieger had been fortunate enough to be in Berlin on the day of the assassination.

    Heydrich, secretly through Krieger, had tried to persuade Frick, the Reichminister of the Interior and technically Himmler's immediate superior, to quietly resign and recommend to Hitler that Himmler succeed him. Frick refused and being an old crony of Hitler's Heydrich could not force him to resign.

    The chances of Himmler dying of natural causes in the next few years were remote and Heydrich was young and ambitious. Thus, a quiet conspiracy was formed to have Himmler die an accidental death. Helmuth was formulating the final preparations in Berlin when the Czechs assassinated him Prague. Helmuth, at Elsa's urging, quickly changed sides quietly eliminating his fellow conspirators. Krieger since then had become an ardent supporter of the Reichsfuhrer.

Elsa was waiting for Helmuth in the great hall of the 14th century castle. Countess vom Rodelbach, Elsa's father only had one child and the creation patent passed the title to her and her descendants, was ten years older than Helmuth. Her first husband, a Guards Officer, died during the closing months of the First World War and her only child Bruno was living with his fraternal grandfather in Munich.

Waiting with her was Standartenfuhrer Albrecht Ehrlich, Krieger's aide de Camp as well as Helmuth's childhood friend. They had grown up the same East Prussian town the sons of the only professionals in the village. They went to university together and officer cadet school. They served in the Army during the first war and both stayed in the Army after the war.

"This message came after you left for your visit with Himmler." Elsa said. "My cousin Hermann is getting nervous about this." Krieger read the telegram and saw that Elsa was right.

"Jung is a weakling." Helmuth rasped. "He wants guarantees."

"He wants a safe position faraway from any shooting." Elsa said crisply.

"Switzerland is neutral." Ehrlich said grimly. "We are not Dr. Ley's Labor Front."

"He is thinking of South America." Elsa said. "He wants someplace warm and faraway from the shooting."

"That shouldn't be hard to do." Elsa said. "Schellenberg wouldn't mind."

"That will be the day." Helmuth said. "Using relatives is never a good idea."

"Hermann was contacted by Skasch." Elsa said dully.

"I don't trust that bastard." Ehrlich said bluntly. "The man is a criminal."

"He has never convicted of a damn thing." Helmuth said flatly. "He is a university professor and a man of letters."

"You speak too kindly Helmuth." Elsa said. "The man is dangerous because he is clever."

"You two might be right." Helmuth said wryly. "Adlerberghof will be his first and last mistake."

"You have become obsessed with this List." Elsa snapped. "MI6 and the OSS are not stupid."

"It exists." Krieger said bluntly.

"It could." Elsa said. "However, never on paper, not lists like that."

"Something they would do because it is so illogical." Helmuth said. "The British are not amateurs Elsa or stupid."

"This could be a trap." Elsa warned. "It has all the earmarks of another Velno Bridge."

Helmuth shook his head. "Adlerberghof will be cut off from the outside world once we arrive. I have anticipated that this could be a trap."

"Dangerous." Elsa hissed. "You'll not be dealing with sheep there."

"Albrecht's duty will be to see that Skasch does not leave Adlerberghof alive." Krieger said bluntly. "It should be enjoyable work for Albrecht."

Elsa lit a cigarette. "Few will shed tears over the fate of Skasch, but you still have another problem Helmuth."

"I know von Tanz." Helmuth hissed bitterly. "He has been a painful nemesis for years."

"The duel has to stop." Elsa said.

"By adding a few lines on the list I will accomplish that." Krieger said. "Von Tanz will fall as a traitor."

"The Abwehr has done business with Skasch in the past." Elsa said. "They might know about the list."

"I have confirmed the fact that they don't." Helmuth said. "If you want the big prize you have to take the big risks. Once I have the List I have power Elsa. Once I have the power everything is within my grasp."

"You mean everything my dear Helmuth, with no limits?" Elsa hissed with delight.

"I said that." Helmuth said. "Unlike Heydrich I will not hesitate to remove any object in my way."

"All objects Helmuth?" Elsa asked bluntly.

"Any and all objects Elsa." Helmuth rasped. "I see fresh opportunities a head of us and Germany. New thinking is needed."

[2]
20:00 hrs

Twickem-Hallesy
Austen-Halton Manor

Mannerling lit his Canadian woodsman pipe while he waited in the small private library in the South wing of the mansion for Colonel Tremayne to escort him to Sir Peter's private office. Colonel Tremayne had left him coffee and some American donuts.

Mannerling was a Canadian by birth and the second son of a RCMP Inspector. Mannerling's older brother, Phillip, had been killed in the First World War; an IRA terrorist had killed Thomas, his youngest brother, a RCMP corporal, in 1938.

Mannerling had been a Mountie, but resigned in 1929 over an incident involving the killing of criminal suspects. After being asked to resign, Mannerling joined the Canadian Army. In December 1934, Lieutenant Mannerling met Sir Peter Austen-Halton for the first time in Ottawa and went to work for him.

Only a handful of people in His Majesty's Government knew exactly what Austen-Halton's little section did. Government officials preferred not to know or find out what he did. Mannerling's job was to fight in the gutters and keep the garbage from seeping up disturbing the public. When Austen-Halton's section became part of the SOE Mannerling went with him.

The bucolic village of Twickem-Hallesy was located north of London. The Austen-Halton Manor house was nestled deep in the forest on what once had been one of King Henry II's private game preserves. King Henry VII granted the game preserve and 300 acres of land around it to Austen-Halton's direct descendant after the Battle of Boswell Field and the title of Baron of Twickem came with the land.

After two hours, Colonel Tremayne silently ushered Mannerling into the private office and left. Sir Peter was standing by the fireplace poking the dancing flames with a poker. Sitting in the large overstuffed dark red leather chair was the American general Crawford from the OSS.

"You know General Crawford, Major." Austen-Halton said turning from the fireplace to face Mannerling. "Please be seated."

"We have met in London sir." Mannerling said as he sat down in the third chair.

"General Crawford has been briefed on your special talents Major." Sir Peter said. "So there is no reason to be coy." Halton passed a large manila envelope to Mannerling. "Read the contents Major."

"Verbal will be sufficient." Mannerling said.

"You should read the contents Major." General Crawford said gravely. "It is very important that you understand."

Mannerling read the contents, placed the papers back into the envelope, and looked at the photograph. "I know this officer."

"You met him on the morning of August 19 in Dieppe France." Sir Peter said.

"Who the hell is he?" Mannerling asked coldly.

"Captain Jefferson D. Colquhoun." Crawford said removing a cigar from his cigar-case.

"You promote sniveling cowards in the American Army General?" Mannerling asked icily.

"The promotion was coming prior to his journey to Dieppe." Crawford said. "His family is politically powerful."

"Your Army believes in court-martials?" Mannerling asked.

"Major, stop being impertinent." Sir Peter said sharply.

"Captain Colquhoun was under a great deal of strain that day." Crawford said flatly.

"So was I sir." Mannerling said. "Why isn't he under arrest now?"

"Politics plan and simple Major." Crawford said. "You understand politics Major Mannerling. You people don't shoot Lords do you?"

Mannerling remained silent his mind falling back to August 19. Operation Jubilee on paper was very simple. The Allies would mount a large raid in force aim at Dieppe to gather intelligence, destroy shore installations while testing new equipment. Another part of the plan was for the Luftwaffe to be drawn into a trap set by the RAF. Canada would supply the bulk of the attacking force to give them practical combat experience. This attacking force would be supplemented with Royal Marine Commandos and 50 American Rangers. About 8,000 men would land stay a few hours then leave.

On reaching Dieppe, everything went down hill. The Germans, sitting behind their fortifications just pounded the hell out of the invading force. The new Churchill tanks foundered on the beaches because their treads couldn't get traction in the gravely sand. The Royal Navy destroyers, who were providing covering fire, were not powerful enough to do any damage to the fortifications without taking brutal punishment from the German shore batteries. The German garrison, hardly first line troops, did not panic and run.

Mannerling, who had attached himself a Royal Marine Commando, managed to get passed the beach with about 12 men. While they were ducking, the Germans Mannerling noticed a squad of Germans dragging what looked like an American officer into a building.

"What's on your mind Major?" The CSM asked.

"Check on that Yank."

"That is a very unhealthy idea sir." The sergeant said sternly.

"Cover my ass Sergeant." Mannerling said. "If things get too hot sergeant take off and save yourself."

Mannerling zigzagged across the street to the building; a small cafe the Germans had dragged the American. Mannerling slowly pushed the door open and entered the café, which was empty. Mannerling could hear a German yelling at the top of his voice in English coming from the kitchen. Mannerling silently moved to the kitchen door and listened.

The German officer was a very bad interrogator but he was getting information quite easily from the American lieutenant whose name was Colquhoun. Mannerling eased the kitchen door open slightly to get a view of the inside. The American was sitting in a chair with his hands tied behind his back and his face was slightly bruised. The German officer stood in front of the American asking questions in English. Behind the American was a German with his hands on his shoulders, the German Sergeant was at the stove cooking something ignoring what was going on behind him.

Mannerling pulled back the bolt of his Sten-gun and entered the kitchen. "Hands up!"

"What the hell is this?" The German lieutenant snarled.

"Raise your hands Herr Leutnant." Mannerling said motioning with his Sten-gun. "Cut the Yank loose and you'll live to make general."

"Drop your weapon major." The Lieutenant said. "You are loosing this battle."

"Okay, untied him lieutenant." Mannerling said bluntly. "Do it now!"

"Honecker shoot this pig." The Lieutenant said in German. Mannerling swung the Sten over and pulled the trigger. Honecker hit the wall and slowly slid down leaving a path of blood on the wall. Mannerling swung the Sten back and killed the lieutenant.

"You understand German." The Sergeant said his hands still pointed upwards.

"Yes." Mannerling answered. "Untie the Yank."

"The lieutenant was right about one thing Herr Major." The Sergeant said moving towards the American.

"What's that?" Mannerling asked.

"You're loosing." The Sergeant said.

"Pick him up and carry him." Mannerling ordered.

"Where are we going Herr Major?" The Sergeant asked.

"We head for the beach Herr Feldwebel." Mannerling said. "What did the Lieutenant do to him?"

"Nothing really tough." The Sergeant said. "A few slaps and he started to talk."

"Head for the beach and don't try anything stupid." Mannerling snapped.

"Not me." The Sergeant said. "My ambition is to make civilian."

"Major Mannerling." Crawford said. "Are you listening to us?" Mannerling shook himself free from the memory.

"Sorry sir." Mannerling said as he relit his pipe. "Who is this Dr. Bodesky?"

"He works for our psychology section." Crawford said.

"He is a headshrinker as the Americans say." Mannerling said. "You obviously know about Colquhoun's history, so why Bodesky?"

"We needed an evaluation." Crawford answered.

"Why bother?" Mannerling said. "He is a coward."

Sir Peter removed a cigar from the cigar humidor. "Dr. Bodesky as well as Dr. Phillipton believes that the Dieppe incident may have been isolated."

"Bullshit." Mannerling said plainly.

"How much do you agree with Edward?" Austen-Halton said as he lit his cigar.

"If you have doubts about Colquhoun, why select him?" Mannerling asked. "I'm to replace him?"

"No." Sir Peter said.

"Why am I here?" Mannerling asked.

"You are to see that Colquhoun is captured." Crawford said plainly.

"You want him to break." Mannerling hissed. "Why?"

"Read Colquhoun's orders." Crawford said handing him to Mannerling.

"Any thinking general at OKW knows that the war is lost." Austen-Halton said in a cold voice. "It is only a matter of time. Some want the carnage to stop."

"This Krieger doesn't strike me as the humanitarian type." Mannerling said crisply.

"Some SS are intelligent." Austen-Halton said.

"Hitler isn't going to surrender today, tomorrow or in one hundred years." Mannerling said bluntly. "I can't see us helping the rats to escape a sinking ship."

"It is called self-preservation." Crawford said. "This is the first law of nature."

"Outrage isn't why Krieger is defecting." Mannerling said. "I see a large cash prize at the end of the tunnel."

"We hope that Major Colquhoun believes Krieger is defecting for noble reasons." Crawford said. "We will reinforce that notion."

"I get the feeling that I didn't read the whole document." Mannerling said cautiously.

"Krieger isn't defecting." Austen-Halton said flatly.

"Damn." Mannerling said looking at Austen-Halton icily. "You left out a whole chapter. Why this little trip to Nazi land?"

"Cover." Crawford said. "This is an elaborate ruse."

"Interesting for what reasons are we doing these gentlemen?" Mannerling asked.

"You and Boyden Orr are going to kill Krieger." Sir Peter said. "That is your specialty."

Mannerling slowly relit his pipe. "Kill him?"

"That is what you do isn't Major?" Crawford said blandly.

"Yes." Mannerling said unflinchingly. "Why is Colquhoun going in under the impression that he his rescuing him?"

"We have to give you a clear shot." Austen-Halton said firmly.

"Why the charade for this mission this time?" Mannerling asked. "You don't need nine men to kill one maggot."

"Others want Krieger dead." Austen-Halton said dourly. "They can't appear to have any part of this."

"Why should we care?" Mannerling hissed.

"These people are a means to an end." Austen-Halton said. "War breeds strange bedfellows."

"There is something missing." Mannerling said brusquely. "Do you intend to tell me or do I walk around in the dark?"

"We are giving you a clear shot in Adlerberghof." Crawford rasped.

"Sorry General." Mannerling said. "SS officers may be fanatical, but they aren't generally stupid sir, so why would Krieger go to Adlerberghof?"

"He is going to Adlerberghof to buy a list of allied agents on the continent." Austen-Halton said in his dull voice. "Dr. Skasch, who is selling the list, is a notorious underworld creature."

"The list is false." Mannerling said. "Does Skasch know this?"

"No." Austen-Halton answered.

"I'll assume that Colquhoun knows nothing of this." Mannerling said.

"Correct." Crawford rasped.

"Won't he get a bit pissed off after I blow the kraut's head off?" Mannerling hissed.

"He won't see you." Austen-Halton said.

"Why won't Colquhoun see me?" Mannerling asked.

"That is simply because you'll be dead major." Sir Peter said offhandedly. "Colquhoun will see you die."

Mannerling emptied out his pipe and refilled the pipe with tobacco. He slowly lit the pipe. "Dead you say? I rise up from the grave no doubt?"

"Nothing so melodramatic Major will be required." Crawford said. "You'll be told how you'll die later. After your resurrection you make contact with the German resistance."

"Boyden?" Mannerling asked.

"He'll be acting independently of you." Austen-Halton said. "Only you will know about Boyden."

"We might not get a shot." Mannerling said.

"You will get the opportunity." Crawford said. "Colquhoun will be betrayed."

"Why?" Mannerling asked.

"That doesn't concern you." Sir Peter said. "You're primary mission is to see that Krieger dies."

"He will." Mannerling said dryly.

"Tell me Major." Crawford said unsmilingly. "In your line of work are there any rules about or compunctions about killing a woman?"

"There shouldn't be." Mannerling said icily. "Women are actually better killers. Are you saying that one is involved?"

"Krieger's wife will be there." Austen-Halton said.

"Is she dangerous?" Mannerling inquired.

"She is very dangerous." Crawford said. "You have the go ahead to kill her."

"Both?" Mannerling hissed.

"Yes." Austen-Halton said. "Colonel Tremayne will drive you back to the Royal Gloucester. Relax for a few days. Tremayne will ring when we want you back."

[3]
22:00 hrs

Brandenburg
Abwehr Training Center

"I thought I would find you here General." The short white-haired man in the uniform of a Vice- Admiral of the Kriegsmarine said as he entered the small cramped office in the basement. "You have a wife von Tanz."

"Magda is not in Berlin sir." Generalmajor Herbert von Tanz said. "She is also is very understanding."

"You should enjoy reading this." The Admiral said handing a paper to Von Tanz, "I found it purely by chance."

Von Tanz took the paper and read it; Von Tanz noticed that this was an original document.

"This will be very helpful sir." Von Tanz said.

"I personally dislike Krieger." The Admiral said. "However, professionally it would be a disaster for the intelligence services."

"I doubt that it exist sir." Von Tanz said. "The Allies would not put it on paper."

"When did the truth matter to them?" The Admiral asked.

"This is more or less a death warrant sir." Von Tanz said coolly.

The Admiral smiled briefly. "Mueller would not have shown you that. The Gestapo doesn't believe there is a serious Resistance movement."

"Why use the cover of the Abwehrpolizei instead sir?" Von Tanz asked.

"If the list is real the Abwehrpolizei would do the investigation." The Admiral said. "This is just a warning to watch your back and cover your trail better; Mueller will not give you a warning and I can't protect you if it goes that far Herbert."

"You want this to stop sir?" Von Tanz asked. "This can be halted."

"No." The Admiral said. "Whatever you have planned Herbert you are committed. The Allies, like Mueller, does not believe there is any resistance to Hitler so you must complete your mission." The Admiral paused. "However, from this point on you'll be totally on your own. The penalty for failure is death for you and your wife."

"I understand sir." Von Tanz said dryly.

"Then you'll understand when I say that I was never here." The Admiral said. "Burn that nonexistent paper too."

Chapter Four
December 1, 1942
20:00 hrs

Berlin
32 Koenigstrasse

Von Tanz lifted back the curtain and looked up and down the street the directly across the street. "You have your people ready?"

"Lars will meet me in Stuttgart." Major Anton Gerhardt said. "I'm not too comfortable with Dietrich."

"This concern is a little late." Von Tanz said firmly. "Dietrich is committed now."

"I know why you selected him sir." Gerhardt said dourly. "I don't see Generaloberst Dietrich as a friend of our cause under any circumstances, he is too old school to change."

"The General could be helpful." Von Tanz said. "Carl wants to impress his father."

"I have to be honest sir." Gerhardt said sharply. "This is not the mission for Carl to prove his manhood."

"It's too late for that." Von Tanz said dryly. "What are your feelings working with the enemy?"

Gerhardt lit a cigarette. "They have the same objective as us. I don't have to like them I suppose."

"I imagine the feeling is mutual." Von Tanz said wryly. "British intelligence is not in the soul-saving business or are we Major?"

"That is an understatement sir." Gerhardt said plainly realizing that the British and the Americans were obviously taking advantage of the situation. Under similar circumstances they would be doing the same thing."

"You must make it clear to your associates if you should run into any trouble Anton." Von Tanz said firmly. "There is no way I can help you."

"That much trouble sir." Gerhardt said. "I plan to be beyond your help since I will be dead."

"I'm not planning for you to die." Von Tanz said. "This will be a simple mission Major. Krieger's own ambition will do him in. He will grab this golden opportunity to be the next Heydrich."

"Being dead in some godforsaken village in the Alps is not high on my list sir." Gerhardt said firmly. "Will you monitor the situation?"

"I will not be associated with this in anyway major." Von Tanz said. "When do you leave for Stuttgart?"

"I was planning on tomorrow sir." Gerhardt said.

"Will Franz meet you there?" Von Tanz asked.

"I have no idea about him sir." Gerhardt said. "He moves about like a ghost."

"What about young Dietrich?" Von Tanz asked seriously. "I would allow you to replace him if we had the time."

"He should be fine." Gerhardt said dryly. "He is not a field operative."

"I never said he was Anton." Von Tanz said. "His father has decided on an object lesson for his wayward son."

"This is no walk in the park sir." Gerhardt said bluntly.

"Just don't get yourself killed Major." Von Tanz said dourly. "That would greatly distress me."

"That would greatly upset my wife if I did that sir." Gerhardt said. "If I have to may I send Dietrich back?"

"If comes to that Anton." Von Tanz said. "Send him to Munich and tell him to contact me when he gets there."

[2]
10:00 hrs

Tweedmuir Scotland
RAF Station

The Air Officer Commanding of the RAF station, Group Captain Roger Witcombe, escorted his guests into the nearly deserted Officer's Mess. Witcombe was a large ruddy looking man with wavy red hair. He had flown with the Royal Flying Corps during the first war and stayed in the newly formed Royal Air Force. Witcombe saw active service in the Third Afghan War and policing Iraq. In the 1930s Witcombe became an instructor at Cranwell and when he thought about retiring his old flying companion, Austen-Halton, arranged to have him command the once abandon base in Tweedmuir.

"Major Colquhoun and his people are settling in nicely." Witcombe said with a half-smile on his face. "Since we are in the middle of nowhere they have no choice."

"That's why we use this place Roger." Austen-Halton said.

"Is there anything wrong sir?" Witcombe asked.

"No, nothing is wrong at your end Roger." Sir Peter said. "Is the bomber ready?"

"Yes." Witcombe said. "How the hell did you get the Air Ministry to part with it sir?"

"We bought it." Crawford said. "Colonel Burton has the two pilots in the village."

"Do you want Colquhoun?" Witcombe asked.

"Bring him to your office Roger." Austen-Halton said.

Colquhoun was surprised that Austen-Halton and Crawford had made the long trip from Twickem-Hallesy to Scotland. Neither man struck him as the sentimental type.

"Did I forget to sign a requisition for toilet paper?" Colquhoun asked.

"War is a fluid situation." Crawford said. "Things change constantly. Being a sarcastic wit is not what is needed."

"Change how sir?" Colquhoun asked.

"This concerns Krieger." Austen-Halton said.

"I don't have to love him to get him out alive." Colquhoun said flatly.

"Circumstances make its necessary to give you more information Major." Sir Peter said lighting his cigar.

"I already know too much about the bastard sir." Colquhoun said flatly.

"Krieger is a Nazi." Austen-Halton said plainly. "However, he is Our Nazi."

"What?" Colquhoun hissed. "That bastard works for us?"

"He is one of Halton's best men." Crawford said.

"Then why all this, is this costume drama?" Colquhoun growled sharply.

"That is why we are here Major." Sir Peter said in a cold voice. "Your mission is to fail Major."

"You people are insane." Colquhoun said bluntly.

"That is not the point Colquhoun." Crawford said stiffly. "Obedience to orders is."

"Why select me to handle this mission?" Colquhoun asked firmly.

"The answer should be obvious even to you Colquhoun." Crawford said in a dull voice looking directly at him. "You have one failure already."

"So I am expendable sir." Colquhoun rasped.

"Only if you want to be expendable, you don't have to die." Crawford said. "This will be your only chance to get your career out of the toilet Major."

"You are risking seven men's lives for nothing?" Colquhoun hissed. "What gives you that right?"

"We are fighting our war." Crawford said bluntly. "There are no rules in our war."

"Why is this man so important?" Colquhoun rasped.

"*Albatross* is very important to us." Austen-Halton said firmly. "He is helping to shorten this war. He is being hounded by an Abwehr general by the name of von Tanz." Sir Paul paused. "This failed attempt to kidnap him will prove his loyalty."

"But why is the money needed?" Colquhoun asked.

"War is won on many fronts," Crawford said. "Nazis are very expensive people to bribe Colquhoun."

"Noble as it sounds you're still risking seven lives." Colquhoun said.

"We picked your team Major." Crawford hissed wryly. "They all have screwed up in there military careers. This is their only chance for redemption."

"Dying is the only way to erase a black mark?" Colquhoun rasped.

"We are not sending you out to die." Austen-Halton said firmly. "All of you should come back from this theater of the absurd." Austen-Halton relit his cigar. "Krieger won't know what is going on and will make his performance more realistic."

"Unfortunately the other krauts will be playing for real." Colquhoun said tersely.

"Do what you have to." Crawford said. "This is still war."

"Who thought of this harebrained scheme?" Colquhoun asked tartly.

"Your knowing that will not help you on this mission Colquhoun." Crawford said stiffly. "You will be the only one in your little group to know the entire truth."

"Marvelous." Colquhoun hissed. "What if I get killed?"

"Captain Mannerling will continue the mission without your special information." Sir Peter said sternly. "Then it will be every man for him self if further trouble happens down the road."

Colquhoun had a cold shiver run down his spine as he lit a cigarette. "There is more isn't there?"

"Astute observation on your part major for once, there are more you should know of an unpleasant nature." Crawford said glumly.

"I'm waiting for the punch line sir." Colquhoun said sourly.

"We must save Krieger from his enemies." Austen-Halton said.

"Why?" Colquhoun said. "He is still a traitor no matter how you look at it."

"Albatross" Austen-Halton said in a low voice. "Is not a German, he is as English."

"Is this what this von Tanz has on him?" Colquhoun asked.

"A crud named Skasch is supposed to be selling a list of allied agents to Krieger." Austen-Halton said. "You'll be impersonating him. There is no list Major. Von Tanz hopes to catch Krieger with the list and find his name on the list."

"What about this Skasch?" Colquhoun quipped.

"He is quietly removed by the Russians." Crawford said flatly. "The removal will be permanent."

"Krieger and Skasch have never met." Austen-Halton said flatly. "Nor does von Tanz know what Skasch look like."

"Just follow orders this time Colquhoun." Crawford said sternly. "Then everyone comes out alive and a hero."

[3]
13:00 hrs

Tweedmuir
Officer's Mess

"I see nothing has improved here sir." Mannerling said putting down his coffee mug. "You people should learn how to make coffee with the Yanks here."

"The coffee seems fine to me." Austen-Halton said.

"This tastes like it was make from the residue of an outhouse." Mannerling said in a dry voice. "However, you didn't order me here to critique the bloody coffee."

"That is a very astute observation Major." Crawford hissed. "There has been a new wrinkle added to this venture."

"Why doesn't that surprise me?" Mannerling said as he lit a cigarette. "What or who this time?"

Sir Peter removed a cigar from his traveling pocket humidor and lit it. "The Russians have changed the dimensions of this operation."

"How deep are the Russians involved in this party?" Mannerling asked.

"They are deeply involved." Crawford said angrily. "In my opinion they are too involved."

"Involved how?" Mannerling asked.

"Colonel Mikhailov has informed us that they have a deep undercover agent involved in this." Sir Peter said in his matter-of-fact voice. "He has been deep for over twenty years."

"How is he involved sir?" Mannerling asked. "The Russians are a paranoid bunch of crazies. Is he on the fringes of this?"

"I'm afraid not." Sir Peter said glumly. "He is in the middle of this insanity."

"Don't tell me he is goddamn Krieger." Mannerling snarled.

"That would make it easier for us." Austen-Halton said. "No he is not *Albatross* either."

"Who is he then?" Mannerling asked.

"Our Russian friends won't tell us." Crawford said.

"How the hell will I know?" Mannerling asked.

"He will contact you if he has to." Crawford said.

"What about Colquhoun?" Mannerling asked. "Is he on this page?"

"Only you and Orr will know about him only exception is under extreme circumstance." Sir Peter said flatly.

"What about our German friends?" Mannerling asked somberly.

"Under no circumstances are they to know." Crawford said. "They are dealing with us only, the Russians are not involved."

"Okay." Mannerling said. "How will I know him?"

"He'll contact you." Sir Peter said.

[4]
14:15 hrs

London
Soviet Embassy

The three men sat at a table in the private dining room of the Ambassador. Major General Pushkin removed the cigarette from the gold cigarette case and lit it. "How did our Allies take the news Colonel?"

"Not as shocked as I expected them to be." Mikhailov said flatly.

"Explain that Comrade Colonel." Sergeyev said bluntly.

"It is very hard to explain Comrade General." Mikhailov said clearly.

"Try to explain Colonel." Pushkin rasped. "We are all university graduates."

"They seem to know about the existence of *Boris*." Mikhailov said dourly. "There was no surprise on their faces or in their eyes."

"Austen-Halton's face would remain granite even if he was on fire." Pushkin said pouring the vodka into a large glass. "I don't know the American well enough to comment."

"General Crawford was a policeman before the war." Sergeyev said passing Mikhailov a cigarette.

"Militia, they allowed him to be a general? The Capitalists are truly doomed having a militiaman as an intelligence officer." Pushkin quipped sarcastically.

"The New York City Police are not the People's militia." Sergeyev said. "Crawford served with their Flying Squad, their idea of Special Branch." Sergeyev looked at Mikhailov. "Did Crawford register any surprise?"

"None, absolutely expressionless, Crawford had dead eyes." Mikhailov said.

"The British had to assume that we have deep agents in Germany." Pushkin said. "It would be abnormal if we hadn't."

Mikhailov lit the American cigarette. "Who will control *Boris* Comrade General?"

"Moscow Central will, Colonel." Sergeyev said firmly.

"Do you know who *Boris* is in this play?" Mikhailov asked.

"His identity is irrelevant to your part in this operation." Pushkin said straightforwardly.

"Sergei Alexandrovich you will pack your suit case with civilian clothes and return to Twickem-Hallesy." Sergeyev said standing up from the table. "Our friends have been told you will be returning tonight."

"How long will I be there Comrade General?" Mikhailov asked.

"You will remain until there is a resolution either way Sergei Alexandrovich." Sergeyev said. "Just be observant and polite, after all they are Allies."

Pushkin poured himself another drink watching Mikhailov leave the room. "Is he the right man for this?"

"He hasn't gone Spanish Yuri." Sergeyev said firmly. "Sending someone else would only arouse suspicion with our Allies." Sergeyev poured himself a drink. "They are already distrustful of us."

"I meant is Moscow getting sentimental?" Pushkin hissed. "One slip could be dangerous for him."

"Moscow has no tears Yuri." Sergeyev said coldly. "There is no reason for *Boris* or Sergei to learn anything. This is not a touch of sentiment on Moscow's part, just an unfortunate coincidence." Sergeyev drank his drink in one gulp. "Moscow only wants the survival of *Boris*."

"Someone should tell him." Pushkin said critically. "Mikhailov is a good officer; something like this could ruin him."

"That is Moscow's job, not ours." Sergeyev said.

"You have become a cold-hearted bastard Semyon." Pushkin said bluntly.

"Showing a sentimental side Yuri?" Sergeyev quipped. "Comrade Beria won't like that."

[5]
17:35 hrs

Tweedmuir
AOC Office

Mannerling lit his woodsman's pipe and tossed the wooden match into the ashtray. "Do they wonder around at night Roger?"

"They are confined to a barracks on the far side of the base." Roger said. "My RSM runs a tight ship Edward and Colquhoun knows his men shoot to kill."

"Sounds like you have them under control Roger." Mannerling said. "Now tell me where in hell did you get the JU-52?"

"Just bloody luck I'm afraid." Witcombe said. "She was doing a weather check up north when they ran into a freak storm and crashed in a field. Some farmers found her relatively intact and contacted the RAF."

"What happened to the crew?" Mannerling asked.

"The coroner said they had been electrocuted." Witcombe said. "Lightning must have hit the plane. She managed a fluke to land at all. I always need aircraft for my airline and Boysenberry has been fixing her up."

"I need a place to hide Roger." Mannerling said wryly.

"No need old friend." Roger said. "I have a nifty Luftwaffe uniform that will fit you; the R/O sits up front."

"Are Crosbie and Daulton flying the mission?" Mannerling asked.

"The front office is bringing in two Luftwaffe POWs to fly this mission." Witcombe said.

"Really, that is hardly comforting Roger." Mannerling said sardonically. "Did Sir Peter or Crawford bother to tell you why?"

"They mumbled something about the XX Committee." Roger said stoking up his pipe. "It seems they plan to have my JU-52 fly on to Hertzberg Luftwaffe base."

"What the bloody hell for?" Mannerling asked.

"I make it a policy not to ask too many questions." Witcombe quipped. "However, I heard the sum of £ 25,000 each has been deposited in the Rothmann Bank, an incentive to return."

"Who are they? Goering's long lost sons?" Mannerling growled damningly. £ 25,000 pounds was ten years salary for him.

"I don't know." Witcombe said stiffly. "Are you heading back to London?"

"No." Mannerling said. "I have a room in the village and Johnson will drive me to the train depot."

Chapter Five
December 3, 1942
17:00 hrs

Stuttgart, Germany
Wulfbrau Gasthof

Gerhardt watched the bluish-white smoke from his cigarette as it swirled slowly toward the naked light bulb that hung over the bed of his third rate Gasthof room. Gerhardt closed his eyes realizing that this room was paradise in comparison to the frozen countryside of Russia that he had left nine months ago.

Gerhardt's career as a field intelligence officer ended outside of Leningrad nine months ago courtesy of a Red sniper having an off day. The bullet had struck him just above the hip chipping the top of the bone scattering bone fragments all over the place. Fortunately, for Gerhardt, they flew him to Riga for proper medical treatment.

Hauptman Gerhardt returned to active duty five months later with only a slight hardly noticeable limp. For six weeks, Gerhardt supervised the record section at the Home Army depot in Leipzig. Later he was transferred to a subsection of the Brandenburg section of the Abwehr commanded by von Tanz and promoted to major. It did not take long to realize that von Tanz's section was not composed of ardent Nazis. Gerhardt also quickly learned that they were very sympathetic to the officially nonexistence resistance. This sympathy only expressed with in the confines of the section, von Tanz had hand picked each man in the section.

Gerhardt had been an eyewitness to the 'pacification' of Russia by the SS. The Einsatzkommando would just drive into a village, town or city. They would round up all the Russians in the place and then just shoot them. Any local Army commanders, who had any objections, where told to mind their own damn business, if they pressed the matter, they were transferred to another sector with a notation on their records were made. In some isolated case, Gerhardt heard that the Army did manage to stop the killing, but the reprieve was short lived lasting only until the Army moved out.

Gerhardt sat up on the bed, crushed out his cigarette, and lit another. Von Tanz had made it very clear to him that detection meant death, not a quick death, but a long lingering death at the hands of the SD. There was no way that Gerhardt could explain to the SS why four Abwehr agents were escorting seven enemy agents near the Swiss border. Gerhardt would make that part very clear to them. Gerhardt had already made up his own mind that he did not intend to be taken alive by the SS under any circumstance.

A light rap came from the door. Gerhardt slid his hand under the pillow and removed the pistol pulling back the slide of the P-38.

"Enter." Gerhardt said pointing the pistol at the door. The door opened and the familiar shape of Lars Lang entered the room. Korvette-Kapitan Lang looked out of place wearing an Army uniform. Lang had been Gerhardt's partner since his arrival at the section.

Lars Martin Luther Lang was two years older that Anton and had been a naval officer since 1928. He had the normal tour of duty of a junior naval officer in the minuscule German navy until 1933 when he became one of the naval attaches assigned to President von Hindenburg. He served in that capacity until the elderly president died in August of 1934. The new Fuehrer dismissed all the military attaché and Lang ended up on the old battleship *Deutschland*. Later in the year, Lang moved to OKM (High Command Navy) in Berlin.

Lang stayed in Berlin until 1938 when assigned to the new heavy cruiser *Prinz Eugen*. When the cruiser left port for its war station in late August 1939 Oberleutnant zur See Lang was missing. He was in the naval hospital in Kiel recovering from a ruptured gall bladder. Lang did not return to full active duty until early 1940. Lars, bored with his desk job in Hamburg, volunteered for the U-boat service. After training in the Baltic, he was assigned to Lorient France.

Lang stayed with the U-boats until March of 1941 rising to the rank of First Watch Officer when his promising career with the U-boats ended. His boat was recharging its batteries on the surface in the Bay of Biscay when a British Sutherland flying boat found them and blew them out of the water. Only six men besides Lang survived.

After five months in hospital, Lang found himself in Southern Russia. Assigned to the naval task force ordered to get the docks in Odessa into working condition to receive supplies from their ally Bulgaria. Lang found the Bulgars to be thoroughly disgusting in their zeal to steal everything that was not nailed down.

Lang, like many of his fellow military officers, closed his eyes and ears to the excesses of the Nazis until he hit Russia. Lang tried to stop an SS Lieutenant from shooting some Russian dockworkers for no reason. The SS officer knocked him down and proceeded with the execution. When the Lieutenant turned, around to deal with the bothersome naval officer Lang shot him between the eyes. Lang rescued by his men from the other SS and turned over to the naval authorities. The SS demanded that Lang be turnover to them, but the Admiral convinced them that Lang was insane. Lang transferred out of Russia and buried in the historical section of OKM in Berlin until January 1942 when he quietly transferred to the Abwehr.

"The automobile is ready Anton." Lang said flatly. "'34 Mercedes-Benz painted a lovely Wehrmacht gray. Franz is waiting in the cafe for us and rover-boy." Lang looked around the room. "Where in hell is the hero?"

"There is no need to wait for Carl." Gerhardt said as he buttoned his tunic jacket.

"I don't like the sound of that." Lang said gruffly.

"Papa wanted him." Anton said.

"The general said he was important." Lang said sternly. "Besides, he knows too much for him to be away from us."

"One doesn't argue with a Generaloberst." Anton said crisply.

"Hell, the whores in Stuttgart will have a rest." Lang said sourly.

"He can't say a damn word without putting a noose around his neck." Gerhardt said lighting a cigarette.

"That really makes me feel good." Lang said cynically.

"You look quite good in feldgrau." Gerhardt said.

Lang smiled. "A Kriegsmarine officer might look a bit odd to the Grenzpolizei near the Swiss border."

"You might belong to the Swiss Navy." Gerhardt said.

"I'm not that good of an actor." Lang said. "Where do we meet our playmates?"

"Woodcutters shack ten kilometers from the drop zone." Gerhardt said.

"That sounds delightful." Lang said. "Did they give you a name?"

"I am *Praetorian*." Gerhardt said. "His name isn't important."

"Was it was wise to let Dietrich wander away?" Lang asked.

"Majors don't generally argue with General officers." Gerhardt said bluntly.

"It's all of our lives Anton." Lang said in a tart voice. "You had other choice."

"Killing him would serve no useful purpose." Gerhardt said bluntly. "The General would know who killed him the moment he heard. The body of a general's son would bring the SIPO."

"He has no guts." Lang said. "He'll spill his guts the moment the Gestapo sneezes at him."

"He won't betray us." Gerhardt said confidently. "Dietrich is too afraid of dying."

"A coward does strange things." Lang hissed. "Survival is the name of the game Anton and he knows that."

"Coward is too strong a word." Anton said flatly. "Carl is just a man afraid of facing the truth. He has just realized that there is something else in the world besides Adolf Hitler and that is scaring the hell out of him."

[2]

As they left the seedy Gasthof room Anton hoped that Lang half believed his story about Carl. General von Tanz had not ordered the lieutenant back to Berlin; Carl just disappeared. Gerhardt had a good idea why Dietrich bolted- family honor.

Carl Henrik Ludwig Dietrich was from an old-line military family dating back to the days of Frederick the Great. His great-grandfather Manfred was the first in the family to hold a commission in the Prussian Army and was killed at Waterloo in 1815. His grandfather Ludwig, as a Major in the Colonial Army, was killed putting down a native revolt in Tanganyika in 1905; his father rose quickly in the Army- Generalleutnant in 1911; General of Infantry -1914; and promoted to Generaloberst in October 1918 by the Kaiser on recommendation of his friend Paul von Hindenburg. Carl was the product of his father's second marriage to a much younger woman. All of his stepbrothers during the First War died.

Why his father forced him to become part of this only Carl knew. His attempt to play the hero was a failure when the pressure became too much. The simple fact that the Gestapo was not breaking down the Gasthof room door told Gerhardt that he was not attempting to be the belated hero either. As a precaution, Gerhardt informed the local military police commander that Colonel General Dietrich's son was missing. Gerhardt told the commander that Carl had a severe drinking problem and often wandered off. Gerhardt asked the commander to keep him under house arrest incommunicado if they found him. Gerhardt stressed the fact that Carl was mentally unstable and nothing he said would be true. The military police commander said he understood the problem and asked Gerhardt if Dietrich had served on the Eastern Front. Gerhardt told him yes and the military police commander seemed satisfied. He could not worry any more about Dietrich now.

Oberleutnant Fredrich Franz was drinking ersatz hot chocolate in the small cafe a few blocks from the Gasthof. Gerhardt and Lang saw the Mercedes-Benz parked out front with the proper Wehrmacht number plates and decals identifying the automobile as belong to the 177th Infantry Regiment and Oberst Mueller in particular. Franz was not part of von Tanz's section. Neither Gerhardt nor Lang knew if Franz was his real name or even if he belonged to the Abwehr.

"Is it stolen?" Gerhardt asked sitting down at the table.

"You cut me to the quick Herr Major." Franz said mockingly. "That classic automobile is own by my third cousin's second husband."

"Oberst Mueller will not miss the tags?" Lang quipped.

"No." Franz said. "Traveling a little light Herr Major?"

"Carl was recalled to Berlin." Gerhardt said.
"Things are developing quickly." Franz rasped. "He is not that stable Herr Major."
"He is not going." Gerhardt said. "I'll explain later."
"That should be entertaining on our long drive." Franz mused. "Are you ready?"
"Yes." Gerhardt said.

[3]
17:40 hrs

Potsdam
Dietrich Estate

The estate was a gift from King William-Frederick to Generaloberst Dietrich's grandfather in lieu of ennobling him. The great house was the center place of the Dietrich family and they in turn kept the estate pristine in appearance. Despite being a military family the Dietrich's were patrons of the arts and the great house was adorn with great work of arts and the music of Mozart.

Colonel General Maximillan Wilhelm Dietrich's military career began as an officer cadet during the Franco-Prussian War at the age of 15 and by 1911 was a Generalleutnant in command of the 112th Infantry Division. By the end of the war, Dietrich was promoted to Colonel-General and given a command in southern Germany before Austria-Hungary surrendered. Dietrich was offered a position in the Reichwehr as a Generalmajor, which he refused and retired.

During the post war years, Dietrich kept in contact with the old and new officer corps. Unlike von Hindenburg and Ludendorff, Dietrich avoided active politics. However, he was a keen observer of the political climate in Germany. The General was wise enough to keep his personal opinion of Hitler and the regime to himself except to a few friends who thought like him. Dietrich was now a sick and tired 87 year old man whom rarely left the estate, but had not lost his senses. Dietrich's closest associate and confident was the estate manager Oberst Hans Maatz, who had served as his adjutant during the First World War. In order to see the General one had to go through Maatz.

Maatz entered his private office in the carriage house near the great house to find an unwanted and unexpected visitor.

"Carl." Maatz hissed. "What in hell are you doing here?"

"I need to see my father Hans." Carl said stiffly ignoring the fact Maatz was a retired colonel.

"Your father is not receiving visitors." Maatz rasped. "Dr. Anspach's orders I'm afraid."

"I'm not the manure salesman." Carl snapped. "I am his son goddamnit."

"Quite right Herr Leutnant." Maatz said coldly. "Who is a serving officer in the Wehrmacht 800 kilometers from where he is supposed to be."

"Committing suicide is not part of my orders." Carl said bluntly. "Take me to the house now!"

"That is impossible." Maatz said bluntly. "Even if he wasn't ill you know the General would not see you." Maatz paused and lit a cigarette. "You are not with Major Gerhardt."

"I never wanted to be in on this madness Maatz." Carl snarled frustratedly. "I was forced to go and you damn well know it."

"Turning tale and running is not the answer either." Maatz said. "The General gave his word."

"This is treason." Dietrich said bluntly.

"The General doesn't see it that way." Maatz said. "This is a matter of honor to him now."

"I just don't care." Carl rasped.

"If you don't care Herr Leutnant you know what to do." Maatz hissed. "Denounce the General."

"He might be crazy, but he is still my father Herr Oberst." Carl snapped. "That is why I must explain it to him."

Maatz crushed out the cigarette and promptly lit another one. He then walked over to the wall size portrait of Frederick the Great. "I thought committing suicide was against your religion Carl?" Maatz turned and faced Dietrich.

"Suicide Herr Oberst?" Carl quipped. "What the hell are you talking about?"

"You tell your father that you have deserted your post he will shoot you himself." Maatz said bluntly.

"I'm his son for Christssake!" Carl muttered.

"Family Honor my young Dietrich." Maatz said plainly. "Weren't you listening to him when he talked about the family?"

"He droned on for hours about that dribble." Carl hissed. "By the age of ten I stopped listening."

"A little family history Herr Leutnant it might save your life." Maatz said grimly. "Your Great Grand Uncle Leopold, a colonel in the Guards shot your Great Grand Uncle Gert for leaving his post at Waterloo."

"For what reason did he shoot him Maatz?" Carl asked somberly.

"Gert went to the field hospital to check on his son Manfred." Maatz said. "He had no orders to go to the field hospital which was technical desertion." Maatz crushed out the cigarette as he walked back to his desk. "Court-martial found Leopold innocent, but twenty years later Manfred walked in the War office and emptied a revolver into Leopold. Manfred was tried and hung."

"The moral?" Carl hissed.

"The General will kill you." Maatz said plainly. "My suggestion is to find Major Gerhardt and complete your mission."

Dietrich shook his head. "What Gerhardt is going to do is doomed to fail. I rather get shot by my demented father than fall into the hands of the SD."

"You know the plan Carl." Maatz said. "Is there a chokepoint?"

Carl lit a cigarette. "I can't do it alone. Gerhardt is a tough man Maatz."

"I have contacts." Maatz said coldly. "They will help you with this problem."

"Military?" Carl asked.

"They are ex-military Carl, very good ex-military." Maatz said stiffly.

"Expensive no doubt Herr Oberst?" Carl hissed.

"They have a set price Carl." Maatz said. "They will not barter for a lower price."

"Make the deal Maatz." Dietrich said bluntly. "My father, what will he know?"

"He will know nothing." Maatz said. "Is killing Gerhardt necessary?"

"It shouldn't be necessary to kill our own people." Dietrich said.

"I'll arrange for travel orders for you Carl." Maatz said. "Stay here until I make the necessary arrangements."

"You still have prewar liquor." Carl. said. "I'll be content."

[4]
18:00 hrs

Tweedmuir
Team Barracks

    Larsen went to the pot-bellied stove and poured himself a cup of coffee. "Do you want coffee Major?"
    "No." Colquhoun said. "How can you drink that stuff?"
    "Taste as good as camp coffee." Larsen said dully.
    "You said camp coffee Captain?" Colquhoun asked. "Boy scouts don't drink coffee."
    "During summers I worked as a ranch hand on my uncle's ranch in Montana." Larsen said.
    "So you are a real cowboy Larsen." Colquhoun said. "How did you end up in the infantry?"
    "I took ROTC in college." Larsen said. "In 1940 it was a good idea when it looked like the draft was coming into the picture." Larsen sat down at the table. "You graduated from the Point."
    "I belonged to the Class of '38 Captain Larsen." Colquhoun said.
    "The name is Sam." Larsen said.
    "I'm not your friend." Colquhoun said. "I don't want to be your friend. I just want to finish this mission and get out alive."
    "You did volunteer sir." Larsen rasped. "I volunteered."
    Colquhoun should his head as he it a cigarette. "You volunteered for this insanity?"
    "Yes." Larsen said.
    "Have you any combat experience?" Colquhoun asked cynically.
    "I have been shot at before." Larsen said. "I served as a County Deputy Sheriff before I graduated from College."
    "Crawford didn't tell me what unit you're from Larsen?" Colquhoun asked.
    "The Rangers Major." Larsen said. "I broke my arm two weeks into training and have been pushing papers ever since."
    Colquhoun crushed out the cigarette and poured himself a shot of Scotch. "Everyone have their uniforms fixed?"
    "Witcombe has a very good tailor in residence." Larsen said. "The men don't like this part of the mission."
    "I don't give a damn if they do." Colquhoun said. "What does Captain Madden say?"
    "The man is a Royal Marine." Larsen said bluntly. "He just obeys orders without question."
    "I want the German lessons to increase to six hours a day." Colquhoun said in a blunt voice. "They have to eat, think, and act German."
    "Have your friends from told you anything about the contact?" Larsen asked.

"We don't need him until we get into the village." Colquhoun said. "Our rally point is the Donner barn."

"One question Major if I may?" Larsen asked somberly.

"Okay one question." Colquhoun answered as he lit another cigarette.

"You obviously have no faith in this mission Major." Larsen said firmly. "So why in hell did you volunteer?"

"Whatever gave you the idea that I volunteered?" Colquhoun grunted.

[5]
21:45 hrs

Twickem-Hallesy
The Manor house

Colonel Tremayne entered the living room and approached Crawford, Sir Peter and Lord Crosland.

"You are looking grimmer than usual James." Lord Crosland said as he lit his pipe.

"Lieutenant Griffin at the gate has a bit of a problem sir." Tremayne said.

"What sort of problem Colonel?" Lord Crosland asked.

"He has a Russian Colonel wanting to come to the house sir." Tremayne said. "He is not on the list."

"Did Griffin bother to tell you his name?" Sir Peter asked.

"Griffin says it is Colonel Mikhailov." Tremayne said. "He has a sealed letter."

"Call the gate and tell Griffin to escort him to the house." Lord Crosland said. "Then call London Control."

"What the hell are the Russians up to?" Crawford asked grimly.

"We'll find out soon enough." Sir Peter said.

Colonel Mikhailov entered the living room and sat down in the chair Lord Crosland motioned him to sit in. "Has London called back gentlemen?"

"They were very prompt." Sir Peter said. "You have a letter?"

"Yes." Mikhailov said removing the envelope from inside his uniform coat pocket. "Just gives the written details of the verbal orders you received."

"We like everything to be in proper form." Lord Crosland said. "How long will you be here?"

"I will be here until the operation is completed gentlemen one way or another." Mikhailov said.

"This is a highly unusual request Colonel." Crawford stated. "You people haven't been interested in joint operations."

"This is because we have involved *Boris* in this venture." Mikhailov said flatly. "Moscow has made a formal request that London and Washington cooperate."

"I see no problems Colonel." Lord Crosland said. "Colonel Tremayne will bring to your room. For security purposes you will please confine yourself to the manor house."

"I fully understand." Mikhailov said standing.

Crawford lit one of Austen-Halton's cigars violently. "Those bastards are up to something."

"Of course they are up to something." Lord Crosland said. "That has always been their nature. Stalin wasn't helping the Republican side in Spain because he believed in democracy."

"Do we have any idea who the hell this *Boris* is?" Crawford asked. "He is like an itch I can't scratch."

"We have nothing on him." Sir Peter said. "Germany after the First War was a very easy place to mingle."

"How much to we tell him?" Crawford asked.

"Only what is needed." Crosland said sternly. "Peter, you best inform Greene to keep his eyes open for increase Soviet activity."

"That will not please our Swiss friends." Crawford said. "They like their image of being neutral."

"Greene has full confidence in his Swiss contact." Sir Peter said. "I have full confidence in Greene."

"Just watch what you say around Mikhailov." Crawford said. "I find the Soviets overly touchy."

"Quite." Sir Peter said. "You will find Colonel Mikhailov a keen observer of the human condition."

[6]
23:30 hrs

Dietrich Estate

Maatz pour Weiss a drink, bourbon neat from the General's pre-war stock. "How much will it cost?"

"Myself and four men Colonel you are talking $10,000 American." Weiss said. "How dangerous will this be?"

"Moderate." Maatz answered.

"Any killing required?" Weiss asked sitting down.

"I want no live witnesses to contradict Herr Leutnant Dietrich's after action report." Maatz said icily.

"Who am I suppose to kill, if it is not a state secret?" Weiss asked somberly.

"Seven allied agents." Maatz said matter-of-factly.

"Is his majesty coming?" Weiss asked.

"Yes." Maatz said. "He is to be protected at all times."

"I find this interesting all of this Herr Maatz." Weiss said. "Where and when?"

Maatz lit a cigarette. "The where is Adlerberghof and the when is six days from now."

"You couldn't find anyplace more remote?" Weiss hissed. "The place is in the middle of nowhere."

"We did not pick the place." Maatz said. "Is there a problem?"

"I see none." Weiss said flatly. "The price will have to go up."

"How much will it be my old friend?" Maatz asked.

"The price is now $15,000 dollars in American money." Weiss said. "Use the Rothmann Bank in Zurich to transfer the money. The Reichbank watches currency very carefully and we don't want the Kripo nosing around."

"Rothmann's is a Jewish banking house." Maatz rasped.

"They are Swiss my friend." Weiss said. "They move foreign currency all the time."

"That is courting danger." Maatz hissed.

"Living without danger is boring my friend." Weiss said. "Tell his majesty I'll meet him in Munich in two days. He'll need traveling orders and a new identity."

"I'll handle that." Maatz said. "I'll send a telegram to your hotel by 9:00 AM."

Dietrich entered the room and moved directly to the bar and poured himself a large drink then sat down. "How do you know a creature like him Maatz?"

"Weiss was a storm trooper during the war." Maatz said. "After the war he join the Free Corps and latter the Black Reichwehr. His little group hired out as guards to political parties to protect rallies."

"He didn't raise an eyebrow about the Allies." Dietrich said. "I can't believe he is the resistance."

"He isn't." Maatz said grimly. "This is strictly business to him."

"If the Gestapo offered him more money, would he betray you?" Dietrich asked.

"He would." Maatz said honestly.

"How can you trust a man like that?" Dietrich asked sharply.

"Weiss is an honest man." Maatz said. "Finish your drink Carl that is your last one until this is over."

"What the hell are you talking about?" Carl hissed.

"Weiss will not tolerate a cowardly drunk." Maatz said bluntly. "I don't want to report to the General that he has a dead hero."

An Honorable Betrayal

Chapter Six
December 6, 1942
21:00 hrs

Tweedmuir, Scotland
RAF Base

    Seven men dressed in plain flight-suits walked slowly towards the lone plane on the runway. They were two hours behind schedule because the German JU-52 had developed engine trouble and took almost two hours to fix. The usual chatter of a flight crew was absent and the men approached the bomber in silence. The chief mechanic gave the okay and they headed for the plane.

    Two men stood by the bomber's hatchway. The man chewing on his cigar standing on the left was Colonel Larry Burton, USAAC, one of Crawford's men. On the right was Group Captain Witcombe. The Group Captain ran the SOE's taxi service that brought agents in and out of Occupied Europe. The usual form of taxi was the Lysander, but the target was beyond its range and it could not handle seven men.

    The first man in line was Captain Harry Madden, Royal Marines. The captain was a professional soldier of more than thirty years. He had come up through the ranks obtaining his commission during the final months of the First World War. The interval between the two wars had not been kind to Madden. The end of the war dropped him back to second lieutenant and it took him twenty years to get back to captain. Madden had been on seven commando raids since the beginning of the war. Madden had avoided a general court-martial for striking two enlisted after a mission by volunteering for this assignment.

    Following him was Lieutenant Lionel Carey, Royal Engineers. Carey looked like a typical college student. His specialty was blowing things up that did not belong to him. Carey used this talent when he was not on raids to open safes. Scotland Yard caught trying to open a safe in a private bank two months ago. They gave him the choice of forty years at hard labor or going on this mission. Carey took the deal simply because he could keep his commission because the Army would transfer him to the Sudan when he came back.

    The third man was Flight Officer Gerald Browne, United States Army Air Force. He was a qualified pilot and radio operator. Browne could make a radio out of anything. Despite his calm demeanor, Browne had fought in Spain with the Abraham Lincoln brigade. Browne was actually a volunteer for this mission.

    The fourth man was Staff Sergeant John Gregg, United States Marine Corps. Gregg spoke fluent German, French, and Italian. His peacetime occupation had been a high school teacher in Maine. Gregg refused a commission when he joined the Marines in 1936. Gregg served in the Far East for three years were he developed a violent streak against prostitutes. Gregg was waiting execution for the murder of a prostitute in London when they made the deal. The British authorities were not too pleased to let Gregg slip through their hands.

    The fifth man was Corporal Peter Reed, United States Army. Reed was an eighteen-year veteran of the Marine Corps/Army. He had fought in the 'Banana Wars' in Central America and a few years in China. Reed was an expert tracker and sniper. Reed's problem was with the bottle and women, married women. The Army was charging Reed with adultery with an officer's wife.

    The sixth and seventh men were Colquhoun and Larsen. They stopped at the hatch.

    "The weather will be clear over the target." Burton said.

"What about snow?" Larsen asked.

"You'll be in the mountains." Burton said. "It could snow anytime."

"Cloudy would have been better." Colquhoun said.

"The JU-52 allows you fly lower." Witcombe said. "Pilots dislike flying into mountains Major and the Germans won't give it a second thought."

"The JU-52 avoids anti-aircraft fire." Larsen said.

"You'll follow the commercial neutral flight corridor into Switzerland." Burton said in a flat voice. "Then you'll veer off course into Germany."

"The Swiss will send up fighters." Colquhoun said.

"I have good pilots." Witcombe said. "There will be radio silence. Good luck."

Burton and Witcombe watched in silence as the bomber sped down the runway and launched itself into the black sky.

"This is very weird Witty, even for you." Burton grunted lighting a cigar.

"Strange." Witcombe conceded. "The bomber was schedule for the scrap heap; Batton's men did a magnificent job to get it flying."

"How did Mannerling draw this hand?" Burton asked.

"Who the bloody hell knows." Witcombe said. "Colquhoun has no idea he is aboard."

"Did they tell Mannerling about the bomb?" Burton asked wryly.

"The bastards most likely did not." Witcombe rasped. "That wouldn't make Mannerling happy."

"What about the pilots?" Burton hissed.

"No." Witcombe said. "They are expendable because they are German."

"You lied to them." Burton grunted.

"Damn right." Witcombe said. "Will Grafton be ready to fly into Switzerland when Bern gets the word?"

"Yes." Burton said. "He wants to fly the damn Mosquito, but he has to use the Hudson"

"Just hope Grafton can land the damn thing in the snow." Witcombe said.

"Grafton can land anything anywhere." Burton said. "Want some coffee?"

"I think something stronger is needed." Witcombe said.

[2]
21:30 hrs

Bern, Switzerland
Hofbraun Gasthof

Jung felt the power that was now in his hands as he waited in a third floor room in the Hofbraun Gasthof. He had picked the Hofbraun because it was central to both of them and considered neutral territory. This was the first time in their tempestuous relationship that Jung clearly held the upper hand.

The telephone rang and Jung answered. It was the desk clerk informing him that Skasch was on his way up. Skasch entered the room without knocking; judging from his expression the Herr Professor was not a happy man.

"Is there insanity in your family Hermann?" Skasch growled.

"There is none that I know of Herr Professor." Jung said.

"This better be damn good Hermann." Skasch rasped. "You took me away from a very profitable venture. Your little package will not be delivered until my bank says the money has been transferred."

"There has been a change of plans Viktor." Jung hissed with a crooked smile crossing his face. "There are important changes Herr Doktor I afraid."

"Changes my dear Hermann?" Skasch rasped. "I decide what is important not you Hermann."

"Krieger wants you in Adlerberghof by the ninth to finish the transaction in person." Jung said pouring himself a brandy before sitting down.

"Impossible." Skasch hissed bluntly. "I'm not leaving Swiss territory for Germany. Franco has forgiven me and I'm wintering in the South of Spain starting on the eight."

"Go to Spain poorer and possibly unhealthier." Jung said with a pompous flair as he lit a small cigar. "We have good friends in the Guarda Civila and they have long memories."

"Are you threatening me Hermann?" Skasch growled.

"Krieger doesn't make threats Viktor." Jung said. "He wants you in Adlerberghof on the ninth."

"I still have the papers." Skasch said. "You'll never find them."

Jung smiled. "You don't seem to get the message. Krieger will be your only customer. You will find that no one else will buy them"

"You are forgetting yourself Hermann." Skasch said firmly. "My organization is not built of weaklings; you know who you are talking to."

"You are a man without a country or friends except us." Jung said coldly.

"Berlin will be very interested in your financial dealings." Skasch said sharply.

"Tell Berlin." Jung said without fear. "You'll be dead shortly after Berlin gets the message. The Countess is my cousin."

"Then I have other ways of dealing with you." Skasch warned.

"Walk over to the window Viktor." Jung said. "Look beyond the police shadow you'll see that you have picked up a second shadow." Skasch went to the window, looked out, and saw what Jung was talking was worried about.

"Who is he?" Skasch asked. "Is he Gestapo Hermann?"

"We believe NKVD." Jung said. "They have decided to talk to you about many things."

"We are even." Skasch said.

"What do you think the NKVD would do to you if they found out that you killed their courier?" Jung asked.

"I could go to the Federal police for protection." Skasch said.

"Trotsky had protection." Jung said.

"The Swiss police are better than some Mexican body guards." Skasch rasped.

"They are hardly your friends." Jung said flatly. "They'll want to know why you need their protection; a Swiss prison is still a prison."

"I see your point Hermann." Skasch said. "Do I still get my price?"

"We are not Communists Viktor." Jung said.

"I'll bring my bodyguards." Skasch said.

"Certainly, bring them." Jung said. "We want you to feel comfortable."

"The worm has turned I see." Skasch hissed.

"It has." Jung said smugly. "You may go now."

Jung watched Skasch storm out of the room. Hermann poured himself another brandy quite happy with himself. He had placed the great Viktor Skasch into a box with only one exit. This victory over the arrogant bastard would be complete after Ehrlich killed him on the ninth. Jung went over to the window and watched the great professor leave the Gasthof followed by the police shadow. The second shadow lit a cigarette and waved to Jung then left in the opposite direction.

[3]
20: 45 hrs

London
Army/Navy Officer's Club

Austen-Halton motioned the Captain to sit down and signaled the steward for three large whiskeys. Captain Boyden Thomason Orr was the illegitimate son of an impoverish Irish Earl. His father did manage to send him to Oxford for an excellent education. Orr joined the colonial police in Kenya, but found the police service boring and too stuffy for his taste and transferred to the Territorial Army while he studied for his masters' degree at Cambridge. Lord Crosland was a friend of his father and the Admiral brought him into the group before the war broke out. This was not an act of kindness on Crosland but practical act on his part. Orr like Mannerling was a cold methodical killer.

"You understand your orders Orr?" Austen-Halton asked plainly.

"Very well sir." Orr said wryly. "Mannerling knows I'm going to be there. I'm not in the mood to get shot by Edward by accident sir."

"Mannerling never shoots anyone by accident Orr." Austen-Halton said.

"The major is the only one who'll know that." Crawford said. "Neither the team nor the Resistance will."

"What about this farmer Donner?" Orr asked.

"Deuxieme Bureau." Austen-Halton said. "He is an Alsatian planted there during the last war."

"That is a comforting thought." Orr said. "Who is he working for, DeGaulle or Giraud?"

"He is one of DeGaulle's boys." Crawford answered.

"What did you have to give him?" Orr asked.

"They have him some minor points in Africa." Sir Peter said. "He just needed his ego stroked. Colonel Henri of the Deuxieme Bureau and I had already made a deal, but DeGaulle found out some how and started to make noise."

Orr lit his pipe. "What about Swiss?"

"You are an Irish businessman, McCray & Sons." Austen-Halton said.

"Why am I in Switzerland?" Orr asked.

"You are buying Swiss watch movements." Sir Peter said. "Gunnarsohn of the Swiss Security Police will give you the blink. Greene and Withgate will get you to the border by the fastest transportation possible."

"What is my particular mission?" Orr asked.

"Your mission is twofold Captain." Crawford said. "In the event that Mannerling is killed you are to kill Krieger. If the plan proceeds as scheduled, you are to aid Mannerling in the performance of his mission. Under no circumstances are you to allow Colquhoun to be killed."

"That is cold-hearted." Boyden said. "That in it self is really out of our hands Sir Peter."

"It has to be that way." Austen-Halton said. "What counts is that Krieger must die and die in as much dishonor as possible."

"That is understood sir." Orr said.

"Do you have any morals about killing women Captain?" Austen-Halton asked.

"I balk at children Sir Peter." Boyden said.

"No children." Crawford said flatly. "You might have to kill a woman"

"Is she involved with this sir?" Orr asked.

"She is Krieger's wife Captain." Austen-Halton said. "Remember the female is more deadly than the male."

[4]
21:00 hrs

Berlin
Zentral Bahnof

Ehrlich opened the first class train compartment as Hauptscharfuhrer Klugge, Krieger's enlisted aide, switched on the overhead light. The compartment was empty and Ehrlich signaled Krieger that he could enter after they holstered their weapons. The colonel and the sergeant never took any chances with Krieger's life, because several times after the Roehm Purge there had been attempts to assassinate Krieger, but Ehrlich and Klugge had stopped the attempts.

Krieger was wearing the uniform of a Waffen SS Gruppenfuhrer, Ehrlich and Klugge were wearing Waffen SS uniforms to blend in. The sergeant put down the bags and left the two officers alone.

"Who are we this time Albrecht?" Krieger asked sitting down.

"You are Gruppenfuhrer/Generalmajor Hosmer." Ehrlich said. "Waffen SS inspector general's office."

"That is very good." Krieger said. "I've never been in the Waffen SS.

"I'm surprised that the Countess did not insist on traveling with you sir." Ehrlich said as he opened the brandy bottle.

"She'll meet us in Adlerberghof later." Helmuth said flatly. "Corporal Nordmann will be driving her down."

"Is that wise sir?" Ehrlich asked.

"Elsa has made up her mind." Krieger said dully. "What is the schedule?"

"We should arrive in Jaegerfeld about 4: 00 AM barring any trouble." Ehrlich said in a flat voice. "Then it shall take us about three hours to drive to the village. The closest help would be Jaegerfeld."

"Does Jung know I expect him to be there?" Helmuth asked.

"He does." Ehrlich said. "The fat weasel was not too pleased."

"One must take chances to be on top." Helmuth said.

"Not foolish ones sir." Ehrlich said. "Jung is not that positive of Skasch's honesty in this deal."

"That is a given." Krieger said. "But there is a war going on."

"Jung is not that trusty in this either." Ehrlich said bluntly.

Krieger smiled to himself. Jung had attached his star to him a long time ago. If he should fall, Hermann would fall with him. Jung was long on greed, but short on guts when it mattered.

"He is a relative." Krieger quipped. "The risks are well worth the prize Albrecht. We secure this list and it becomes a gold-plated invitation to succeed Heydrich."

"Your enemies will try to stop you." Ehrlich warned angrily.

"They'll try." Krieger said. "I understand their nervousness since more than one is on the list."

"You should have allowed me to investigate this fully." Ehrlich said stiffly. "This cockroach Skasch could be selling you a deliberate fake. We know Skasch deals with the Allies on occasion."

"The sample he gave was valid." Krieger said. "The list may be a fake, but it is the threat of its existence is what makes it so powerful."

"That knowledge would make you a target for everyone." Ehrlich hissed.

Krieger lit an American cigarette. Despite Ehrlich's disdain of Jung, Hermann was a trained investigator. Jung had confirmed Skasch's overblown story on how he got the documents. The American courier had died in a Gasthof fire in Zurich; the British courier had strolled into a trolley in Geneva; the Soviet courier drove his car off a cliff. The highly efficient Swiss Federal police as well as the canton police failed to make the connection that before each accident Skasch's man Muth was in the area. Muth was the best cat burglar in Europe, thus the Allies always found their precious documents or thought destroyed. Nor did the Swiss police make the connection when Muth decided to take a swim in Lake Geneva under the ice.

Helmuth knew that the list only had a limited life span. It would not take long for the Allies to figure out what was happening once their people started to disappear. Helmuth was under no illusions that Skasch would try to sell the information that he had the list to the Allies. The Americans might be squeamish about killing Skasch out right with out proof. The British and Russians would not give it a second thought; killing was part of the work. Killing Skasch in Adlerberghof would buy him a few more weeks. By that time, he would have been able to bring the list to Himmler's attention and allow the Reichsfuhrer to present 'his' discovery to the Fuehrer as a gift. That would force Himmler to name him Heydrich's successor almost immediately. Once there Helmuth would be able to settle old scores without worry. He would find Jung a safe position somewhere out of the country with a large expense account.

[5]
22:00 hrs

Bern, Switzerland
Gasthof Raumbeau

Skasch slammed the lid of his suitcase after packing his clothes still angry at his humiliation at the hands of Jung. He had badly underestimated Jung thus allowing him to gain the upper hand. Skasch lit one of his Turkish cigarettes knowing what he had to do now. Hermann may have won the battle, but he would win the war. The British would pay well for this information and provide him with transportation to Spain.

Skasch walked out of the Gasthof and headed for the train station. He would contact the British intelligence resident agent, Major Sidney Greene in Geneva. He would deal with Greene and be heading for South America, a few thousands pounds richer.

When he stepped off the curb, Skasch realized that his police shadow was missing. Skasch put his hand into his overcoat and wrapped it around his Mauser. The black automobile came out of an alley and sped by him. Two flashes of light blinked from the rear window. Skasch reeled back staggering a few steps before collapsing.

The black automobile stopped and two men wearing ill-fitting top coats emerged from the backseat of the automobile. They moved directly to the fallen Skasch. The first man kicked Skasch in the ribs yelling at him in Russian. The second man removed a pistol from his pocket and fired three times at pointblank range at Skasch's head.

The police detective, who had been following Skasch, wobbled out of the alley yelling at the two men. The first man raised his weapon, but the second man pushed down his arm and pointed to the automobile. They ignored the yelling policeman and quickstepped to the waiting automobile. The police officer, wiping the blood from his eyes, fired at the moving automobile.

[6]
23:12 hrs

Bern
Central Morgue

Colonel Gunnarsohn from the Swiss Federal Security Police lifted up the morgue sheet and slowly shook his head. He then looked over at the Bern police detective with the bandaged head. Gunnarsohn then looked at the man standing in the shadows.

"Plate number Kahn?" The Colonel asked flatly lowering the sheet.

"No rear plate." Kahn said bitterly. "I was hit from behind Colonel. It was a planned killing."

"You are correct Kahn." The Colonel said. "Are there any witnesses?"

"I doubt it." Kahn said. "The gunshots didn't even bring out the curious."

"Inspector Zeman is handling the investigation." Gunnarsohn said. "It wasn't your fault Kahn. Go home and rest."

"Skasch going out that way was a total surprise." Kahn hissed. "I never thought it possible sir. Do you have any suspects?"

"Give me a copy of the last national census." Gunnarsohn said. "Viktor Skasch had no friends. We'll keep this quiet a few days and sees who celebrates"

Kahn left the morgue leaving the colonel and the civilian. Gunnarsohn lit his cigar.

"Satisfactory?"

"Quite." Major Greene said.

"Only Skasch was supposed to be hurt Major." Gunnarsohn said firmly. "Damaging Kahn was not in the bargain."

"A cash bonus will be anonymously sent." Greene said.

"I want the Major gone." Gunnarsohn said bluntly.

"Already flying to Stockholm as we speak Colonel Reyeski sends his apologies." Greene said flatly. "Do I have my 72 hours?"

"Yes." Gunnarsohn said. "After that the news will be released."

"Will Skasch's organization survive him?" Greene asked.

"He was the only one left." Gunnarsohn said coldly. "He killed the others off to avoid dividing the pot. How much was that going to be?"

"I heard 3 million Swiss francs." Greene said.

"Good payday." Gunnarsohn said flatly.

Chapter Seven
December 7, 1942
02:30 hrs

Germany
The Drop zone

There was nothing Colquhoun or the others could do but watch in silent horror. The explosion had died quickly in the cold December air. The JU-52, which had dropped them only a few minutes later, had been circling the drop zone to come in again to drop equipment and Captain Larsen who would drop the equipment, just disintegrated into a giant orange reddish ball of twisted wreckage plunging towards the earth.

The Major watched the bomber crash into a hillside about five miles from the drop zone. The bomber was now a blazing beacon for any German troops in the area. The crashed plane was least of Colquhoun's worries. As the team jumped, a crosswind came up and scattered the team all over the place. The old barn, which was the rallying point, was now two miles away. The team had orders to go to the old barn immediately if separated.

Colquhoun rolled up his chute and buried it in the snow along with his jumpsuit. The uniform under the jumpsuit was that of the dreaded Geheimefeldpolizei, Secret Field Police also known as the Headhunters. Unlike the regular military police, the GFP worked for the SS. Colquhoun checked the Walther P-38, the only weapon he had because of the bomber crashing.

It would take Colquhoun almost an hour to get to the barn in the deep snow. Donner's farm was a further two hours away. Colquhoun checked his identity card, put on the field jacket, picked up the attaché case, and started to walk. Colquhoun glanced over his shoulder at the red glow of the burning bomber thinking about the pilots and Mannerling; the way things were going, they might be the lucky ones.

[2]
03:47 hrs

The Barn

The old barn was located in a clearing between two stands of pine trees .The barn, used by the local farmers, for their cows during the spring and summer. From the lack of footprints in the snow, Colquhoun knew he was the first to arrive. He would wait for an hour before striking out for Donner's farm; he wanted to get there before dawn. The others would find his sign and head for Donner's without waiting.

Colquhoun had been in the barn for about fifteen minutes listening to the silence when the tranquility was shattered. Colquhoun drew his pistol as the noise became louder; what ever was making the noise did not seem to care about how much noise it was making.

The barn door swung open violently and a figure of a man staggered into the barn and collapsed to the ground. Colquhoun closed the door and moved cautiously towards the moaning man. Colquhoun pressed the barrel against the man's head and turned him over.

"Gregg!" Colquhoun hissed. The saw that he was still in his jumpsuit and a large hole was in the man's chest just below the collarbone. Gregg adjusted his eyes and recognized Colquhoun.

"Ambush…ambushes…them." Gregg wheezed as dark blood flowed from his mouth.

"Who... damnit!" Colquhoun rasped.

"Krauts... They... Wer...." Gregg coughed his voice trailing off as he slipped into death.

The Major lowered Gregg to the ground; nothing he could do for Gregg, he needed a doctor and a lot of luck. Gregg must have stumbled into a German patrol going to check the burning bomber before he could get out of his jumpsuit. Colquhoun stood and pointed his pistol at Gregg, but after a few seconds, he holstered the pistol. Gregg was beyond pain and a gunshot might bring Germans to his location.

Colquhoun was one-step out of the barn when a rifle shot cracked kicking up the snow in front of him. Colquhoun froze keeping his hands away from his body. From the trees Colquhoun saw the gunman approaching him, were wearing civilian clothes.

"Stay perfectly still Herr Colquhoun." A voice called out in English from behind him. "Use your left hand and removed the pistol with your thumb and index fingers. Toss it away from you-do anything else and Weiss will shoot you in the right knee cap."

"More shooting will bring the Army." Colquhoun snarled.

"No Army patrols in this sector." The voice said coldly.

"Who the hell are you?" Colquhoun hissed.

"I said now Captain!" The voice ordered.

From the forest, four men emerged herding Carey, Reed, Madden and Browne towards them. Colquhoun saw that Madden was the only one not in his jumpsuit. Only Madden looked at Colquhoun when they lined up next to him. A few minutes later a German officer appeared.

"You're the voice?" Colquhoun hissed looking at him.

"You are very wise not to act stupid." The Lieutenant said. "No sense in dying for a lost cause Colquhoun." The Lieutenant lit a cigarette. "I'm the only one who speaks English Herr Major."

"My name is Voss." Colquhoun said sternly. "GFP, you have a lot to explain Herr Leutnant."

"Your name is Colquhoun." The Lieutenant said lighting a cigarette. "Major Jefferson Davis Colquhoun, OSS. Major Gerhardt will not find you."

"Who the hell is he?" Colquhoun hissed.

"Time is running out Herr Major." The Lieutenant said crisply. "Playing stupid will only get you killed along with your men." The Lieutenant paused. "I know everything."

Colquhoun remained stoically silent as he looked at his men. Carey had a deep purplish welt across his left cheek; Reed a crimson stream ran from the corner of his lower lip; Madden had a bruised upper right cheek and closed left eye. They had not come easily by the looks of it.

"Herr Major." The Lieutenant said. "Your men tried to be brave, but one broke so to speak. The trail was very easy to follow. Is he dead?"

"Yes." Colquhoun said.

"He was stronger than I thought he would be." The German said wryly.

"Are you Gestapo?" Colquhoun rasped.

"Hardly, since you are still breathing." The Lieutenant said. "I need to know all your contacts and the exact target."

"I thought you knew everything?" Colquhoun hissed.

The Lieutenant tossed his cigarette to the ground. "Let's not play the fool at this late stage of the game. I'm not that interested in killing you Major. Tell me what I want to know and you'll be set free."

"Sorry." Colquhoun hissed.

"You would be treated as POWs." The Lieutenant said.

"I am Colquhoun, Jefferson D.; I'm a Major in the United States Army." Colquhoun said flatly.

"You want to be shot as a spy Herr Major?" The Lieutenant snarled.

"Tell him to stuff it sir." Madden snorted. The Lieutenant turned his attention to the Royal Marine.

The Lieutenant drew his pistol and pressed it against Madden's chest. "Then you tell Captain."

"Damnit man bugger off." Madden said calmly. "You know bloody well I'm not going to tell you a bloody thing now or ever."

"Is dying for honor that damn important to you English?" The Lieutenant hissed. "There is no honor in dying for nothing."

"Piss off." Madden said defiantly. Without a moment's hesitation, the Lieutenant squeezed the trigger of the Luger. Madden was lifted off his feet and tossed backwards. Captain Harry Madden, Royal Marines, was dead before he hit the ground.

"My patience wears thin Major Colquhoun." The Lieutenant said aiming the pistol at the major. "I admire courage, but your mission has failed. Krieger will live while you die for nothing."

"Do what you have to." Colquhoun rasped. "Kill us or try to bring us in."

"Perhaps I won't have to." The Lieutenant said dryly tapping his lips with the pistol barrel. "The Englishman will tell me everything."

"That will be a neat trick." Colquhoun said stiffly. "You killed him."

"He was a big man." The Lieutenant quipped firing the Luger at Madden jerking up an arm. "You see, he moves."

"Christssake he is dead." Colquhoun growled.

The Lieutenant walked over to Madden and stood over him. "I can get him to a hospital quickly."

"He is dead." Colquhoun rasped.

"I can have the body shipped home." The Lieutenant said. "How would his family react to a mutilated body? The Red Cross will get all the grizzly details about how you failed to save his life by just talking."

"You are a bastard." Colquhoun snapped. "He is dead!"

"Are you a doctor?" The Lieutenant hissed. "I'll illustrate a point for you."

The Lieutenant raised his pistol and took deliberate aim at Madden. "Corpses don't bleed Herr Major." Two quick shots coming from the barn shattered the night air. The first shot smashed into the Lieutenant's face killing him instantly. The second shot dropped the one called Weiss. The Major dove for Weiss' weapon as Carey flung himself at the closes guard to him. Browne tackled the third guard and quickly broke his neck. Colquhoun brought up Weiss' rifle and shot the fourth guard. Reed finished off the guard Carey jumped by cutting the man's throat with the switchblade he had hidden.

"Gregg is dead this time for certain." Reed said flatly coming from the direction of the barn. "He saved our butts."

"What difference does that make?" Carey rasped. "That smart-ass bastard knew everything major. I smell a trap."

"He was working alone." Colquhoun rasped.

"How the hell do you know that?" Browne asked sharply.

"He had only four men." Colquhoun said. "The German Army would have has a damn company."

"The kraut was waiting for us." Reed said bluntly.

"You suggest something?" Colquhoun asked.

"The border isn't that far away." Carey said.

"We finish the mission." Colquhoun said icily. "Nothing has altered that."

"You just don't get it Major." Browne hissed. "We might still have a Judas down the road."

"He is dead." Colquhoun said.

"Suicide is for the Japs." Carey hissed.

"I'm not planning to do that." Colquhoun said bluntly.

"What about them?" Reed asked.

"We leave them." Colquhoun said. "Any krauts finding them will assume that Madden and Gregg killed them."

"What if we don't want to go?" Browne asked.

"I see plenty of room for another hero." Colquhoun said in an icy cold voice.

"I hope this Donner has some coffee." Carey said. "And some damn heat."

"Let's move before it starts to snow." Colquhoun said.

Chapter Eight
December 7, 1942
02:30 hrs

Germany
The Drop zone

Mannerling went out the bombardier's hatch the moment he saw Colquhoun's parachute opened and the bomber veered left. Mannerling waited until he was far away from the plane before opening his chute. The bomber would complete it circle and make a drop of the equipment and head home. Mannerling had secured a note to the equipment telling Colquhoun that he was having parachute trouble. Mannerling looked up at the bomber as his chute opened to see the bomber explode into a fireball.

Mannerling frantically searched the ground below for an AAA battery, but saw nothing. Mannerling's eyes searched the sky for an enemy fighter, but the sky was empty. Mannerling watched the bomber glide towards the ground and slam into a hillside. As he watched, the bomber burn on the hillside Mannerling knew how the bomber died.

Mannerling's landing zone was a small clearing about two miles from Colquhoun's drop zone. His German contacts were to meet him in a thicket of pine trees. Twenty minutes after landing Mannerling heard someone coming towards him and he removed his pistol. Three flashlight beams hit him from three different angles.

"*Augustus.*" A voice called out.

"*Praetorian.*" Mannerling answered. The flashlights went out and three figures moved towards him. Mannerling saw that two of them had weapons drawn.

"Major Anton Gerhardt." The man in the middle said with a British accent to his English. "May I introduce Leutnants Lang and Franz?"

"Mannerling." Mannerling said. "You're a little short."

"There was a change of plans." Gerhardt said. "We better get moving."

"What happened to the bomber?" Franz asked somberly. "No flak batteries or Luftwaffe in this sector."

"There was a change of plans." Mannerling answered flatly. "It blew up."

"Your colleagues are living very dangerously." Gerhardt said. "Not a good start."

"I was only a passenger." Mannerling said. "Call London if you have a complaint."

"It makes little sense in doing that." Franz said icily. "They can't help us."

"Do you have enemies in London Herr Major?" Lang quipped.

"Perhaps Lang I do." Mannerling said wryly.

"We better get the hell out of here." Franz said. "That blazing bomber can be seen by a blind man."

"Damnit Major." Mannerling growled. "Who in hell is in charge?"

"I am." Gerhardt said bluntly. "Franz is understandingly annoyed- a bomber blowing up was not in the plan."

"Plans have to be fluid." Mannerling said. "I didn't want a goddamn funeral pyre leading every German soldier in the area here. We have to check to see if they made it to the barn."

"Dangerous side trip Herr Major." Lang said. "We might not be the only ones in the damn woods tonight."

"I'll go myself." Mannerling growled.

"The hell with that idea Mannerling, so don't get anxious." Gerhardt said bluntly. "We can't have you turn up missing."

"We have to know if Colquhoun is alive or dead." Mannerling said. "Krieger is coming to see Skasch."

"Lang and I will check the barn." Gerhardt said. "You go with Franz to Adlerberghof."

"That sounds reasonable." Mannerling quipped.

"Come with me." Franz said dryly. "I'll drive."

[2]
04:30 hrs

The Barn

"Damnit, this doesn't feel right." Lang whispered as they saw black lumps lying in the snow in front of the barn. "This isn't in the fucking script Anton."

"Circle to the left." Gerhardt said flatly understanding Lang's misgivings about the situation. "I'll go to the right-you flush anyone out shoot first."

"That was my intention." Lang said pulling back the bolt of the MP-41. "He might not be alone."

"Move it Lars." Gerhardt ordered.

They circled the barn and found that they were the only living people in the area now. Lang pulled the identity disc from the body just inside the barn. "This one is Gregg."

"This one is Madden." Gerhardt said standing holding another identity disc. "It looks as if a small party headed towards Donner's."

"This Major Colquhoun is not the jellyfish London made him out to be." Lang said in an icy voice. "We can't contact him now."

"We weren't to contact him anyway." Gerhardt said. "It seems he is following the plan at least."

"Not bad for someone who is supposed to be paralyzed with fear." Lang said in a curt voice.

"He has done everything right so far." Gerhardt said moving towards the body of the German officer. Gerhardt lifted the body over with his foot. "Damn."

"Schiess!" Lang hissed. "The price has gone up my friend. You don't have to worry about Dietrich now." Lang looked around. "Who the hell are the others?"

"They are most likely hired help." Gerhardt said blandly removing Dietrich identity disc. "Low level thugs or do you recognize any of them?"

"The one next to Carl I've met." Lang answered. "His name was Weiss."

"Who was he?" Gerhardt asked.

"Freelance." Lang said. "In the old days he was with the Freikorps and the Black Reichwehr."

"Berlin knows?" Gerhardt asked.

"This isn't Berlin's work." Lang rasped. "Weiss didn't ask questions and he wasn't cheap."

"Who hired him?" Gerhardt asked flatly.

"Someone with money" Lang said dryly.

"What is Carl's connection to this?" Gerhardt asked.

Lang lit a cigarette. "What in hell was he trying to prove with this? With his connections he could have saved his neck."

"Wipe out Colquhoun and he stopped us." Gerhardt said sternly. "This was a noble gesture on his part."

"He failed miserably." Lang said. "He likes Krieger?"

"Hell no, this was family honor." Gerhardt said softly.

"Someone is bound to find them." Lang said. "Local police will take fingerprints and send them to Stuttgart."

"Not until spring." Gerhardt said. "This is high mountain pasture and nobody will be here until then."

"Our Englander is going to love this." Lang said damningly. "This mission is about as solid as quicksand Anton. We better wrap this up quickly before we join the newest hero of the Fatherland."

"Yes." Gerhardt said without argument.

"We better take the identity disc." Lang said dully. "Why make it easy for the bastards Anton?"

[3]
03:00 hrs

Donner's Farm

Donner poured them two cups of real coffee and sat down at the kitchen table. "You understand the danger?"

"Yes." Orr said tasting the coffee. "Real."

"Of course it's real." Donner said his twirling his long Petainish mustache. "The Grenzpolizei could pay me a visit anytime and a smuggler without real coffee, sugar would arouse their suspicions more than twenty Jews in the barn."

"Why haven't they arrested you?" Orr asked.

"I perform an occasion errand for the local border police commandant." Donner said.

"How did the French latch on to you?" Orr asked looking at his watch.

"I am French." Donner rasped. "When the Germans took Alsace- Lorraine in '71 my father was too slow to get out. The Germans drafted me in 1915 and I deserted in 1916."

"How did you get here?" Orr asked.

"Colonel Saxe recruited me in 1917." Donner said. "I escaped from a French prisoner-of-war camp in June 1917. The Crown Prince pinned the Iron Cross 2nd Class on me personally." Donner poured another cup of coffee. "After the war I bought this farm."

"Wonderful." Orr said. "Where is my hiding place?"

"In the attic my friend." Donner said. "It is relatively soundproof, but don't start jumping around while they are here."

"I'll be silent as the dead." Orr said.

"Your friends will be here in about two hours." Donner said. "Then the fun begins right?"

"You could say that friend." Orr said. "This coffee is good."

[4]
05:30 hrs

Near Donner's Farm

Colquhoun lowered the binoculars and rubbed his tired eyes. In the far distance was the town of Adlerberghof lit up like a Christmas tree making the scene look like something out of a Rockwell picture. "What do you think?"

"I'm waiting for 'Silent Night' to come drifting up the valley any minute now." Carey said sourly.

"It is a good ten miles." Browne said.

"The book says nothing about committing suicide Major." Carey rasped.

"Nobody is waiting here to machine-gun us." Colquhoun said in a grim voice. "From the condition of the roads no one has been in or out of the town."

"That proves only that our friends didn't come from there." Carey said in a damning voice. "That kraut officer knew too much."

"He wanted us." Browne said. "The border isn't that far."

"We go to Donner's." Colquhoun said flatly. "If anything has gone sour he should know."

"When do we get rid of these damn kraut uniforms?" Reed asked.

"We dump them at the farm." Colquhoun said hollowly. "Then they can shoot us for being spies."

"Hell Major." Carey hissed. "These bastards will just kill us or the hell of it."

"It is too late to cry now." Colquhoun said flatly.

"Damn the bastards who thought this one up." Reed muttered.

"Let's go visit this Donner." Browne said. "He will have a nice warm house and food and we might get some sleep."

[5]
05:45 hrs

Twickem-Hallesy
Manor House

Colonel Tremayne entered the private library on the second floor and waited for Sir Peter to turn from the fireplace. "Yes, James?"

"Greene has signaled sir." Tremayne said. "He confirms what Colonel Mikhailov reported about Skasch. The Swiss are keeping the news of his death quiet for 72 hours sir."

"I consider that a major victory Colonel." Crawford grunted from his chair in the shadows. "They haven't lied to us in 48 hours." Colonel Sergei Mikhailov was the GRU liaison officer from the Soviet military mission to London. Neither the OSS nor the SOE were certain how much control the NKVD had over him.

"What about Adlerberghof Colonel?" Sir Peter asked somberly.

"From Operation *Roundup*, *Praetorian* and *Centurion* have landed." Tremayne said drably.

"What about details?" Austen-Halton asked as he lit a cigar.

"What sort of trouble Colonel?" Crawford asked bluntly.

"They had trouble at the landing zone." Tremayne said dryly.

"What sort of trouble Colonel?" Crawford asked.

"Captain Madden, Captain Larsen and Sergeant Gregg are dead." Tremayne said. "No more details."

"That is not a good sign." Austen-Halton said wryly. "Have Greene make further inquiry Colonel." Tremayne nodded and left the room. "Could Colquhoun suspect something?"

"I would be cautious right about now." Crawford said. "How much do you trust your German friends?"

"*Albatross* trusts them." Sir Peter said. "He hasn't stayed alive this long by being stupid." Austen-Halton relit the cigar. "Colquhoun is the one who has surprised me. He has shown unexpected resourcefulness. Perhaps your people were wrong about him?"

"He'll break." Crawford said coldly. "Dr. Craig says that as the pressure builds he will start to unravel. The Gestapo has the methods to break him and he'll talk."

"Nothing is certain." Sir Peter said blandly.

Chapter Nine
December 7, 1942
02:30 hrs

Saugenbruk, Germany
Train Station

    Krieger looked at his watch as the train slowly entered the wrecked depot. The train could go no further since the RAF destroyed the tracks in front of them. The train stopped and the conductors herded the passengers off the train into the slightly damaged terminal. Klugge found them a bench and went out into the crowd to gather information. The sergeant returned twenty minutes later with information from the stationmaster. This was the first time the RAF had bombed them.
    "When will the tracks be fixed?" Krieger asked Klugge.
    "The Bahnschutzpolizei officer says that they won't start working on the tracks until morning sir." Klugge said. "That's only and if though. This is a spur line off the main track sir."
    "That is unacceptable." Krieger said sharply. "Find that BSP officer and tell him I want to speak to him."
    "Is that wise sir?" Ehrlich asked. "The railroad police don't know how to keep their mouths shut."
    "Klugge I need your help." Krieger said. "Find an automobile."
    "Does it have to be done legally sir?" Klugge asked.
    "Anyway you can Sergeant-Major." Krieger said. "Buy it, borrow it or steal it Sergeant-Major."

[2]
03:00 hrs

Stahlwald

    The Countess received her guest in the manor hall. The guest was a tall good-looking man in his mid-thirties. He had the bearing of a military man despite the Party uniform. Bruno Vochner was one of the new Party elite. He bore no wounds from the Party's early battles and was a university graduate. Vochner was a senior party leader in this district. Though Bruno was a newcomer to the Party's tribal wars, his father wasn't. The elder Vochner had been a power broker in the Old Prussian Kingdom before and after the war. He kept his son in university while he cultivated the Nazi elite.
    "How many men can Eidernau muster on short notice?" She asked coldly.
    "He could gather up perhaps twenty, Countess." Vochner answered plainly. "Your husband could have three times that many without cost."
    "This is private, Bruno." The Countess said. "Tell him the standard fee plus a bonus."
    "When and where do you want them?" Bruno asked.
    "Four hours heading for Adlerberghof." The Countess said. "He's to stay out of town."
    "That is a long journey." Bruno said. "The police are cracking down on unnecessary travel by civilians. Their faces are well known to the Orpo and Kripo."
    "Auxiliary police are exempted." The Countess said. "You'll supply them with the required permits and uniforms."

"That will cost money." Bruno said.
"I want the best." The Countess said coldly. "No drunks or cowards."
"I always provide the best for you." Bruno said.
"What about your support with Bormann?" The Countess asked.
"Bormann is pragmatic." Bruno said. "He bends with the wind."
"Bormann is a coward Bruno." The Countess said. "He serves only the winners my old friend."
"If you win Bormann will be with you." Bruno said dryly. "Lose my dear Elsa and Bormann will show no mercy."
"Where will you be Bruno?" The Countess asked coldly.
"Always on the winning side my dear." Bruno said.

[3]
06:30 hrs
Donner's Farm

Colquhoun's sixth sense awoke him an instant before he heard the barn door creaked open. Colquhoun reached into his overcoat pocket and removed the P-38 Walther. The old man entered the barn armed with a shotgun. The old man turned and faced Colquhoun and his men.
"I can get most of you." The old man said in German. "This has a wide bark."
"Ease off the trigger old man." Colquhoun said. "Or you'll be dead."
"Too damn cold to talk here." The old man said. "You better come into the house and get warm."
"Are you Donner?" Carey asked.
"Yes." The old man rasped. "I have hot food waiting for you."
Donner placed the shotgun on the rack over the kitchen door and then faced his guests as he removed his coat. "Would you tell your heroes to put away their weapons?"
"Put them away." Colquhoun said but keeping his out.
"Sit down." Donner said in English. "I'll put the coffee on."
"Before you do that I need something from you." Colquhoun said bluntly pointing the pistol at the old man's head.
"You're not English." Donner said removing his pipe from the shirt pocket and lit it.
"I'm American." Colquhoun replied.
"You both like your little childish games." Donner grunted dourly.
"A 9 mm bullet is no game." Colquhoun said harshly.
"*Richard III.*" Donner said placing a half a shilling on the kitchen table. "*Ajax.*"
"*Hunchback.*" Colquhoun said placing his half of the coin next to Donner's coin and slid the halves together. "*Richard III.*"
"Are we through with the games?" Donner hissed.
"Start the coffee." Colquhoun said.
Donner leaned back in the chair after they had eaten breakfast. "Krieger will arrive in town on the 8th. He normally travels with his aide Standartenfuhrer Ehrlich and his enlisted orderly Hauptscharfuhrer Klugge."
"He has a Sergeant-Major for a batman?" Carey quipped. "How big is this bastard?"

"He is one of Himmler's inner-circle." Donner said. "He bears a striking resemblance to the late Heydrich. As for Klugge he is more of a bodyguard than orderly."

"Are they in on this?" Browne asked.

"I doubt it." Donner said.

"All high ranking SS have watchdogs." Reed said.

"Not all." Donner said. "The one you really have to worry about is Krieger's wife, the Countess."

"Will she be here?" Colquhoun asked.

"Most likely she will be." Donner said. "She makes Lady MacBeth look like a school girl."

"We need to rest." Colquhoun said flatly.

"What about transportation?" Reed asked. "This Skasch isn't going to walk in."

"The automobile is in a storage shed 2 kilometers from here." Donner said. "I'll bring it up here around 4 PM."

"Reed you go with him." Colquhoun ordered. "You pick it up now."

Chapter Ten
December 7, 1942
06:00 hrs

Adlerberghof

"This is very quiet and peaceful." Mannerling said grimly. "They don't believe in blackout?"

"The closest military or economic target is Jaegerfeld." Gerhardt said. "The Army has a training command for mountain troops and one factory produces ammunition. They keep the lights on so the bombers don't bomb them."

"That sounds reasonable." Mannerling said as he lit a cigarette.

"Who are you? Gerhardt asked starting up the car.

"Hauptsturmfuhrer Gert Fleischer." Mannerling said dully. "Security Police."

"We should impress the locals even the Mayor." Gerhardt said.

"What are Lang and Franz doing?" Mannerling asked somberly.

"They are cutting the telephone/telegraph lines." Gerhardt replied in a matter-of-fact voice. "The SW transmission tower will also lose power."

"They can repair it?" Mannerling asked.

"They don't work very well here under normal conditions and when the generator is destroyed it doesn't work at all." Gerhardt said. "In the winter the telephone/telegraph Lines go down often; takes days or weeks to repair."

"Where are we going now?" Mannerling asked as they headed back to the staff car.

"Wake up the Chief of Police." Gerhardt said.

"Why?" Mannerling asked.

"It will be the easiest way to meet the Burgermeister." Gerhardt said in a dry voice.

[2]

The town of Adlerberghof was really made up of three small villages, nestled in a small valley in the Southern Alps. During the Thirty Years War, they joined for mutual protection against marauding mercenaries from both sides. The villagers petitioned the Holy Roman Emperor who placed the villages under his protection. When the German Empire formed in 1871 Adlerberghof officially became a town with a Burgermeister and town council.

The surrounding area held very little military or industrial importance during the Imperial era or now. Adlerberghof became a popular ski resort for the growing middle class of Imperial Germany at the turn of the century. The First World War damaged the tourist industry and it was recovering during the early days of the Nazi regime. Since the outbreak of the war, most of the Gasthofs closed. Most of the people went to work in the factories in Jaegerfeld or into the Wehrmacht.

The citizens remaining were quiet and very nonpolitical. The local Home Guard commander, a seventy-year-old former captain, wore his old Imperial uniform sans the Nazi emblems. Only a handful of people actually belonged to the Nazi Party; most of the people had voted for the Catholic Center Party before 1934.

The Nazis were the Burgermeister, Kurt Schiller; People's Court Judge, Hugo Kohlberger; Chief of Police and Landwacht, Otto Heinz, Schiller's brother-in-law. Kurt Schiller was the most dangerous. He was young, daring and well educated, Law degree from Leipzig University. Schiller had been a person of substance in Berlin, but exiled to Adlerberghof for some unknown reason. Schiller's Party rank was Oberdienstleiter and he was very anxious to end his exile.

[3]
06:45 hrs

Adlerberghof
Polizeidienststelle

    Otto Heinz moved swiftly for a fat man as he moved to his desk and sat down. Heinz usually slept in the backroom when he took his turn on night duty and was not accustomed to having anyone interrupt his sleep. Heinz buttoned his uniform collar adjusting the Pour Le Merit that hung from his neck. It was hard to believe, but Heinz had been in the air force during the last war and had shot down thirty enemy aircraft before the war ended.
    "I am the President of the Gendarmerie and Landwacht." Heinz rasped officiously to the two men who had awakened him. "No strangers have entered Adlerberghof Herr Major." Heinz lit a cigar. "It is my duty to know these things."
    "You fail to understand Herr Heinz." Gerhardt said cautiously. "We are not looking for strangers."
    "Address me as Herr President." Heinz rasped in a serious voice. "You have names then Herr Major?"
    "How many military age men are in town?" Gerhardt asked.
    "There are very few now." Heinz answered. "They are exempt from military conscription. Are you looking for deserters?"
    "That is our business." Gerhardt said.
    "The Army has no jurisdiction here." Heinz snapped. "Everything that happens here is MY business."
    Gerhardt threw down his identity card on the desk. Heinz picked up the card and read it. Gerhardt watched Heinz's round face go completely blank followed by a deeply puzzling frown.
    "I, Leutnants Lang and Franz are Abwehrpolizei." Gerhardt said in a dry voice. "Hauptmann Fleischer is from SIPO."
    "Why come here of all places?" Heinz hissed.
    "We are looking for dangerous people." Gerhardt said firmly.
    "From here?" Heinz quipped.
    "Are you refusing to help Herr President?" Gerhardt asked crisply. "Or are you always this thick?"
    "You'll have my fullest support." Heinz said firmly.
    "We'll be here for a few days." Gerhardt said. "We'll be at the Gruenling Gasthof. I want your people to stay out of our way during our investigation."
    "Anything you want." Heinz said.
    "Your cooperation will be noted Herr President." Gerhardt said.

[4]
10:00 hrs

Donner's Farm

"They are mixed lot." Donner said as he poured Orr a cup of coffee and placed the brandy bottle on the table.

"I didn't pick them." Boyden said. "Are you certain Krieger will be here?"

"The clerk from the Gruenling has a loose mouth after a few drinks." Donner said in a dry voice. "They are holding rooms for them."

"How many will be in the party?" Orr asked.

"Five." Donner said.

"We know of four." Orr said seriously. "Where did five come in?"

"The fifth is coming in from Switzerland." Donner said.

Orr lit a cigarette. "How do you know this?

"They are using the old smuggler's route." Donner said. "My friend Oskar is bringing him in. They don't want anyone to know that he will be in Germany on the 8th."

"You have a name?" Boyden asked.

"Jung." Donner answered. "Hermann Jung."

"Goddamnit!" Boyden rasped.

"What's wrong?" Donner asked.

"Jung is Krieger's man in Bern." Boyden said. "Damn."

"So what is the problem?" Donner asked as he lit the alpine pipe.

"London was not anticipating on Jung coming here." Orr said grimly.

"It would be logical assumption." Donner said uncorking the brandy bottle. "What is the problem?"

"Jung knows the real Skasch." Orr said.

"Yes, I see your problem." Donner hissed. "But there is not a damn thing you can do about it. Colquhoun will just have to kill him."

"I'll have to contact London." Orr said.

"Not until four." Donner said. "You better rest until then; hell breaking loose can wait until then."

"Can you contact your friend Oskar?" Orr asked.

"I could do that." Donner said. "But Jung not arriving could cause Krieger to change his plans."

"Damn, always problems." Orr hissed. "Damn it."

[5]
10:20 hrs

Gasthof Gruenling

The door of the room crashed open and Heinz entered the room with two tough looking young men carrying MP-38s. Heinz signaled to the occupants to remain seated.

"I am Schiller." The young man in a Party uniform said briskly as he entered the room followed by two more toughs. "You are under arrest."

"We have been expecting you Herr Burgermeister." Gerhardt said dully lighting a cigarette. "With less theatrical flare though."

"I outrank you Herr Major." Schiller snapped. "I'm the sole authority in this district and my town is not going to be searched."

"Sit down Herr Schiller." Franz ordered in a cutting voice his eyes meeting the Mayor's eyes. "That is not a suggestion."

"Who the hell are you to give ME an order?" Schiller snapped rattled by Franz's apparent lack of fear.

"We are the Gestapo." Franz said cold bloodedly holding up his right wrist to show the warrant disc."

"You told Heinz Abwehrpolizei." Schiller hissed glancing at the dumbfounded Heinz.

"We lied." Gerhardt said flatly showing his warrant disc. "I told you to sit down Herr Schiller. Then order your pet monkeys to lower their weapons and leave." Gerhardt paused and lit cigarette. "One shot fired and you'll be dangling from a rope in less than 12 hours."

"You are a sonofabitch Gerhardt." Schiller rasped.

"We don't need them here." Gerhardt said. "Tell them to leave or they'll be on the Eastern Front by tomorrow. You and Heinz stay."

Schiller signaled them to leave as he sat down opposite them. The befuddled Heinz sat down next to him.

"This place is pretty far a field for the Gestapo?" Schiller hissed. "I can call Stuttgart and have this verified?"

"Standartenfuhrer Donier." Gerhardt said. "I'll give you the number of his private line."

"The telephone/telegraph lines are down again." Heinz said.

"We need to talk alone now." Gerhardt said flatly. "My companions will entertain Heinz at the bar."

"Do as he wants Otto." Schiller said.

"Kurt, let's not be stupid." Heinz snarled.

"Do it." Schiller said. "I'll be all right."

The Party, by happenstance, sometimes produced a few totally devoted and fanatics who could not be bought. Kurt Peter Schiller was one of those elite members of the Party. Schiller was a college student when he joined the Nazi Party in 1929. He was not a Brown shirt, but liked being with them and one of his drinking companions was Horst Wessel.

Wessel was a well-known pimp in Munich who had joined the SA to fight the Communists. The future mayor was at the brawl where the 'Hero of the Revolution' Horst Wessel, while fighting the Communists, got himself killed. Schiller, however, knew the truth that Wessel had died fighting over the favors of a whore. The Party needed a hero and spread the story that Wessel had died at the hands of the Communists and the Zionists. Schiller's fervor in proclaiming Wessel a Nazi hero brought him to the attention of Joseph Goebbels. The Nazi propaganda chief brought him to Berlin and secured him a position with the Party's newspaper in Berlin. Schiller understood hard work and quickly rose to be one of Goebbels' chief aides within six months.

In 1932, Schiller commissioned a Hauptsturmfuhrer in the Sturmabteilungen, through Goebbels influence. He wanted someone with intelligence to keep a watch on the SA. By 1934, Schiller was an Obersturmbannfuhrer and well known in high Party circles in Berlin for his zealousness in his believes in the Fuehrer and the Party.

Ernst Roehm, Chief of the SA, was not enamored with Schiller because he knew that Schiller was Goebbels' spy. Schiller joined Goebbels and others to destroy Roehm. His reward for his participation in the 'Night of the Long Knives' in June 1934, Himmler made Schiller an Ehrenfuhrer in the SS.

The Party rewarded him by making him a Kreisleiter in Berlin. However, the Party, found out that Schiller actually believed in the Party rules and regulations. This made him very difficult to deal with by the more pragmatic Party leadership in Berlin. Schiller refused to hire Party hacks, misfits, or relatives for his district. He infuriated the hierarchy by not looking the other way when Party members committed crimes in his district.

This on going difficulty finally came to a head after 'Kyrstalnacht' in November 1938. In his district, Schiller followed orders and confiscated the insurance money due the Jews. However, Schiller distributed the money to the people of his district instead of the Party's coffers.

Schiller's immediate superiors tried to force him to reverse what he had done, but Schiller stopped them by having the Gestapo arrest them. Goebbels, hearing rumors that certain people where planning a more drastic and direct solution, had Schiller transferred to Party Headquarters in Munich.

The Party bosses in Munich were not overjoyed to have him in Munich either. They found him to be the same pain-in-the-ass as he had been in Berlin. Out of desperation, Party officials sidestepped Goebbels by going Hess's deputy Bormann after the war had begun. The shadowy Bormann found out that Schiller had failed his military physical. The whispering campaign began and Bormann, through Hess, got this word to Hitler.

Goebbels interceded and secured a promotion an appointment to the sub-Gau district of Adlerberghof and Burgermeister. Goebbels assured his young friend that this was only temporary and once the war was over, he would be back in Berlin.

Schiller lit a cigar. "You do have a satisfactory explanation of why you are here Major. I still have friends in the Gestapo in Berlin."

"Your charming town has been selected for a top secret meeting between a government representative and an envoy from a neutral country." Gerhardt said handing Schiller an identity card from the Reichssicherheitsdienst.

"Damn." Schiller hissed swallowing slowly. The State Security Service only protected the Fuehrer and very high-ranking government and Party officials. "I have received no instructions from Berlin or Gauleiter Ernst."

"None will arrive." Gerhardt said flatly. "The Gauleiter doesn't know nor will he know."

"That will be a first." Schiller said not hiding his dislike of Ernst. "But, why tell me?"

"You are the town's leading citizen." Gerhardt said. "We could not operate tripping over your people and Heinz's."

"Heinz?" Schiller asked.

"He obeys orders." Gerhardt said. "He is not the man to be in command."

Schiller nodded his head in agreement knowing his brother-in-law had his limitations. "What do you want me to do?"

"Nothing Herr Burgermeister, I want you to do nothing." Gerhardt said flatly.

"Nothing Herr Sturmbannfuhrer is odd?" Schiller quipped in a puzzled voice.

"Everything must appear to be normal." Gerhardt said. "Once everyone is in town we seal off the town. Your men can help with that."

"I'll need photos." Schiller said. "To avoid accidents or unwanted incidences of the fatal kind."

"A much needed precaution." Gerhardt said handing Schiller photographs of Colquhoun, Browne, Carey and Reed. "The neutrals, the names they will use will be false."

"What about our side?" Schiller asked.

"Obergruppenfuhrer Helmuth Krieger." Gerhardt said.

"I understand." Schiller said.

"You understand that any failure on our part Schiller will result in our mutual liquidation." Gerhardt said bluntly. "Adlerberghof would suffer the same fate of Lidice."

"Let's hope for success." Schiller said grimly remembering the vivid description Oberst Jherling, base commander in Jaegerfeld, had given him of the fate of the small Czech village after Heydrich had died of his wounds. The SS killed all the males over 16; deported the women and children to concentration camps; blew up and bulldozed the village.

"That will be acceptable." Gerhardt said.

[6]
11:00 hrs

Twickem-Hallesy
Manor House

The man in the dark suit wearing wire-rimmed glasses listened attentively to Sir Peter and the man from the Treasury, only addressed as Mr. Fletcher; explain what they wanted from him and his bank.

"This sounds highly irregular gentlemen." Milton Rothmann said in a soft voice.

"The War Powers Act gives His Majesty's Government full authority here Mr. Rothmann." Mr. Fletcher said sternly.

"I'm not disputing that Mr. Fletcher." Rothmann said. "Why not use the Bank of England instead of a small private bank?"

"We can't admit that counterfeit currency is in circulation on a massive scale." Mr. Fletcher said. "You have examined the five pound note?"

"For all practical purposes they are real." Rothmann said flatly. "I have no doubt that I have several thousand pounds worth in my bank in London alone."

"The Bank's reputation must be above dispute in all matters." Sir Peter said.

"This is why you want a small private bank owned by Jews to take this risk." Rothmann said coldly.

"The Germans would find it very difficult to believe that the Bank of England would do what we planned." Sir Peter said. "They would suspect you instantly if this unraveled."

"His Majesty's Government realizes that we are asking you to take a great risk in regards to your bank's reputation." Mr. Fletcher said firmly. "Therefore I am empowered to inform you six months after the completion of the mission you will be raised to the peerage as a Baron."

"Will it be a Life peerage?" Rothmann asked.

"The government has agreed that it will be hereditary." Mr. Fletcher said,

"Will my brother Reuben be included?" Rothmann asked.

"He shall receive a baronetcy which is automatically hereditary." Mr. Fletcher said.

"You may inform the government my brother and I will cooperate." Milton Rothmann said flatly.

"His Majesty's Government is appreciative of your family's cooperation." Sir Peter said dryly.

"The American government appreciates your assistance Mr. Rothmann." Crawford said.

"The bank's name will not be mentioned." Rothmann said.

"This will never reach the ears of the press and all documents will be sealed for 50 years." Sir Peter said. "Colonel Tremayne will drive you back to London."

"Everything set?" Crawford asked as he lit a cigar.

"Greene will contact *Albatross*." Austen-Halton said lighting his cigar.

"Will this work?" Crawford asked dourly.

"Mr. Rothmann has received something that had always been out of his grasp." Mr. Fletcher said. "What's one more Jewish Lord of the realm? I will leave you gentlemen to what you do best."

"You people are very hard to warm up to." Crawford said chillingly.

"Fletcher is from the old school Henry." Sir Peter said. "He dislikes Jews and they dislike him, but they can work together if need be."

"I had one helluva time convincing the Treasury Department to give me the money." Crawford said. "They dislike having that much bogus cash floating around."

"If Colquhoun should fail for any reason Krieger won't be able to explain two million dollars in American currency in a Jewish owned bank in Switzerland." Austen-Halton rasped.

"Even if he does escape this by some miracle, the bastard still loses." Crawford said coldly. "It's all bogus. You have a criminal mind Sir Peter."

"Thank you." Austen-Halton said with a slight smile.

"What are the Rothmanns really getting out of this?" Crawford asked.

"They get respectability." Austen-Halton exhaled a long column of smoke. "Not bad for some ghetto Jews from Poland."

"Glad to see someone is getting a head." Crawford rasped.

Chapter Eleven
December 7, 1942
08:00 hrs

Enroute to Adlerberghof

"Give your report on Adlerberghof Albrecht if you don't mind Colonel." Krieger asked as he lit a cigar in a slow deliberate manner. "Does this flyspeck have any value to the Greater German Reich?"

"Not really sir." Ehrlich said flipping open a small black notebook. "No industry, just farmers and shopkeepers. The Burgermeister and the Police Chief are Party members."

"Only two paragons of virtue?" Helmuth laughed coyly.

"There is a troika." Ehrlich said. "Kurt Schiller is the mayor; Otto Heinz, police chief; Hugo Kohlberger is the People's Court judge."

"This Schiller sounds familiar." Krieger said.

"You met him in Berlin, 1937." Ehrlich said. "His devotion to the Party's rules was what got him exiled to Adlerberghof. His self-righteousness stomped on too many toes."

"Why is he still alive?" Helmuth asked dourly.

"Goebbels is his mentor." Ehrlich said flatly.

"Now, I remember him." Helmuth said dryly as he relighting the cigar. "How many people do they have?"

"Ten regular policemen exempted from military service." Ehrlich said gravely. "There are 50-60 members of the Landwacht."

"Can we separate Heinz from the Mayor?" Helmuth asked.

"Heinz is Schiller's brother-in-law." Ehrlich said. "The Chief is a real live war hero from the last war- Blue Max. Schiller has a private bodyguard of 15 SA."

"Has the Burgermeister lost his guts?" Helmuth asked.

"Schiller is a tough uncompromising bastard in any type of fight." Ehrlich said. "One of the few SA officers Hitler trusted in '34. He personally killed five of his SA colleagues during the Purge in Berlin. He is a devout Nazi which means trouble."

Krieger crushed out his cigar. "It might be necessary to eliminate Schiller and Heinz if they refuse to be cooperative Albrecht."

"Would that be wise with Goebbels' interest in him?" Ehrlich asked frankly.

"Skasch will be blamed for any killings." Krieger said flatly. "Himmler will smooth things out with the Dwarf."

"Schiller will not be easy to kill." Ehrlich said.

"Elsa has contacted our Old Freikorps friend, Hauptmann Willi Eidernau." Helmuth said grimly. "He will bring enough men to insure that we control the town and any events."

"Then we are set." Ehrlich said with a smile.

[2]
09:45 hrs

Twickem-Hallesy
Halton Manor

Colonel Sergei Alexandrovich Mikhailov was no stranger to the manor house. Unlike other Soviet intelligence officers, Mikhailov mixed well with his British counterparts and now the Americans. Austen-Halton was reasonably certain that Mikhailov was not NKVD agent or informer within the GRU.

"Are you satisfied so far?" Sir Peter asked after Mikhailov had finished reading the various reports.

"As far as the report goes." Mikhailov said wryly. "However, Moscow has heard disturbing rumors that this whole operation has been designed to save one man."

"As usual Moscow got it wrong Comrade Colonel." Crawford said not hiding his great dislike of the Soviets. "Krieger is as much a danger to you as he is to us."

"Moscow has no tact at times." Mikhailov said firmly as he lit a Russian black cigarette with an American Zippo lighter. "But, Moscow was told that nothing would be hidden."

Sir Peter adjusted his crippled arm. "Quite true, but it was supposed to be quid pro quo Colonel." Austen-Halton relit his cigar. "Then we learn of *Boris*."

"Whose existence, if we had known, would have negated the need of this mission?" Crawford said gruffly.

"Officially I deny all of this." Mikhailov said coldly.

"Unofficially, what do you say?" Austen-Halton asked pouring a cup of coffee.

"He is a deep agent, very valuable to Moscow." Mikhailov answered.

"Let's not engage in senseless fencing Sergei." Austen-Halton abraded. "In all honesty we will need his help."

"I am not his control." Mikhailov said bluntly. "He has no control per say."

"How is he contacted?" Crawford inquired. "I can't believe you people don't have a line to him."

"*Boris* is independent of Central Control." Mikhailov said flatly.

"Damnit, you don't expect us to swallow that crap?" Crawford growled. "The NKVD and the GRU don't work that way. You're people can't go to the latrine without someone reporting it upstairs."

"True." Mikhailov answered. "The NKVD and GRU operate that way."

"Stalin doesn't have to follow the rules." Austen-Halton said sternly.

"Da, that is correct." Mikhailov said.

"You'll have to inform him that we need to use him." Austen-Halton said flatly.

"Committing suicide is not on my list of things to do Sir Peter." Mikhailov said.

"You have a glib tongue." Crawford hissed.

"I'm not supposed to know about him." Mikhailov said.

"However, you do." Austen-Halton said. "Stalin wouldn't allow you to be above ground unless he wanted you to know."

"I would have to talk to him directly." Mikhailov said bluntly. "The people who surround him don't like strangers breaking into the circle."

"You are a clever man." Crawford said bluntly.

"Stalin will need a damn good reason." Mikhailov said.

"If he wants him to stay alive he'll let him help us." Crawford said bluntly. "We don't intend to leave survivors."

"We are Allies." Mikhailov said. "We have a mutual goal in defeating the fascists."

"That is the immediate goal Comrade Mikhailov." The General said. "We have no friends Sergei, only enemies."

"This is the only way to save *Boris*?" Mikhailov asked crushing out his cigarette.

"Our people will kill him if they don't know." Sir Peter said. "How would Comrade Stalin take that Colonel?"

"He would take it very badly." Mikhailov said. "I'll inform Moscow immediately."

"Use our wireless." Austen-Halton said. "We can scramble the signal."

[3]
09:45 hrs

Berger Gasthaus
Room 2

"Schiller believes you?" Lang asked looking out the room window towards the police station.

"Perhaps he is a good actor." Gerhardt said undoing his necktie.

"Nobody is that good." Lang said sourly.

"We better be that good." Mannerling said. "Or we better start running."

"I'll give him an hour, maybe two before he sends someone to Jaegerfeld to check my story." Gerhardt said as he lit a cigarette.

"That could be unhealthy." Mannerling said dully. "What are your plans?"

"Franz will handle that." Gerhardt said.

"Schiller might send more than one." Mannerling said.

"Jaegerfeld is closer." Gerhardt said. "It will take 72 hours or more to get to Munich and back. We should be gone by then."

"Damn well better be." Mannerling said firmly.

[4]
9:55 AM

Burgermeister's Office

Schiller looked at the large wall map that hung behind his desk in his office staring at the Swiss-German border.

"What in hell did Gerhardt tell you Kurt?" Heinz asked sharply.

"I'll tell you latter." Schiller said. "Where are Stupnagel and Aufwasser?"

"At home, no beer halls open at this hour." Heinz answered. "They worked the night shift."

"I want you to visit each man." Schiller said. "Stupnagel is to go to Jaegerfeld and send a telegram to Berlin. He is then to go the Jherling to wait the answer."

"What about Aufwasser?" Otto asked.

"Aufwasser is to go to Stuttgart and deliver a letter to Reichkriminaldirektor Fuchs." Schiller said.

"Why seem him?" Heinz growled. "Why in hell go to him Kurt?"

"He is a rare commodity these days an honest man." Schiller said turning away from the map. "You are to pay them 1000 Rms each- no commission for you."

"Damn, if you don't trust our visitors." Heinz rasped. "Kill them."

"I am covering my options." Schiller said. "All your men are to be on duty 12 on/ 12 off until further notice and no practice blackouts."

"They'll notice that." Heinz said.

"Good." Schiller replied.

"Any chance we can get the Army here?" Heinz asked.

"Very slim chance Otto I am afraid." Schiller answered plainly. "Our best bet is Fuchs."

"Why must it be him Kurt?" Otto asked.

"I told you." Schiller said. "He is an honest man, a rarity today."

[4]
09:45 hrs

Adlerberghof
Nordland Hill

Colquhoun viewed the town 2.5 kilometers away from a mound of pine trees called by the locals Nordland's Hill. He had decided that he and Reed would take the room reserved for them at the Gruenling Gasthof; Browne and Carey would stay at Braunfuch diagonally across the street from the Gruenling.

The Gruenling Gasthof was located on a small knoll in the central area of the town by the small lake. The Braunfuch was 100 meters away. The Gasthofs both built in 1898, out of granite. The Gruenling was actually the winter home of the local baron until the brief socialist revolution toppled the King in 1918. The baron fled to Spain and never returned. His family sold the property to a Jew name Patz, who also bought the Braunfuch.

The Gruenling and Braunfuch were the only Gasthofs allowed to be open because Judge Kohlberger, the Volksgerichtshof judge owned them. In 1935, Kohlberger had the government seize the property for taxes and Kohlberger bought them for a few hundreds marks each. His son-in-law ran both hotels before the war, but he was now in the Army and the judge allowed his dim-witted step-son-in-law Prezhauffer to run them.

Colquhoun nodded to Reed to start the car and head for the town knowing that the original plan had gone to hell. London had never contemplated losing three men before they reached here. Colquhoun knew that every plan had flaws that would not show up until it was too late to correct. Colquhoun and the others knew that continuing was the only way they could possibly survive this mess.

Colquhoun glanced down at the attaché case knowing this was a ticking time bomb. Inside the case was $50,000 American dollars in $100 bills. This was the down payment due Krieger to cover his expenses. This was his biggest worry overall because stopped by police Colquhoun had no logical explanation for the cash without Reichbank clearance and with a clearance they would call the Reichbank to confirm it The local police would have no choice but to call in the Sipo or Gestapo after they got the answer.

Colquhoun and Reed entered the Gasthof lobby. Colquhoun found a chair and sat down while Reed rang the desk bell. After a few minutes, the desk clerk emerged from the back room. He was a surly little bastard who said his name was Prezhauffer.

"Who are you?" Prezhauffer asked tartly. "This is a private Gasthof not open to the general public."

"We have a reservation." Reed said sharply.

"What is your name?" Prezhauffer asked sourly.

"My name is Reisler." Reed answered. "I'm Dr. Skasch's assistant."

"Is he Viktor Skasch, Bern Switzerland?" Prezhauffer hissed.

"He is Herr Dr. Skasch." Reed said. Curtly.

"I need to see your passport Passports and visas?" Prezhauffer asked. Reed handed him the documents

"Everything is in order." Reed said.

"Sign the cards." Prezhauffer said. "Police regulations and we keep the passports."

"That is standard procedure." Reed said flatly.

"We have no porters." Prezhauffer said handing Reed the room key.

"We are neutral not weak." Reed answered.

Reed unlocked the door of 209 and they walked in. Reed locked the door from the inside leaving the key inside the lock. "Sleep or watch?"

"I'll sleep." Colquhoun said placing the attaché case on the table. "Browne and Carey will watch the front from across the street. They will ring if anyone shows up early. I want to meet him and get the hell out of here quickly with as little fuss as possible."

"That sounds reasonable." Reed hissed collapsing into a chair. "This place reminds me of a bad Boris Karloff movie."

"Going to be just as bloody as when we get through." Colquhoun said grimly. "We kill Krieger's companions."

"Do we bother to ask to see if they are going?" Reed asked dourly. "No sense in leaving bleeding bodies around if we don't have to."

"Ask once." Colquhoun said. "But don't wait to long for the answer."

"What about the wife?" Reed hissed.

"She objects." Colquhoun said. "Krieger gets a quick divorce."

"That is fine with me." Reed said.

"Keep the pistol hidden until the last moment." Colquhoun said flatly. "I don't want trouble with the local police. We'll have a long journey without someone chasing us bent on revenge."

"Hick cops don't scare me Major." Reed said.

"I grew up in a small town Reed." Colquhoun said. "Policemen and firemen are usually related in small towns. Killing one of them is an attack on all of them."

[5]
09:55 hrs

Berger Gasthaus
Room 4

Mannerling lowered the custom-made rifle as Gerhardt entered the room.

"Are you as good as they say Mannerling?" Gerhardt asked somberly as Mannerling placed the rifle on the bed.

"Yes." Mannerling replied lighting a cigarette.

"Make?" Gerhardt asked sitting down in the chair next to the bed.

"This is .375 magnum H&H rifle Herr Major." Mannerling said dully. "It was custom-made for the Earl of Somerville for the Graf von Sunderberg in 1910. The telescopic sight is German/Swiss and the ammunition is from Slovakia."

"I see nothing English." Gerhardt said. "How did you get it?"

"The late Graf von Sunderberg had the unfortunate luck to be in East Africa at the outbreak of the First War." Mannerling paused. "He was not as lucky Lettow-Vorbeck and got himself killed. Sir Peter's brother brought the rifle home in 1915."

"It has come full circle." Gerhardt said unbuttoning his collar. "Have you test fired it?

"I'll have to do this cold." Mannerling said. "All I need is a target."

"I try to arrange that." Gerhardt said coldly. "You could kill him before he gets into the Gasthof?"

"Easily." Mannerling said. "Unfortunately the manipulators of this bizarre plan want nothing that simple."

"An unknown assassin." Gerhardt said. "That will drive Berlin nuts."

"We better have someone in the Gasthof to shepherd our friends out of the Gasthof." Mannerling said drably. "They might try to become too late the hero."

"There will be no heroes." Gerhardt said flatly. "We better get all the rest we can. "

[6]
15:00 hrs

Jaegerfeld
Mittfeld Gasthof

"Why not push on to Adlerberghof Herr Schimdtz?" Jung asked as they settled in their room at the Mittfeld Gasthof in Jaegerfeld. Schimdtz was one of Krieger's numerous aide-de-camps.

"Instructions Herr Jung." Schimdtz said hollowly. "We stay here until the General arrives in Munich."

"This makes no sense." Jung said. "I thought the General would go straight to Adlerberghof?"

"The General won't arrive there until after dark." Schimdtz said. "Driving on mountain roads in winter is very dangerous."

"This is dangerous for me." Jung said grimly.

"No one is looking for you." Schimdtz said. "The General should be here by 8 PM."

"You don't know Skasch." Jung hissed.

"I'll call room service." Schimdtz said. "We should be back on the road by 20:00 hrs."

"I thought you said it was dangerous driving at night?" Jung hissed.

"For him not you Herr Jung it is dangerous." Schimdtz said.

Chapter Twelve
December 8, 1942
01:00 hrs

Bonn
Majestic Hotel

    The hotel Majestic was a first class hotel and had originally been built for the King of Bavaria in the late 1880's as a summer home for foreign nobility. The Countess had invaded the hotel shortly before 5:00 PM yesterday and took control of the whole top floor.
    Eidernau knocked on the door and entered. The Countess lowered the newspaper as she fitted a cigarette into the gold and ivory cigarette holder
    "He is at the Mittfeld." Eidernau said flatly. "He'll leave in two hours."
    "Will there be moonlight?" The Countess asked seriously.
    "There will be a full moon starting in about 30 minutes." Eidernau said.
    "Are your men ready?" She asked coldly.
    "We are waiting for final instructions." Eidernau said.
    "Move up to Adlerberghof using the old lumber road." The Countess said. "You will wait at Ingeldmann's lumber mill for Ehrlich's signal. Spread your men out to surround the town."
    "Should any of the townspeople see us there?" Eidernau asked somberly.
    "Kill them." The Countess said. "That goes without saying for Skasch's men."
    Eidernau shook his head as he lit a cigarette. "Skasch's gang is a myth Countess. He killed off most of them and the rest simply vanished."
    "He might still have a bodyguard." The Countess said.
    "You really don't need all this firepower Countess." Eidernau said. "If all we do is freeze our asses off."
    "You are being paid." The Countess said. "Just do what you are told."
    "Of course it is your money." Eidernau rasped.
    "Exactly Herr Eidernau my money." The Countess said. "After this is finished I might still need your unique services Willi."
    "I'm always available for a price." Eidernau said.
    "My husband's career may still need to have barriers removed." The Countess said in an icy tone. "How do you feel about Ehrlich?"
    "I would consider him a friend." Eidernau said.
    "Could you kill him for 250,000 Reichmarks?" The Countess asked chillingly.
    "He's not that much of a friend." Eidernau quipped. "What about Klugge?"
    "He knows his place." The Countess said. "If the sense of loyalty comes leaves him, kill him too."

[2]
01:30 hrs

London
USSR Embassy

    Major General Sergeyev swirled the vodka in the glass then swallowed it as he looked at his young friend. "Could they have been bluffing Sergei?"

"Austen-Halton is a Cheshire cat." Mikhailov said. "Crawford is not that good an actor. They know about *Boris*."

"What good is that my friend?" Sergeyev hissed. "All they have is a name."

"Krieger is not leaving Adlerberghof Alexi." Mikhailov said flatly. "The British are as cold-blooded as we are and the Americans are learning quickly."

"You have to accept what will be Sergei." The General said.

"They want our help." Mikhailov said.

Sergeyev poured himself another drink and lit the American cigarette in a slow deliberate manner. "Moscow has agreed to expose *Boris* to our temporary allies."

"Moscow will allow him to die a senseless death?" Mikhailov asked bluntly.

"*Boris* has been living on borrowed time for years." Sergeyev said coldly. "You must think of yourself Sergei. Officially you know nothing about *Boris*."

"He is Stalin's friend." Mikhailov said firmly.

"Don't be a damn fool." The General said turning up the radio. "Stalin, he has no friends."

"I will do this on my own." Sergei said. "I have a separate control."

"Good luck my young friend." Sergeyev said grimly.

[3]
02:00 hrs

Adlerberghof
Gasthof Gruenling

Prezhauffer lighted the cigarette as he glared at the two men at the front desk. "Are you both staying?"

"Only Herr Jung will be staying." Schimdtz said bluntly

"I'll need a fire started in the room." Jung quipped. "Central heat is not available in these old places."

"That will be 100 marks extra." Prezhauffer grunted. "The wood isn't free."

"Add it to the bill." Schimdtz said bluntly.

"It will take about twenty minutes," Prezhauffer grunted. "Wait here."

Jung lit a cigarette. "Why are you leaving?"

"I have no orders to stay." Schimdtz said.

"How the hell am I supposed to get back to civilization?" Jung asked irritated by not knowing.

"Perhaps the General will give you a ride back?" Schimdtz hissed with a half-smile. "Or perhaps this is your new posting?"

"You are hardly amusing Herr Hauptman." Jung said. "Without you I have no protection from Skasch "

"You have the advantage of surprise Herr Jung." Schimdtz said. "He won't be expecting you."

"Has he left yet" Jung said.

"No idea." Schimdtz said flatly. "That Wagner's job to keep tabs on him Herr Jung."

"I'm still uneasy about this Schimdtz." Jung said damningly. "Skasch is a dangerous man."

"After today he will no longer be dangerous to anyone." Schimdtz said "Do you need this?" Schimdtz showed Jung a PPK.

"I have my own weapon." Jung said.

[4]
02:45hrs

Bern Switzerland
Skasch's Hotel

"There goes Melville." Withgate said "And his shadow Wagner."

"I told Melville to head directly to the train station." Greene said tampering down the tobacco in his pipe bowl.

"Wagner will board the train." Withgate said. "Alan doesn't look a bit like Skasch close up."

"Gunnarsohn's people will pick him and the driver at the station." Greene said.

"On what charges will Gunnarsohn use sir?" Withgate asked flatly.

"Illegal procession of a fire arm will do." Greene said firmly.

"Wagner may be a slug, but he is a slug with diplomatic immunity." Withgate said turning from the window. "Once he calls the embassy the border guards will be notified. Von Huess is not an idiot sir."

"Gunnarsohn's men will hold Wagner and the driver for 24 hours." Greene said. "Von Huess will not suspect anything. Wagner most likely has orders not to report unless trouble occurs."

"Von Huess is the type who will call border control." Withgate said. "He trusts no one."

"The telephones lines to the German embassy will have difficulties." Greene said with a half-smile. "The Federal Post Office will be uncooperative."

"What about the wireless?" Withgate asked.

"It will be jammed." Greene answered.

"How long will this all last sir?" The Captain asked.

"5-6 hours at the most." Greene said. "Melville will pass through customs as Dr. Viktor Skasch that will be reported to Standartenfuhrer von Huess."

"How will Melville get back?" Withgate asked.

"He has another mission to complete." Greene said looking at his watch. "We should be leaving for Rielmort é now."

[5]
04:00 hrs

Stuttgart
Central Police Headquarters

Kriminalinspektor Arthur Wulff walked down the staircase to the offices of the Criminal Police. He stopped at the table and poured himself a cup of what they called coffee nowadays and headed for the office with the yellowish light shining out into the hallway.

"Did you bother to go home sir?" Wulff asked his superior officer in the Kripo, Reichkriminaldirektor Janus Fuchs. The Reichkriminaldirektor looked up at Wulff brushing off the cigar ash from the old grayish sweater and adjusting his glasses

"I went home for supper Arthur." Fuchs said with a smile at his young assistant. "My wife baked today and she gave me cake."

"It's 4 AM sir." Wulff said. "This could have waited sir."

"It is easier to conduct police work without Strupp." Fuchs said. "Have some cake Arthur. What brings you here?"

"The duty sergeant called in the 4th District called me." Wulff said sitting down.

"Why?" Fuchs asked.

"Sergeant Jaeken had a letter for you." Wulff said. "He knows I work with you now."

Fuchs leaned back in his chair, lit his pipe, and blew a long column of white smoke into the air. "Interesting… Delivered by the Post?"

"No by hand." Wulff said. "The man's name was Aufwasser from Adlerberghof."

"Don't know him." Fuchs said. "Is he still here?"

"No." Wulff said. "He went on to Munich."

"Adlerberghof is too small to concern us, but it sounds familiar." Fuchs muttered. "Interesting... you read the note?"

"It is an invitation to visit Adlerberghof by the Burgermeister." Wulff answered.

"His name is Schiller." Fuchs said.

"Yes, you know him sir?" Wulff asked.

"We've met in the past." Fuchs answered.

"I would prefer Innsbruck or Salzburg." Wulff lamented. "Not cheerful little Adlerberghof."

"Why does he want me to go to Adlerberghof?" Fuchs asked.

"He has a problem." Wulff replied. "We'll be out of our jurisdiction and Strupp likes things legal."

"He'll enjoy the idea of me being far away Arthur." Fuchs said. "For as long as possible."

"This is political." Wulff rasped.

Fuchs smiled. "This is the Third Reich Arthur, it is always political now. The Police Law gives the Kripo national jurisdiction." Fuchs relit his pipe. "The same law allows for preventive arrest which gives us the power to stop crime before it happens."

"What crime sir?" Wulff asked. "Do you know this Schiller sir?"

"I know him Arthur." Fuchs said firmly. "He must be in deep shit to ask me for help?"

"How many men do you need sir?" Wulff asked.

"You and Oberwachtmeister Grau are the only ones I need." Fuchs said. "Have Grau sign out a car."

"What about Strupp sir?" Wulff asked.

"He'll be in at nine." Fuchs said. "We'll leave at noon."

[5]
07:00 hrs

Adlerberghof
Gasthof Gruenling

Krieger's automobile pulled up in front of the Gasthof after a torturous drive through the mountains to the town. Ehrlich and Klugge entered the Gasthof followed by the General. Klugge went directly to the front desk and rang the bell.

"We have reservations." Klugge said to the bored looking clerk who emerged from the back room. "We have two adjoining rooms with bath."

"The Gasthof is closed." Prezhauffer grunted rubbing his eyes

"The rooms are under the name of Jung." Klugge said tiredly.

"Herr Jung is here, but he said nothing about your party." Prezhauffer said.

"Look again." Klugge hissed unsnapping his holster flap.

"I don't have too." The clerk hissed. "If you have complaints go over to the town hall and complain to Judge Kohlberger, the owner."

"Is there a problem Sergeant-Major?" Ehrlich asked stepping up to the front desk as he removed his gloves.

"This fool lost our reservations sir." Klugge answered.

"Have you?" Ehrlich asked.

"The Gasthof is closed." Prezhauffer said. "Complain to the owner."

"I don't care who the owner is." Ehrlich said softly as Klugge placed his P-38 under the clerk's chin. "We have two adjoining rooms; if you don't find the card the Sergeant-Major will splatter your brains all over the ceiling."

"That is murder." Prezhauffer gulped.

"The SS never commits murder." Ehrlich said crisply. "What about our rooms?"

"My mistake sir, they were misfiled." Prezhauffer squealed. "Frau Ober took the reservations." Prezhauffer handed Ehrlich two keys. "They are Rooms 230 and 232."

"Has Herr Skasch arrived?" Ehrlich asked.

"Yes." Prezhauffer said.

"Inform Herr Jung to come to the General's room in an hour." Ehrlich said bluntly, as he turned around. "We'll have breakfast in fifteen minutes."

"Make certain that the coffee is hot." Klugge said placing a 1000 Reich mark note on the desktop. "Real coffee, understood?"

"Yes." Prezhauffer said.

Room 230
One hour later

Jung entered the room looking quite ill at ease as he closed the door. Klugge pointed to the chair by the fireplace. Krieger emerged from the bedroom and sat down opposite Jung.

"Coffee Hermann?" Helmuth asked. "This is real coffee."

"No thank you." Jung said. "My stomach is bothering me."

"Nerves." Krieger said.

"The doctors say ulcer." Jung said.

"Relax." Krieger said. "Does Skasch know you are here?"

"No." Jung said dourly. "I'm not that clumsy."

"Even the best have a bad day." The General said.

"My police source in Bern tell me that something happened two nights ago involving Colonel Gunnarsohn of Swiss Intelligence." Jung said flatly.

"We are not the sole worry of Swiss Security." The General said bluntly.

"The Russians put a tail on him." Jung said. "You know how crazy they are."

"Skasch is here." Krieger said. "The Russians are crazy, but always inept so stop shitting your pants."

Jung lit a cigarette. "Why am I here?"

"Simple Hermann." Krieger said. "You are the only one who can identify Skasch."

"What?" Jung hissed.

"Skasch is a clever weasel as you well know." Helmuth said. "He has used doubles in the past."

"He is the only one left." Jung said dryly.

"He has people with him." Helmuth said.

"Hired help." Jung said. "Too much money for him to trust anyone, but himself." Jung crushed out the cigarette. "When do you plan to do this?"

"Tonight at 7." Krieger said.

"Do I have to stay?" Jung asked.

"Once you do your part, you may leave." Krieger said. "Klugge is delivering the invitation at this moment."

[6]
08:45 hrs

Gasthof Gruenling
Room 218

Colquhoun looked at the Sergeant Major with a grim expression seeing that Klugge was a determined man. "Why not now?"

"7 PM Herr Skasch." Klugge said.

"I don't like it." Colquhoun said. "I want it earlier."

"This is not a negotiation Herr Skasch." Klugge said bluntly. "The General considers this a private matter."

"Does he have everything?" Colquhoun asked.

"Yes." Klugge said. "The General suggests that you stay in your room until then."

"Understood." Colquhoun said. "Anything else I should know?"

"Just be on time." Klugge said.

Reed closed and locked the door and lit a cigarette after Klugge left the room. "This I don't like."

"What in hell are we going to do?" Colquhoun rasped flatly. "I can't play this game for too much longer."

"Night is to his advantage." Reed said.

"His game." Colquhoun hissed. "His rules and he knows I have no choice."

"Do you trust this bastard?" Reed asked.

"He has to be cautious." Colquhoun said. "After all he is walking a tightrope soaked in grease."

"My heart bleeds." Reed hissed. "What the hell do you think we're doing major?"

"Juggling hand grenades with the pins pulled Reed." Colquhoun said tartly. "You better get out your mirror and signal Browne and Carey."

[7]
10:00 hrs

Berger Gasthof

"Night?" Gerhardt asked anxiously. "Are you certain Franz?"

"Prezhauffer is the snoopiest hotel employee I have ever met." Franz said as he lit the cigarette hanging from the corner of his mouth. "He is also the most talkative desk clerk for a price."

"Has he been listening in on us?" Mannerling asked.

"Even Prezhauffer isn't that stupid." Franz said dully.

"Will night be a problem for you?" Gerhardt asked Mannerling bluntly.

Mannerling removed the telescopic sight from the rifle. "It will make it harder, but not impossible." Mannerling said. "I might have to be closer?"

"How close are you talking about?" Gerhardt asked.

"I'll need at least100 to 200 yards closer perhaps." Mannerling answered.

"That shouldn't be too hard I suppose." Gerhardt said. "Can you do it?"

"You are being vague." Franz said toughly. "Can you kill him?"

Mannerling lit a cigarette. "Killing him is not the problem Herr Leutnant; it's the getting out alive which is the trick."

"What is the alternative?" Gerhardt asked.

"We might have to do this the old fashion way." Mannerling said. "Face-to-face."

"Krieger might not kill Colquhoun." Gerhardt said. "After all the major is a good hostage for him."

"I doubt it." Mannerling said. "Krieger will realize that he has been set up and he will not want any witnesses around which includes us."

"The old fashion way." Gerhardt muttered. "Glad this was planned out."

"As the Americans say 'situation normal all fucked up.' They are amusing." Mannerling said.

"This means we have to get closer." Gerhardt said.

"Do they know you?" Mannerling asked. "That could complicate things."

"Yes, they know me." Gerhardt said.

"Wonderful." Mannerling grunted.

"If this sours beyond help, I'm wondering how many of the townspeople I'll have to kill to get out of this alive."

"As many as you have to Major." Mannerling hissed.

Chapter Thirteen
December 8, 1942
19:00 hrs

Adlerberghof
Gasthof Gruenling

    Colquhoun knocked on the door firmly. The door slowly opened and they were greeted by a man wearing the uniform of a Waffen SS colonel. In his right hand, he held a Walther P-38. He motioned Colquhoun and Reed to enter. They walked to the center of the room to a table where a brandy bottle and glasses were.
    "Herr Dr. Skasch of Bern." Ehrlich said holstering his pistol. "At last we meet."
    "Then you know why I'm here?" Colquhoun asked slyly.
    "Of course I do." Ehrlich said pouring the brandy into the snifter. "The General has no secrets from me or Sergeant-Major Klugge."
    "The General?" Reed asked.
    "He'll join us in a few minutes." Ehrlich said. "Sit down and relax."
    "We are pressed for time Herr Oberst." Colquhoun said stiffly.
    "Why the rush?" Ehrlich quipped. "You are among friends."
    "This is still unfriendly territory." Colquhoun said trying to avoid a long discussion with Ehrlich. The background information on Skasch was rather lean and the wrong word could prove to be fatal.
    "After this you'll be able to retire in style." Ehrlich rasped.
    "I want to enjoy this new found wealth." Colquhoun snorted. "I understand that the taxes here are murderous."
    "Only a few minutes more." Ehrlich said placing an attaché case on the table and sat down. Colquhoun nodded and sat down wondering why they needed two attaché cases. Reed stood behind the chair acting like a bodyguard.
    Colquhoun stood as the SS General entered the room from the bedroom. Krieger's eyes met Colquhoun's doleful eyes.
    "Herr Doctor." Krieger said offering his right hand. "We finally meet at long last; Hermann has told me much about your colorful career."
    "All lies." Colquhoun said with a smile taking the cold hand firmly. "My hope is that our business can be conducted quickly."
    "My sentiments exactly." Krieger said with a slight smile. "You have the merchandise?"
    "Are you ready to fulfill your part Herr General?" Colquhoun asked.
    "In the next room." Krieger said. "Colonel."
    Ehrlich went to the room that Krieger had entered from and returned with an overweight man with a round face. As he came closer, a scornful expression crossed his face as he looked at Colquhoun.
    "Hermann, you're acting odd." Krieger hissed tartly as the man moved next to the General. "Skasch has come a long way."
    "Skasch?" Jung grunted. "What the hell are you talking about- he isn't Skasch!"
    "What?" Krieger growled.
    Reed brought his pistol up and fired first killing Jung instantly with a bullet through the head. As Jung fell, he knocked the General to the floor. Colquhoun was trying for his weapon

when a loud sound exploded followed by a searing pain in his left shoulder turning him around. Colquhoun collapsed to his knees by the table. Colquhoun saw Reed hit the wall and slide down. The Major fumbled for his pistol his anger growing as he realizing that London betrayed him. Colquhoun felt the recoil of his pistol as he pulled the trigger, but Colquhoun fell into the swirling mass of darkness as three bullets tore into him.

[2]

Gerhardt's Room

"The show is about to begin." Franz said closing the door. "Klugge is bringing Colquhoun and Reed to the room."

"I hope the lights are on brightly." Gerhardt said.

"I think Mannerling could hit a target by candlelight." Franz said begrudgingly. "This could end pleasantly."

"Not designed to end pleasantly." Gerhardt said flatly. "If we are lucky Colquhoun will kill Krieger and save us the trouble."

"When the shit hits the fan, what about our other two heroes?" Franz asked.

"Lang will take care of them." Gerhardt said.

The gunshot caught them by surprise. Gerhardt and Franz were out of the room heading for Krieger's room before the echoes died out. Gerhardt savagely kicked the door open and they rushed in weapons drawn.

Gerhardt leveled his pistol at the kneeling Ehrlich, who was about to finish Colquhoun off. Ehrlich stood needing no words to tell him that killing Colquhoun would be the last act of his life. Ehrlich tossed his pistol to the floor and stepped back. Klugge did the same thing.

"Help him Sergeant." Gerhardt rasped. "Now or I'll kill where you stand." Klugge looked at Ehrlich who nodded. Klugge moved to Colquhoun."

"The other two are dead." Franz said.

"Will he live?" Gerhardt snarled.

"He needs a doctor." Klugge fired back. "Then a lot of luck."

"Keep him alive." Gerhardt ordered.

"Christssakes I'm not a doctor." Klugge rasped.

Gerhardt turned his attention to the smirking Ehrlich. "Give me the excuse to kill you Albrecht."

"I'll not give you that pleasure Anton." Ehrlich said cynically. "You have crossed the line Herr Major. I can wait for your court-martial to see you die legally."

"Where is Krieger?" Gerhardt ordered.

"Go to hell Gerhardt." Ehrlich grunted.

"Where is the General?" Gerhardt said icily moving up to Ehrlich pointing his pistol at the colonel's face. "Dead men make convenient scapegoats."

The smirk left Ehrlich's face knowing that Gerhardt would shoot him without hesitation. "The General is in the bedroom, these pigs tried to assassinate him."

"Really." Gerhardt hissed.

"Why are you here Gerhardt?" Ehrlich demanded.

"Get him." Gerhardt snapped.

"You don't have to bother him." Ehrlich said defensively. "They just tried to murder him."

"My heart bleeds." The Major sneered.

"He isn't up to answering damn fool questions." Ehrlich said firmly. "This is an SS operation ... The Abwehr has no jurisdiction over us!"

"I have the weapon Herr Oberst." Gerhardt said wryly.

[3]

"What the hell is going on here?" Heinz growled as his mass moved into the room followed by four of his police officers armed with machine pistols. "Drop the weapons now!"

"This man needs a doctor!" Gerhardt barked.

"Who the hell is he?" Heinz rasped.

"Just get him a doctor Goddamnit!" Gerhardt snapped. "Play policeman later Heinz."

"Paulus, get Dr. Brandt." Heinz ordered. "You three on the sofa, sergeant you stay with the wounded." Heinz glanced at the other two men on the floor. "Do they need a doctor?"

"No." Klugge said bluntly.

Heinz moved in front of Ehrlich and Gerhardt. "Now what in hell is going on here? You scared the shit out of poor Prezhauffer."

"Leave this alone Heinz." Gerhardt warned.

"State Security." Ehrlich snapped. "Get the hell out now while you can my fat friend."

"I don't take orders from you." Heinz hissed. "You have to explain two dead men not me gentlemen."

"Ehrlich shot them." Gerhardt said matter-of-factly.

"You bastard." Ehrlich hissed tartly.

"Where's the big shit?" Heinz asked.

"Heinz, you don't want to get in the middle of this." Gerhardt said. "Talk to Schiller before you do anything stupid, which would be the smart move."

"Perhaps." Heinz said.

"He can't give you a damn thing." Ehrlich said coldly.

"My men will be outside the door." Heinz said. "Anyone sticks his head out the door they will blow it off."

"You are a fool Heinz." Ehrlich growled. "And a marked man."

[4]

Donner's Farm

"You're save now gentlemen." The Stranger said flatly as be brought out a Webley-Scott semi-automatic pistol. "You can breathe again."

"Who in Christ are you?" Carey sneered.

"I'm on your side." The Stranger said not lowering the pistol.

"We're kinda short on trust right now." Browne growled. "Lang sticks a gun in my ribs and pushes us into a car- then we are dumped here." Browne lit a cigarette. "Then I find you here; Donner, where is he?"

"Gone to town." The Stranger said.

"We need a name Mac." Carey demanded.

"Orr."

"Same outfit as Mannerling?" Browne rasped sharply. "We've been had."

"Yes." Orr said. "I think a drink is in order."
"Best thing anybody has said all day." Carey said.
Donner was back at his place by 9 PM and was not at all happy. Donner poured himself a drink.
"What happened at the Gruenling?" Browne asked dourly.
"From what I got from the truly scared shitless Prezhauffer isn't good." Donner said in a low voice. "Reed is dead and Colquhoun is a prisoner as well as being wounded."
"Fucking great." Orr growled. "What happened?"
"Prezhauffer didn't really know for certain." Donner said. "I get the feeling that he doesn't want to know; he is really scared."
"Where does that get us?" Carey rasped. "Mr. Orr?"
"Time for the truth." Orr hissed damningly.
"Somebody better start making some damn sense around here." Browne said in a sharp voice. "I'm getting pissed."
"Gather around the table." Orr said. "What I'm going to say might make you puke."
"Like everything else that has happened so far hasn't?" Carey rasped.

[5]

Schiller's Office

"What the hell is going on?" Schiller asked Heinz as the Chief entered the office.
"Shooting at the Gruenling." Heinz said.
"Was it Gerhardt?" Schiller asked.
"No it was the others." Heinz answered. "Gerhardt is involved some how."
"Damn." Schiller hissed. "This is beginning to make sense."
"What is?" Heinz asked.
"Wendahl found Stupnagel six kilometers outside of town." Schiller said coldly.
"That lazy bastard he promised me." Heinz grumbled. "Shacked up with Sophie Mueller, damn him."
"He never got that far." Schiller said. "Wendahl found him buried in a snowdrift."
"Froze to death?" Heinz asked.
"No." Schiller said. "Gut shot with his throat cut."
"Shit." Heinz rasped. "Did Aufwasser get through?"
"No way of knowing." Schiller said grimly. "Wendahl left the body where he found it and came to me directly. I told him to keep his mouth shut and go back home."
"Now what do we do Kurt?" Heinz asked.
"Tell me what happened." Schiller said. "Then have Moritz find Kohlberger."

[6]

Krieger's Room

After Heinz left the room, Gerhardt got up and headed towards the bedroom. Ehrlich's attempt to stop him was thwarted by Franz jabbing a PPK in the colonel's ribs. Ehrlich knowing that Franz would kill him sat down.

Krieger was sitting on the bed smoking a cigarette as Gerhardt walked into the room. The general looked at him with a blank expression; his uniform stained with blood, but no visible wounds.

"I should have known Major Gerhardt." Krieger hissed. "I should have known that a vulture like you can smell blood."

"Not hard with you Herr General." Gerhardt answered blandly.

"Why are you here?" Krieger asked crisply.

"I'm here on official business sir as always." Gerhardt replied. "Who are they?"

"That is none of your business." Krieger hissed.

"This is not a request Herr General." Gerhardt stated bluntly. "This is official business Herr General."

"I don't answer questions especially from the damn Abwehr." Krieger snapped.

Gerhardt sat down and lit a cigarette deliberately violating the rules of military courtesy twice. "Then you'll leave me with little choice, but to call Berlin."

"That will not be necessary." Krieger said. "We have no need for Berlin."

"Who are they?" Gerhardt asked.

"The fat man is Sturmbannfuhrer Hermann Jung, Ausland-SD." Krieger said. "The other two are Red assassins. They kidnapped Jung in transit here and forced him here. Jung sacrificed himself to protect me; killing them at the cost of his own life."

"Only one of them is dead." Gerhardt said. "The other one is hanging on."

"Major Gerhardt, what the hell are you doing here?" Heinz barked as he barged into the room with two of his men. "Dr. Brandt is here and we are moving the wounded man to another room."

"I need to leave Chief." Krieger rasped.

"Nobody is going anywhere." Heinz snarled. "You are all being held as suspects."

"You're joking." Krieger quipped.

"You're under house arrest." Heinz said. "Schiller wants to talk to you Herr Major."

"I can't." Gerhardt said bluntly.

"Schiller is an impatient man." Heinz rasped. "Your other companions try to interfere they will be arrested."

[7]

The Braunbierkeller

Mannerling slowly sipped his beer watching in a disinterested way the activity across the street at the Gruenling. "What happened?"

"The unexpected happened." Lang said cynically.

"That usually what kills you." Mannerling said dryly. "Are there any worthwhile details?"

"Fortunately for us the police are very talkative." Lang said leaning back into his chair lighting his pipe. "Two are dead."

"May I ask who?" Mannerling inquired.

"My talkative friend says Skasch's bodyguard and someone named Jung." Lang said in a low voice. "Skasch was shot up badly. They have a local doctor taking care of him."

"What about Browne and Carey?" Mannerling asked.

"I moved them to Donner's." Lang said. "They would have tried to be heroes."

"The police know about them," Mannerling said.
"Not interested." Lang said. "Schiller thinks they're hired muscle that ran away."
"Orr?" Mannerling asked.
"Browne and Carey will be introduced to him." Lang said.
"That should ruin their day." Mannerling said grimly.
"This is a flexible operation." Lang hissed.
"It damn well better be." Mannerling said. "From this point on we'll be making it up as we go on."
"I thought that's what we have been doing?" Lang quipped.
"No wonder you are losing the damn war." Mannerling said wryly.
"Humor is not a German characteristic Herr Major." Lang said flatly. "They'll round us up soon enough."

[8]

Twickem-Hallesy
Halton Manor

Austen-Halton slowly puffed on his cigar as he read the message from Greene, who was monitoring Donner's radio signal. "This is all James?"
"Yes sir." Tremayne said. "I have Miller doing the deciphering."
"Keep him on it." Austen-Halton said handing Crawford the message. "Keep me informed James, any time or any where."
"This wasn't in the play book." Crawford said sourly. "We should have killed this Jung when we had the chance."
"The unexpected was always part of this Henry." Sir Peter said.
"I see that Orr isn't brimming over with enthusiasm." Crawford said.
"Boyden is a Scot and they don't brim over about anything." Austen-Halton said flatly. "This does not impede our basic plan."
"You are an optimist." Crawford hissed.
"I am a realist Henry." Austen-Halton said bluntly.
Crawford stood and lit a cigarette. "I just hope these damn head-shrinkers are right about Colquhoun."
"There is another part of message from Greene sir." Tremayne said wryly.
"Just read James." Sir Peter said relighting the cigar.
"Major Colquhoun has been wounded and taken prisoner." Tremayne said emotionlessly. "Reed is dead."
"Damn, what about the others?" Crawford asked.
"They are still alive." Tremayne said. "Greene wants to know if he should send Donner the abort signal."
"That is premature Colonel." Sir Peter said coldly. "Tell Miller good work and keep monitoring the situation Colonel."
"Great." Crawford crushed out his cigarette. "Colquhoun wounded one shitty mess; they'll give him drugs to keep him out."
"The SS are not humanitarians Henry." Sir Peter said. "They will want him to talk. The wounds should lower his resistance." Sir Peter paused. "It should make him easier to break."

"He might die before our grand plan is deployed." Crawford said. "Once he wakes up he'll realizes that he has been had from the beginning."

"Colquhoun is intelligent enough to come to that conclusion." Sir Peter said. "That is why his money is counterfeit; also why Mannerling and Orr are there."

"We have done a wonderful job." Crawford rasped.

"It is very realistic to assume that none of them will survive this mission." Sir Peter said icily. "Or little solace to them to know they died for a noble cause."

"Damn, it would be profane to allow that bastard to live if they all die." Crawford said angrily.

An Honorable Betrayal

Chapter Fourteen
December 8, 1942
20:30 hrs

Adlerberghof
Town Hall

Schiller was sitting behind his massive desk with a hand carved swastika on the front. Sitting at his right was Hugo Kohlberger, the People's Court Judge. Kohlberger was a cold-eyed man in his sixties. He wore a miniature Iron Cross First Class in his lapel above his Nazi membership pin.

"You have an explanation what in hell is going on?" Schiller asked in a sharp, but controlled voice.

"State security prohibits what I can say." Gerhardt said sternly.

"I would reconsider that position Herr Major." Kohlberger said icily. "We have three dead men; one severely wounded. The time to be forthcoming is now."

"The other one died?" Gerhardt asked.

"No." Schiller said. "One of my men has been killed."

"Chief Heinz informs us that you apparently know Krieger." Kohlberger said in a flat tone. "Something else you neglected to tell us."

"I had nothing to do with your man getting killed." Gerhardt said. "What else did I fail to tell you?"

"You neglected to inform us about the assassin." Kohlberger hissed.

Gerhardt glanced at the Judge realizing that he was not a typical Party hack, but a very dangerous and clever man. The dossier on Kohlberger said that his family was from the petty nobility that had infested Weimar Germany. The judge was legally a Baron, but he stopped using the title after the creation of the Weimar Republic. Kohlberger had been a lawyer with the Bavarian Ministry of Justice. Kohlberger disliked the limelight and the postwar military intelligence did not keep records on nonentities.

"You gentlemen seem to doubt me, a bit too much." Gerhardt said firmly. "I have to ask why?"

"That crock of shit you served up about the RSD." Kohlberger said. "Krieger doesn't rate the RSD holding his hand."

"I had to try." Gerhardt said.

"Who the hell are you?" Schiller asked.

"We are the Abwehrpolizei." Gerhardt answered.

"This better be damn good why in hell you are here." Schiller snapped.

"It is." Gerhardt said sitting down lighting a cigarette.

"Better be more than good Herr Major." Kohlberger said stiffly. "Accidents can and do happen here."

Gerhardt crushed out the cigarette and lighting another one knowing that he had reached the point of no return. "Two days ago across the border in Inglewald there was a meeting between Skasch and an unknown."

"Unknown?" Schiller asked.

"Our sources could not identify him." Gerhardt said. "Allied or other is their guess."

"Are you certain it was Skasch?" Schiller asked.

"Not 100%." Gerhardt said grimly.
"Who were you following?" Kohlberger inquired.
"We were following Krieger." Gerhardt replied.
"Killing in person isn't Skasch's hallmark." Schiller said hollowly.
"Every man has a price." Gerhardt said. "That includes Skasch."
"What could Skasch gain by killing Krieger?" Schiller asked in a puzzled voice lighting a cigar. "Viktor Skasch isn't a stupid man."
"The British and the Americans are not the Reich's only enemies." Gerhardt said. "Those enemies have the vast resources to buy even the clever and cunning Viktor Skasch."
"Not the fucking Jews again, that is a tired story?" Kohlberger rasped.
"No not that again." Gerhardt said deftly. "This war has cost certain people vast sums, none of whom are Jews. Krieger is adept at grabbing other people's money."
"Krieger was to be made an example of." Schiller hissed.
"What does Krieger say about this?" Kohlberger asked coldly.
"He has decided not to cooperate." Gerhardt said. "His reason for being here was to meet with Skasch for something."
"This smells Kurt." Kohlberger warned. "Berlin might decide that we are involved because of your past."
"We are not involved." Schiller growled.
"Gerhardt has dragged us into this Kurt." Kohlberger said cynically.
"You both are aware of how Berlin thinks." Gerhardt said sardonically. "They do not draw fine lines of distinction or think very rationality. Krieger knows this." Gerhardt paused. "To save all our asses the prisoner must talk before he cuts his throat shaving."
"You have a plan no doubt," Schiller said dourly. "Which involves you?"
"We need the truth." Gerhardt said. "My orders brought me here- call Generalmajor von Tanz in Berlin."
"We'll have to return your weapons." Kohlberger said flatly.
"That would be a gesture of good faith." Gerhardt said. "The prisoner is the only one who will tell us the truth. Unless you want to believe Krieger will tell you the truth?"
"The truth has many faces." Schiller said. "Why should we believe you?"
"I wasn't meeting, secretly, a known criminal near the Swiss border." Gerhardt said flatly. "It was Gruppenfuhrer Krieger."
"How will you protect him?" Kohlberger asked.
"I'll need the police and Landwacht." Gerhardt said.
"I'll inform Heinz to return your weapons and to cooperate with you." Schiller said in a firm voice. "His protection is your total responsibility Major."
"That is understood." Gerhardt said. "I know the price of failure gentlemen."
"Make certain that you do understand the price of failure." Kohlberger said bluntly with no hidden meaning in his voice. "There will be no mercy Herr Major. We do not intend to die for a misguide gesture or mistake."
"I and my men understand this." Gerhardt said. "We don't intend to die for anyone from this shit hole. Once Skasch is capable of talking the truth will be known."
"Berlin doesn't put much stock in the truth Gerhardt." Schiller said.
"Berlin wants resolution to sticky problems." Gerhardt said. "The Reichsfuhrer will want this resolved."

"I really don't give a damn about what Himmler wants." Schiller said. "You solve the problem one way or the other."

[2]

Gasthof Gruenling
Krieger's Room

Krieger lit a cigarette and peered out the window. "That bastard can not be allowed to talk Albrecht."

"There is very little I can do at the moment." Ehrlich said. "Neither Heinz nor Gerhardt are going to let me stroll into the room and kill him. From what I saw he is badly wounded and might not regain conscientiousness."

"I can't depend on that." Helmuth hissed. "Did Klugge bring in the short-wave?"

"It is still in the automobile." Ehrlich said. "You want Klugge to get it?"

"No." Helmuth snarled. "Elsa will be here in the morning, she'll bring hers inside."

"What good?" Ehrlich asked.

"Eidernau has a short-wave." Helmuth said. "Willi would have someone watching this place."

"The list is what is important." Helmuth said dryly. "What about that damn list?"

"Nothing has been said." Ehrlich said. "They haven't found it."

"Why say that?" Helmuth rasped.

"If Gerhardt or Schiller had the list we would be dead." Ehrlich said. "Eventually they will search their room."

"They have $ 25,000 in American currency in my attaché case." Helmuth said. "That alone is more than enough for Gerhardt to arrest us."

"Nothing has been found out yet." Ehrlich rasped. "Gerhardt is the direct threat."

"Not at the moment." Krieger said in a faraway voice.

"Stop living in your dream world." Ehrlich hissed. "Gerhardt isn't here by accident. Your 'friends' in Berlin are involved damnit."

"My dream world, I'm in the real world." Helmuth murmured. "You are forgetting yourself Albrecht."

"The hell I am." Ehrlich snarled. "You are here in this shit hill of a town with a known criminal and illegal currency. You really think Gerhardt is here by accident. Those vultures in Berlin have been waiting for years for you to make a mistake."

"There has been no fatal error yet." Helmuth said.

"You have not made yourself popular." Ehrlich said. "You'll find no allies here; if you manage to dodge Gerhardt, Schiller is still there waiting."

"I'm not dead yet Albrecht." Krieger said. "I intend to dance on their graves with your help and Eidernau's. Willi's specialty is death and he is quite good at it."

"Schiller isn't going to allow his little kingdom to be turned into a killing ground." Ehrlich said flatly.

"Dying will upset my wife." Krieger said sternly.

"We can't upset her can we?" Schiller hissed.

[3]
19:00 hrs

Town Hall
Schiller's Office

    Kohlberger lit his pipe after Gerhardt left the office then poured himself a drink. "Is it wise to trust the Major?"
    "Would you prefer to trust Krieger instead?" Schiller hissed.
    "We better contact Jaegerfeld." Kohlberger suggested. "Jherling has 700 men getting frostbite on their asses."
    "Someone has this place under surveillance." Schiller said flatly. "Stupnagel was no accident."
    "Old Tozoff could get through with little trouble." Kohlberger said. "He knows all the cow paths and nobody is going to sneak up on him."
    "Have Metz contact him." Schiller said. "Have him use the cellar entrance."
    "Sig will want something." Kohlberger said. "The curmudgeon is mad as a hatter."
    "I'll give him a hunting rifle." Schiller said. "We can afford it."
      "You have an alternate to Jherling?" Kohlberger asked firmly.
    "Janus Fuchs." Schiller answered dully.
    "Damn it why involve him Kurt?" Kohlberger hissed. "He does lip service to the Party; he arrested you damnit."
    "Thus he would not be involved in any conspiracy." Schiller said.
    "Gerhardt is still a question mark." Kohlberger said.
    "He is no Boy Scout Hugo." Schiller said. "This situation does not require boy scouts."
    "Fuchs is still a boy scout." Kohlberger asked.
    "He is honest and completely incorruptible." Schiller said firmly. "That is the reason the Party keeps him around despite those virtues."
    "I heard they use him to handle the political and embarrassing cases involving the Party." Kohlberger said in a knowing voice. "He does it quietly and gets results."
    "That is exactly why I want him to be here." Schiller said. "Fuchs is most likely our only hope of getting out of this mess alive."
    "You better have more than him up your damn sleeve Kurt." Hugo said curtly. "The Army would help tremendously."
    "I know." Schiller said. "We have to pray that Jherling has developed a sense of curiosity since we last met."

[4]

Outside of Adlerberghof

    "What the hell is going on Brosch?" Eidernau asked lifting up his field glasses. "I just the highlights Brosch."
    "We heard gunshots from the town." Brosch said. "Then cops are crawling all over the place."
    "Where did the shots come from?" Eidernau asked.
    "The Gasthof, across the square," Brosch said. "Krieger's Gasthof it seems."
    "Anybody try to leave?" Eidernau asked.
    "Car sped out just after the gunfire." Brosch said. "Drehben and Witte killed one man who was too curious about the wires."

"Keep the wires down." Eidernau ordered. "Schimdt is spreading the word to the others not to let anyone out of the town, in, but not out. I'll be at the woodcutter's hut."

Eidernau entered the hut and moved to the stove removing his gloves. "You're nice and comfortable Hothman."

"Good stove." Hothman said handing Eidernau a bottle of schnapps. "Hut is well built."

"The owner might come here to check." Eidernau quipped taking the bottle.

"He did." Hothman said matter-of-factly. "I have him in the drift outback."

"Something happened in town." Eidernau said rubbing the scar on his left cheek, a souvenir from Verdun. "There was shooting in the town."

"Don't like that." Hothman said. "I thought we were supposed to do the shooting."

"I smell trouble." Eidernau said harshly. "I told Krieger to let me go in, grab this piece of paper and kill Skasch- ten minutes."

Hothman lit a cigar. "Take the boys and head for Vienna. I have a contract to remove some diamonds from the ghetto."

"You don't run out on Krieger." Eidernau rasped. "Our special status would be canceled in the blink- of- an- eye. I don't want the GFP tracking me down if I got lucky."

"You are worried about the bitch." Hothman hissed.

"Damn right I'm worried about her. She is deadlier than the male." Eidernau said. "She will be arriving here tomorrow."

"Why the worry about her in the first place, she can't be that bad?" Hothman asked.

"I've seen her in action." Eidernau said. "She is an aristocrat who doesn't mind getting her hands dirty." Willi lit a cigarette. "Several years ago one of those show girls Krieger played around with got a little too familiar. The Countess had me drive her down to Cologne and confronted the girl in her flat. I thought Miller was good with a straight razor; she made him look like an amateur. She peeled that girl's face like a grape. She took photos and had then delivered to Krieger's office."

"Damn." Hothman growled. "What about the girl?"

"She lived." Eidernau said. "The Countess had her arrested for prostitution and violating the Nuremberg Laws. The girl was sterilized and spent two years in Ravensbruk." Willi paused with a stern look on his face. "She hung herself three days after leaving Ravensbruk."

"Better call Bruno to stop her." Hothman uttered firmly.

"He can't." Eidernau said. "We are stuck with her. Have Witte stop her at the crossroads."

"Then what do we do with her?" Hothman asked.

"Have her stay here." Eidernau grunted.

"What about the town?" Hothman asked.

"Untermayer looks the most like a peasant." Eidernau said dryly. "Have him go in and snoop around." Eidernau paused. "Tell him not to get caught."

"We'll need someplace for the men to keep warm in between watches Willi." Hothman said.

"There is a farmhouse about 6 kms from town." Eidernau said. "It's called the Donner farm."

"What about Farmer Donner?" Hothman asked.

"What happened here?" Eidernau hissed.

"That's fine with me." Hothman said. "This better get over with soon, that Vienna job won't stay open for long."

[5]
23:00 hrs

Gasthof Gruenling
Skasch's Room

The throbbing pain ebbed and flowed from dull to sharp down the length of his arm telling Colquhoun that he was still alive. He could feel the splint on his left arm and the pressure of bandages on his body. Colquhoun slowly forced open eyes. The room swirled violently for a few seconds until they focused on the old man sitting next to him. The room did not have the feel or smell of a hospital prison ward.

"Where the hell am I?" Colquhoun asked tilting his head towards the old man.

"I don't speak English son?" The old man said. Colquhoun repeated the question in German this time.

"Gruenling Gasthof, go back to sleep." The old man said briskly

"Who the hell are you?" Colquhoun hissed.

"Dr. Ludwig Brandt." The old man said. "You need rest so go back to sleep."

"Sleep hell." Colquhoun hissed.

"Who are you son?" Brandt asked.

"Viktor Skasch." Colquhoun answered. "Bern."

The old man smiled. "You'll have to do better than that son." Brandt's soft grandfatherly voice became harsher. "I'm afraid you'll have to do much, much better son."

"What?" Colquhoun rasped.

"You are not Lazarus." Brandt said.

"Make sense." Colquhoun snapped. "The name is Skasch."

"Radio Bern announced several hours ago that Dr. Viktor Skasch of Bern was killed in a car crash." Brandt said flatly. "Radio Bern is not Radio Berlin."

"Listening to foreign broadcasts is illegal." Colquhoun said officiously.

"Many things are." Brandt said. "Foreign currency is illegal too." Colquhoun's stomach flipped over several times.

"Who knows this?" Colquhoun asked.

"Very few I image." Brandt said. "Most tune into the BBC."

"What is the damage?" Colquhoun asked. "When can I leave?"

"You are very lucky." Brandt said. "Your left arm is broken in two places; if the hole in your chest was a few millimeters over Offenbach would be working on you in silence."

"What about my colleague?" Colquhoun asked somberly.

"I'm afraid he is dead." Brandt said. "The one called Jung is dead too."

"How long have I been out?" Colquhoun asked apprehensively.

"Only a few hours." Brandt said. "I'll give you something that will ease the pain and make you sleep."

"No." Colquhoun hissed.

"Son, it's too late to worry about anything." Brandt said gripping his right arm. "What you need is rest."

Brandt emerged from the room after his injection had taken affect on his patient. Brandt groped for a cigarette until Gerhardt handed him one.

"Thank you Herr Major." Brandt said politely. "My name is Dr. Brandt."

"I know, Heinz told me." Gerhardt said. "You are the only medical doctor in the area."

"My patient is in fragile condition." Brandt said. "The results of being shot more than once drain the system."

"Will he be able to talk?" Gerhardt asked.

"Not 'til morning." Brandt said. "What is the Army's interest in him?"

"Can he be moved?" Gerhardt asked. "Say to Stuttgart?"

"Depends if you want a live prisoner or not." Brandt said in a firm voice. "Perhaps it will take a week for him to be strong enough to be moved to Jaegerfeld."

"A week you say?" Gerhardt mused.

"Unless it is a corpse you wish to carry down the mountain, very hard to question a dead man." Brandt said adroitly.

"Your patient is a prisoner." Gerhardt said firmly. "There will be a guard in the hallway all night."

"I don't want to know the game you are playing." Brandt said. "I'm not interested in politics Herr Gerhardt."

"That is a good way to be these days." Gerhardt said handing Brandt a packet of cigarettes.

"My sole concern is the patient." Brandt said bluntly.

"Excellent." The Major said. "Under no circumstances are you to allow anyone to enter the room."

"The exception being you I assume." Brandt said with a half smile.

"You are a mind-reader." Gerhardt said. "Do you need a man inside?"

"No." Brandt said. "I always have a Luger in my medical bag; a habit I picked up in East Africa."

"If he should wake, inform me immediately." Gerhardt said.

"Burgermeister Schiller?" Brandt asked.

"Just me Herr Brandt," Gerhardt said. "No one else is that clear."

Chapter Fifteen
December 8, 1942
21:30 hrs

Donner's Farm

Eidernau walked around the kitchen then moved into the living room lighting a cigarette. "An old man did this?"

"Looks like it." Hothman said. "He used a shotgun."

"Durer had his throat cut." Eidernau rasped. "One old man killed five of my best men?"

"He must be a tough old bastard to do all this." Hothman said. "With the wind and the snow blowing now there could have been twenty men here."

"Some one was here besides Donner." Eidernau said flatly. "That would explain a lot about what happened here."

"Do we use this place or what?" Hothman hissed.

"Get rid of them." Eidernau said. "I want five men on watch at all times."

"You expect Donner to come back?" Hothman hissed.

"He might." Eidernau said looking around. "This is his home, if I was him I would be back with some friends."

"Is this worth it?" Hothman asked.

"It better be." Eidernau rasped. "I'm heading back to Jaegerfeld for a few hours. Try not to get everyone killed."

Path to Monastery

"You recognize any of them?" Orr shouted to Donner as they plowed through the snow heading for the old monastery on the mountain.

"No." Donner said stopping.

"Who the bloody hell were they then?" Browne asked tartly holding his arm.

"That doesn't matter." Carey shouted. "Is any one following us?"

"No." Orr rasped.

"What about this god-damn monastery?" Browne asked sharply.

"Only the Abbot can speak." Donner said. "Cloistered monks, with medical training, nobody bothers them."

"Who is going to tell our German friends?" Carey asked.

"I will." Orr said. "Once we get settled at the monastery."

[2]
21:00 hrs

Jaegerfeld
234th Jaeger Regiment

Oberstleutnant Pieter Jherling leaned back in his chair lighting a cigar trying to figure out what his Adjutant, Major Utlaut, had muttered to him.

"What are you muttering about?" Jherling asked. "Speak slowly."

"The military police have given me this curious report sir." Utlaut said.

"Hauptmann Krueger's job is to find problems." Jherling said flatly. "What is it?"

"A security patrol reports that Obergruppenfuhrer Krieger passed through yesterday sir." Utlaut said.

"General Krieger?" Jherling hissed. "Why wasn't I told about this immediately?"

"You were in the field with the second company." Utlaut said.

"Where was he going?" Jherling asked.

"He told Krueger Adlerberghof that is a very curious place for him to go sir." Utlaut said.

"No SS up there?" Jherling quipped.

"It is the hind end of the world, but it is in our Wehrkries sir." Utlaut said.

"The only thing interesting in Adlerberghof is the Burgermeister Schiller." Jherling said.

"Wasn't he some kind of big-shot in Berlin sir?" Utlaut asked.

"That he was Major." Jherling said.

"What happened sir?" Utlaut asked.

"Don't really know that Franz." Jherling said.

"I still find this very odd sir." Utlaut said.

Jherling nodded in silence. The colonel had been in the Waffen SS until 1941 when he ran a foul of Krieger and his aide Ehrlich. Jherling was in line to assume command of Waffen SS regiment, but Ehrlich wanted his brother to have the command. Krieger used his influence with Himmler to secure Ehrlich's brother the command. Jherling protested to GHQ; then he found himself facing a Court of Honor or transfer to the regular Army. Jherling transferred to the regular army it was far better than a punishment battalion was even though he was demoted to major.

"Why pick Adlerberghof Utlaut?" Jherling hissed. "What the hell is there for Krieger?"

"No idea sir." Utlaut said. "Perhaps Schiller is a friend?"

"Unlikely." Jherling said flatly. "I think they don't like each other."

"Perhaps there is a meeting sir?" Utlaut suggested picking up a piece of paper.

"Why say that?" Jherling quipped.

"Reichkriminaldirektor Fuchs and Inspektor Wulff are going there too according to Utlaut said. "That is from the local police sir."

"This sounds like a civilian affair major." Jherling said dryly.

"Fuchs is Kripo from Stuttgart." Utlaut said flatly.

"Is there anything else?" Jherling asked.

"Countess Vom Rodelbach is at the Savoy right now." Utlaut said. "She is General Krieger's wife."

"This is very odd, anything from Schiller Utlaut?" The colonel asked as he rolled the cigar ash off his cigar.

"Telephone & telegraph lines are down." Utlaut said. "Wireless is useless in this weather sir."

"Ready two platoons." Jherling said. "I'll take my command car and two armored cars."

"General Wyess will have to approve sir." Utlaut said. "He has no concept of modern warfare sir."

"Just get him on the telephone." Jherling said. "Lie to the old gentlemen; where is this Fuchs from?"

"Stuttgart." Utlaut said.

"After lying to Wyess I want to talk to someone at police headquarters in Stuttgart."

Jherling ordered. "Then have Konrad and Fogler come here."
"How do I do that sir with the wires down?" Utlaut asked.
"Send a rider." Jherling said flatly. "I want the men in winter camouflage Major."

[3]
23:40 hrs

Adlerberghof
Der Blauwasser Kaffeehaus

"May I ask who side is your friend on?" Gerhardt asked crisply as Orr got up and left Mannerling at the table as the Germans approached.
"He is on our side." Mannerling said. "Name is Orr."
"Are there any other surprises?" Lang asked dourly sipping a cup of real coffee.
"Not from me." Mannerling said frankly.
"What did he want?" Franz asked lighting a cigarette.
"Donner had some unexpected company." Mannerling said.
"Was it the Zollenpolizei?" Gerhardt asked.
"They weren't Customs or Border Police." Mannerling said. "Do you recognize this name?" Mannerling tossed down a billfold on the table.
Franz picked up the billfold and opened it. After a few moments, Franz handed it back to Mannerling.
"His name is Zessenborg." Franz said. "He is muscle for hire, not too bright."
"How good was he?" Mannerling asked.
"Use to be good." Franz said. "Not too particular about whom he worked for." Franz held up the bills to the light. "These are new notes."
"New players have been added." Lang said. "Are any of your people in trouble?"
"All escaped." Mannerling said. "Relocated at the monastery, but they know where about too."
"Wonderful." Gerhardt said.
"What has turned to shit since the last time we talked?" Mannerling said.
"Colquhoun is holding his own according to the local doctor." Gerhardt said. "He can not be moved for perhaps a week."
"We can't keep this masquerade for a week." Mannerling said. "It's already unraveling." Mannerling lit a cigarette. "What is Schiller thinking?"
"He will cooperate at the moment." Gerhardt said. "He is helping with guarding Colquhoun."
"Pragmatic." Mannerling said hollowly.
"Security is a joke around here." Franz rasped. "Schiller's men are not going to stop Krieger's friends."
"The obvious target is Colquhoun." Lang said. "With him dead Krieger can invent any story he wants."
"With us joining Colquhoun," Gerhardt said. "He can wiggle out of this."
"Colquhoun has to survive long enough for this to work." Mannerling said.
Gerhardt look directly at Mannerling. "You can cover Colquhoun's room from the windows."
"I'll need a roost." Mannerling said.

"We'll move to the room directly across from his in the Braunfuch." Gerhardt said. "I doubt they'll try anything during the day time."

"Okay." Mannerling hissed. "Then you better get the train rolling so it can go off the tracks."

"You understand that Colquhoun is expendable." Gerhardt said coldly.

"I do." Mannerling said. "He didn't when he left Scotland, but now he knows he is a pawn."

"Pawns are sacrificed." Gerhardt said.

"He might try for the King." Mannerling said.

"He is not supposed to go for the King." Lang said.

"Colquhoun thinks he is alone." Mannerling said. "He'll go for the King; even the brass hats can misjudge people."

"Then this is all for nothing if he does." Gerhardt said.

"If he kills Krieger it won't be for nothing." Mannerling said. "We'll have to see were our new visitors are hiding in the woods."

"What good is this?" Lang asked.

"Give us a bloody chance." Mannerling said. "If Schiller sent someone for help, we can't wait that long to find out if help is coming."

"There is a possibility that the weather could clear enough to get a wireless message out." Lang said flatly.

"We can't have that happen." Mannerling said.

"It won't." Franz said. "I've been busy, but someone might have spare parts."

[4]
23:30 hrs

Jaegerfeld
Gasthof Savoy

Eidernau looked out of place in the SA Hauptsturmfuhrer uniform because he was not tall, blond, or blue-eyed. Eidernau was an ugly little man; badly disfigured from shrapnel received at Verdun.

"You better have a damn good reason for having stop." The Countess asked coldly.

"There has been unexpected trouble." Eidernau said plainly.

"What sort of trouble?" The Countess hissed. "Explain."

"There has been shooting in the town." Eidernau said. "Schiller sent a messenger to the Army commander here."

"What about this messenger?" The Countess asked.

"He won't be found until spring." Eidernau answered.

"What was the shooting about?" The Countess inquired. "Connected?"

"We intercepted the messenger before the shooting begun." Eidernau said.

"Have you bothered to investigate this shooting?" The Countess asked bluntly.

"Skasch tried to kill the General." Eidernau said flatly. "Your husband wasn't hit, but Jung was killed."

"What about Skasch?" The Countess asked icily.

"Wounded and a prisoner." Eidernau said. "The police are very talkative."

"You left him there?" The Countess asked bluntly.

"That's the unexpected trouble madam." Eidernau said. "The Abwehr is in the town."

"Who is there from the Abwehr?" The Countess asked.

"We believe it is Major Gerhardt from the Brandenburg unit." Eidernau said. "But, he isn't the sole problem. I believe there are others watching the town."

The Countess lit a cigarette. "How many men do you have?"

"Thirty." Eidernau said.

"I'll have Bruno send more." The Countess said. "Keep the town under heavy watch."

"Schiller won't wait forever madam." Eidernau grunted. "Nor will Gerhardt."

"You'll wait." The Countess said. "Did you bring Wassenberg?"

"Yes." Eidernau said. "He has a price."

"What is it?" The Countess asked blandly.

"He wants the reinstatement of his medical license." Eidernau said. "He also wants a commission in the SS Medical Service."

"Tell him yes." The Countess said.

"How do I get him in?" Eidernau asked.

The Countess smiled. "The old Gastborg mine opening is 3 kms West of town; 800 meters inside is the entrance to the tunnel."

"What tunnel?" Eidernau asked.

"The Jew who built the Gruenling Gasthof had an escape tunnel built and staircase." The Countess said. "The staircase goes to Helmuth's room, his picking the Gruenling was not an accident."

"He was a smart Jew." Eidernau said. "Who knows about it?"

"Only he did." The Countess said. "He left in '38."

[5]
23:45 hrs

Road to Adlerberghof

Fuchs lit his pipe and listened to the wind whistle by the windshield as the automobile headed towards Adlerberghof. Fuchs knew that this was a calculated risk and his young associate had the right to be worried. This was either the noblest thing he had done or the dumbest thing in forty years of being a professional police officer.

Fuchs had joined the Prussian State Police at the earliest age possible over the objections of his father, a Lutheran Bishop, who had his career already chosen. He had spent his early career patrolling small villages and towns like Adlerberghof. After seven years of night school and state exams, Fuchs qualified to be an investigator in the Public Prosecutor's Office in Berlin with the rank of Kriminalkommisar.

After deactivation from the Army, as a captain, in December 1918 Fuchs returned to the PPO in Berlin as a Kriminaldirektor. In 1922, Fuchs transferred to the Berlin Metropolitan Police as a detective. He spent most of his time keeping the pot from boiling over.

An Honorable Betrayal

Fuchs's first encounter with Schiller was in 1930. He was now with the homicide section with the rank of Oberregierundkriminalrat investigating a particularly gruesome double homicide in a brothel. The two women, who ran the brothel, had an argument with a customer, who settled his bill with a straight-edged razor. The customer, who had disappeared, left a letter with a return address. Fuchs went to the flat to question him, but Schiller refused to cooperation and tried to escape. Fuchs had to shoot him in the left leg.

Schiller never went to trial for the charges were dropped by the Public Prosecutor's office and his roommate just disappeared. The Police President transferred Fuchs to an outlying district and moving him to the political police. Fuchs's orders were to keep the roving bands of thugs working for the extremist wings of various political parties out of the affluent suburbs.

Fuchs excelled at this task. He tormented the Brownshirts of the NDSAP at every given opportunity; he was equally aggressive towards the Socialist, Catholic and Communist thugs. The Nazis, even after they came to power in Prussia, avoided direct confrontations with Fuchs.

When Hitler became Fuehrer after the death of President von Hindenburg in 1934, Fuchs started to make retirement plans. He knew the Nazis were purging members of the police who were not Party members. Fuchs knew that Schiller was now a high-ranking Party official in Berlin. After a few months waiting for the ax to fall, Fuchs submitted his resignation to the Police President, who refused to accept it three times.

After the third time, Fuchs was ordered police headquarters. Waiting for him was Kurt Schiller; the time for vengeance had arrived. Schiller was extremely upset that Fuchs wanted to leave the police. Schiller reinstated him to the State Police and assigned him to Wittenberge. The meeting lasted less than ten minutes. That was the last time he saw or spoke to Schiller.

In 1939, just before the outbreak of the war, Fuchs was transferred to Stuttgart on his request. His wife's mother became ill and they had to care for her. His mother-in-law died in 1941, but Fuchs elected to remain in Stuttgart instead of returning to Berlin. His wife enjoyed being home and since the children were gone, the house in Berlin would have been too large. Everything was calm and almost routine until the request from Schiller came. This gave Fuchs the chance to stretch his legs and unclog his mind.

Chapter Sixteen
December 9, 1942
02:00 hrs

Adlerberghof
Gasthof Gruenling

Gerhardt answered the door and found one of Heinz's men who told him that Brandt wanted to see him. Gerhardt followed him to Colquhoun's room. Brandt signaled the guard to leave the room.

"You'll have to be brief." Brandt said firmly. "He is still weak, but his mind is clear."

"Do you understand English Herr Doctor?" Anton asked.

"No." Brandt answered. "Why?"

"This is very important Brandt." Gerhardt said. "It is best that you don't know what we talk about."

"I understand." Brandt said. "I'll read the newspaper."

Colquhoun opened his eyes and looked at the German officer sitting next to the bed.

"Who the hell are you?" Colquhoun asked in German. "You don't look like the Gestapo?"

"My name is Gerhardt." Anton said firmly in English. "Speak English only, the doctor doesn't understand English."

"Go to hell." Colquhoun said in German. "My name Victor Skasch from Linz Herr Major, a retired college professor, what in hell is going on damnit?"

"The vultures are circling." Gerhardt said. "We don't have time to play games Major."

"Who the hell are you?" Colquhoun asked cautiously.

"I am from the Abwehr." Gerhardt answered. "You are safe for now."

"Safe?" Colquhoun quipped. "That is relative to your situation."

"*London is warm in the spring.*" Gerhardt said in a firm voice. Colquhoun looked at Gerhardt. Crawford had told him that he would have help in Adlerberghof, but he was not expecting someone like Gerhardt.

"You *mean wet*." Colquhoun said.

"Yes." Gerhardt said.

"I see how long before the bad guys show up here, Herr Major?" Colquhoun asked coldly.

"They are here," Gerhardt said. "My advice is just don't play the hero too long."

"I don't plan on being a dead hero." Colquhoun said grimly his voice trailing off as he drifted back to sleep.

"He'll keep on doing this Major." Brandt said in English. "I'm afraid that he will need a hospital within the next 48 hours."

"You understand English?" Gerhardt quipped looking at the doctor. "That omission could be unhealthy."

"I have no idea what sort of game you are playing Herr Major." Brandt said firmly. "I frankly don't want to know."

"Even a tiny amount knowledge is dangerous in these troubled times." Gerhardt said coldly well aware that Brandt understood what was going on.

"I'm apolitical Gerhardt." Brandt said. "You're colleague should change his cover name."

"Why?" Gerhardt asked.

"Viktor Skasch is dead." Brandt said.

"How could you know that?" Gerhardt rasped.

"I heard it from Radio Bern." Brandt said. "Skasch is… er… was a well-known scholar and the Burgermeister will soon learn of this."

"I thought SW didn't work all that well here?" Gerhardt asked.

"Some of us have older radios?" Brandt said. "What will they do to him?"

"Everything and anything to get what they want." Gerhardt said crisply.

"Barbaric." Brandt hissed.

"That is the only way they know." Gerhardt said bluntly.

Brandt bowed his head knowing what the major meant. "Even they can't question an unconscious man Herr Major."

"They have no rules." Gerhardt warned. "They kill people."

"I have seen what they can do to their own countrymen." Brandt said. "I was visiting my sister in June of '34."

"They'll go after every member of your family." Gerhardt said bluntly.

"I am seventy-eight." Brandt said. "I have no family or close personal friends. What can they do to me, but kill me."

"I can't protect you." Gerhardt said bluntly.

"I've survived native uprisings, internment, epidemics." Brandt said. "I'll survive the Nazis."

"Keep your bag open." Gerhardt said wryly.

[2]
02:15 hrs

Twickem-Hallesy
Austen-Halton Manor

Austen-Halton unbuttoned his collar and lit his cigar as Tremayne entered the living room. Crawford, who had been catnapping on the sofa, rose to a sitting position.

"Knowledge about Skasch is getting out." Tremayne said.

"How much is known Colonel?" Crawford asked.

"Gunnarsohn was forced to say that he was killed in a car accident." Tremayne said.

"Still makes him dead." Austen-Halton said sarcastically. "Why didn't Greene send this first?"

"Gunnarsohn doesn't work for Greene sir." Tremayne said flatly.

"Local?" Crawford asked.

"Radio Bern sir." Tremayne said.

Sir Peter exhaled a large flume of whitish smoke. "That means Berlin will know if anyone at the Foreign Ministry was paying attention."

"They may be a sleep at the switch, but Himmler's people won't be." Crawford said dully. "Do you have any other wonderful news Colonel?"

"It will be snowing in Southern Germany with in the next 12 hours sir." Tremayne said.

"I thought the weather boys said no bad weather." Crawford quipped.

"Unexpected low pressure system moved in." Tremayne said flatly.

"Contact Flemming at Ashenton Station," Austen-Halton said dryly. "Tell him to start *Willful Lies* now. Have the leakage come from Madrid, Lisbon, and Tokyo."

"That should prick up Berlin's ears." Crawford said flatly. "Glad you are our side Peter. Why Tokyo to spread nasty tidbits that Krieger is *Albatross*?"

"The Nazis still think Soviet intelligence is a joke." Austen-Halton said. "This will only reinforce this situation."

"You are a bastard." Crawford said. "I pale in comparison to you."

"You are a first class sonofabitch." Austen-Halton said. "Colquhoun's father is a friend of yours."

"The Senator wanted a hero for a son." Crawford said. "I'm showing them that war is hell. My grandfather was with Sherman during his little stroll through Georgia and he knew what war was."

[3]
02:30 hrs

Adlerberghof
Gruenling Gasthof

"Sir, you should get some sleep." Sergeant-Major Klugge suggested.

"Please, in this place Dieter?" Krieger said tiredly. "I don't want to wake up with my throat cut."

"That will never happen with me around." Klugge said bluntly.

"I know Dieter." Krieger said. "However, Gerhardt is no rank amateur my old friend. Soldiers are expected to die, but not stupidly."

"I'm hard to kill sir." Klugge said flatly.

"Gerhardt is not here by accident." Krieger said. "He is here for a sinister reason."

"Could he know who the impostor is sir?" Klugge asked.

"That is entirely possible Dieter." Helmuth said. "I wouldn't be surprised if he did."

"Why?" Klugge asked.

"Gerhardt is a good soldier." Helmuth said flatly. "He obeys orders from his superiors."

"Which includes killing you sir?" Klugge rasped.

"Yes." Krieger said. "Just peel away the layers until you find von Tanz."

"Why does he hate you so much General, if I may ask sir?" Klugge asked.

"It's hardly personal Dieter." Krieger said. "It is the power they fear, Gerhardt is only a lancet."

Klugge nodded and headed for the door, but stopped and turned about to face the General. "Sir, they don't seem to be too worried about me. I can move around the Gasthof and even outside, unarmed."

"You're point Dieter?" Helmuth asked.

"What if the lancet is blunted or destroyed sir?" Klugge asked coldly.

"You've been in the service long enough not to volunteer." Krieger said seeing that Klugge was deadly serious. "You have a wife and two sons Dieter."

"My sons are serving the Fatherland sir." Klugge said.

"I appreciate the gesture." Helmuth said. "Dead you are useless to me."

"I wasn't planning to get killed sir." Klugge said. "I'm not getting that old."

"No." Helmuth said. "Enjoy your freedom while you can Dieter, find a radio and listen to some music."

"Yes sir." Klugge said.

"Eidernau is out there with his men Dieter." Krieger said firmly.

"I have little confidence that he could find his way out of a latrine sir." Klugge hissed.

"The Countess has complete confidence in him." Krieger said.

"More in Herr Vochner you mean sir." Klugge said matter of factly.

"Vochner does not pick fools Dieter." Krieger said grimly. "Neither does my wife after all she selected me."

[4]
02:30 hrs

The Rotebahr

Mannerling laid the rifle on the makeshift shooting bench and zeroing in the telescopic sight. Mannerling then rolled away to the other side of the window. The Rotebahr had been a tavern before the war but 500 yards from the Gruenling.

"You can breathe now." Mannerling said to Browne.

"Thanks?" Browne said flatly.

"Smoke, but stay away from the window." Mannerling said removing three extra cartridges from a cartridge box and placed them into his uniform pocket.

"Not .303 caliber Major." Browne quipped.

"They are .375 H&H magnum." Mannerling said.

Browne nodded as he watched Mannerling wondering where in hell the British had found him. When Orr brought him here, he was not that surprised that, he was not dead. Browne knew he was not British; the closest thing the British had to an American was a Canadian. Mannerling's return from the dead told Browne that this whole mission was just one long nightmare.

"Damn, do you have enough light?" Browne asked glancing through the dirty window.

"Gerhardt will keep the room lights on and shade up." Mannerling said.

"What did you do before the war Major?" Browne asked somberly. "If you don't mind talking sir, it passes the time."

"Knock off the sir." Mannerling said. "I did this."

"This?" Browne hissed.

"I was a Mountie." Mannerling said in a far away voice. "That was a hundred years ago it seems. What did you do?"

"College, with a law degree in my future" Browne said. "When the draft started I dropped out and joined the Army Air Corps, flunked out of flight school, but became a warrant officer in administration." Browne paused. "I volunteered for the OSS to relieve my boredom."

"I've been doing this for a long time." Mannerling said. "It has never been boring."

"Damn." Browne rasped. "You've been doing this type of ghastly work for a long time, who the hell hires a hit man?"

"I've been a government employee." Mannerling said flatly with a half smile.

"The British government pays you to kill people?" Browne hissed.

"Yes." Mannerling said. "I'm a civil servant and this is all legal under the Official Secrets Act and Defense of the Realm."

"For Christssakes," Browne rasped. "Doesn't seem right some how."
"Governments need someone to clean the sewers." Mannerling said.
"No trials or juries?" Browne quipped.
"None of this is public." Mannerling said. "War only makes it socially acceptable."
Browne crushed out his cigarette. "Do you think Colquhoun knows that he is a patsy?"
"Give him some credit." Mannerling said. "I think he knew that the moment Jung walked into the room."
"Why?" Browne asked.
"The big boys don't want a hero Browne." Mannerling said.
"What do they want then?" Browne asked.
"They wanted a coward." Mannerling answered.
"That went over my head Mannerling." Browne quipped.
"Let's say that the major has a tainted career that needed polishing." Mannerling said.
"I get the feeling that you know the major." Browne rasped.
"I've met him before." Mannerling said. "We are not friends."
"This was set up to fail," Browne said firmly. "Wasn't it?"
"Do anything as long as you win." Mannerling said bitterly.
"You do intend to get him out?" Browne asked seriously.
"If it is humanly possible we'll get him out." Mannerling answered.
"If not major, what do we do then?" Browne hissed.
"The cardinal act of mercy would be to kill him." Mannerling said grimly.

[5]
03:00 hrs

Gruenling Gasthof
Krieger's Room

"I expected you earlier." Krieger said as Eidernau and another man entered his bedroom via the trapdoor.
"It wasn't marked secret entrance." Eidernau said sitting down. "Why are you staying?"
"Running gains me nothing." Krieger said. "Who is your friend?"
"Herr Dr. Wassenberg." Eidernau said lighting a cigar.
"I trust my wife gave you a plan Eidernau." Krieger said ignoring the doctor's outstretched hand.
"Dr. Wassenberg was handpicked by your wife." Eidernau said. "The doctor is a distinguished graduate of Leipzig School of Medicine."
"I don't need a doctor." Helmuth said flatly. "I know who Felix Klaus Wassenberg is, the infamous butcher of Hamburg, and an abortionist."
"Your wife recruited me Herr General." Wassenberg said. "The Countess seems to understand that I performed an important medical function for German society."
"The Ministry of Health revoked your license in '34." Helmuth said. "You're lucky that we weren't in total power or you would be in a concentration camp."
"You have been misinformed." Wassenberg said. "If it wasn't for the goddamn Jews who once dominated the profession at the time no charges would have ever been brought."
"Eidernau, how can this butcher help me?" Helmuth asked.

"I arrange death." Wassenberg said. "By a simple technique the subject seems to die of cerebral hemorrhage. Even the best forensic pathologist couldn't say otherwise."

"So?" Helmuth said. "Why do I need him Willi?"

"He knows how." Eidernau said plainly. "Other wise do you want Ehrlich or Klugge to use the bogus Skasch as a pin cushion?"

Krieger lit a cigarette. "How do you plan to get pass the police guard and Dr. Brandt? I doubt they'll step aside to let this creature kill him."

"The doctor has many talents." Eidernau said frankly.

"I don't want to know the details." Helmuth said somberly.

"You can add realism to your shock." Eidernau said.

"What were you promised Wassenberg?" Helmuth asked.

"The reinstatement of my license to practice medicine and the burning of my police records," Wassenberg said.

"Do you want anything else Herr Doctor that I could help you with?" Helmuth asked

"My commission in the Waffen SS Medical Service restored." Wassenberg said. "The alternative is 500,000 Reichmarks as payment."

"You guarantee he'll die?" Helmuth asked.

"He will." Wassenberg said. "When do you want this to happen?"

"Thirty minutes." Krieger said.

Chapter Seventeen
December 9, 1942
03:30 hrs

Adlerberghof
Gasthof Gruenling

    The police guard leaned against wall watching the rear staircase his back facing the balcony and the French doors. The guard lit a cigarette knowing that he had one of the easier jobs around tonight. The Gasthof was nice and warm with little chance of anything happening.

    Wassenberg moved quietly and slipped over the balcony rail. The police guard was about 4 meters from the doors facing away. Wassenberg moved to the side of the door and checked the door handle; it was unlocked. The doctor removed the PPK from his coat pocket and screwed on the silencer. Wassenberg decided against firing through the door, that the breaking glass could alert someone.

    The sudden blast of cold air caused the guard to turn and face the door. The guard moved his hand for his pistol as three muffled pops sounded. The guard grabbed his throat as he slumped to the floor. Wassenberg walked into the hallway, closing the door behind him. He moved up to the fallen guard and fired another bullet into his brain.

    Wassenberg with catlike smoothness moved towards the target's room. Wassenberg tried the door handle to the room and found it locked. Wassenberg switched the pistol to his left hand and got the master key. He quietly unlocked the door and stepped in. The white-haired old man, who had been sitting in the chair next to the bed, was half way up brandishing a Luger when Wassenberg shot him twice in the chest. The white-haired man collapsed back into the chair quite dead. Wassenberg re-locked the door and went to the table where the medical bag was after seeing on the table. He would cast blame on the old man by using his equipment.

    Wassenberg searched the bag and found a syringe. He fitted a large gauge needle to the syringe and walked over to the sleeping man in the bed. Within two minutes, the air bubbles pumped into the man's veins would produce an embolism, which would then produce death .He, would then place the syringe in the white-haired man's hand and the PPK on the floor minus the silencer. He would then leave by the balcony after locking the door. This would certainly confuse the issue.

    Wassenberg rolled up the sleeve of the sleeping man. Wassenberg pulled back the syringe plunger filling the container with air. The syringe was only a few inches from the man's arm when the first bullet tore into Wassenberg's arm knocking the syringe out of his hand. The second bullet smashed into Wassenberg's heart.

[2]

    The sound of the two rifle shots brought Gerhardt and Franz out of their room as quickly as humanly possible. The Major saw the police guard crumpled in the hallway as the raced for Colquhoun's room. Mannerling would only have fired if there had been a direct threat to Colquhoun.

    They reached room first with two of Heinz's men joining them; one of them kicked the door open. Gerhardt saw Brandt slumped in the chair quite dead, the other man lay sprawled on top of Colquhoun with a large hole in his back, and the bedding was slowly turning a deep crimson. Franz grabbed the dead man and pulled him off Colquhoun than felt for a pulse.

"He is alive." Franz said checking Colquhoun's pulse

"Check across the street!" Gerhardt shouted at the two police officers. "Find the goddamn shooter you idiots, move now!"

"Is he dead?" Franz asked about the stranger.

"Yes." Gerhardt snapped squeezing man's throat for any sign of a pulse after he rolled the assassin off the bed.

"The shit will fly now." Franz rasped. "Schiller is going to ask questions like who shot him, if he had any help they're long gone by now; these stumbled bums couldn't find their ass with both hands."

"It's usually the damn amateur who kills you." Gerhardt said. "Judging from that hole in his back Mannerling did his job."

"A little late for the doctor I'm afraid." Franz said sourly.

"Brandt was out of his line of sight." Gerhardt said. "This is not what I wanted for the old man, not at all Franz." Gerhardt looked down at the dead man. "Any idea who that piece of shit is?"

"His name is Wassenberg, disbarred doctor." Franz said flatly. "In the old days he was an abortionist. He has been making the rounds offering his talents."

"Not as an assassin?" Gerhardt quipped.

"Times were tough." Franz said dourly. "The last I heard he was freelancing for Willi Eidernau."

"Shit." Gerhardt said gruffly. "This makes it goddamn interesting."

"You seem to attract bodies Major." Heinz said entering the room with two men with MP-40s.

"Seems that way Chief." Gerhardt said dryly. "You find the shooters?"

"Brandt?" Heinz hissed. "Schiller has declared a state-of-emergency."

"Did you find them?" Franz asked.

"No." Heinz said signaling his men to raise their mps aiming them at Gerhardt and Franz

"This is a little extreme Herr Heinz." Gerhardt said.

"A state of emergency exist Herr Major." Heinz said. "This time the Schiller wants the right answers."

"Are we under arrest?" Franz asked.

"No." Heinz said. "Schiller wants to talk to you Major. You are free to walk about Franz, but my men have orders to shoot everyone trying to leave the town."

"I'm not leaving." Franz said.

[3]
04:15 hrs

The Monastery

"London hasn't been right at all in this." Orr said lighting a cigarette after Mannerling told him what had happened.

"You got that right." Mannerling said. "This was not amateur hour."

"They want Colquhoun dead." Orr said.

"Krieger wants him dead." Mannerling said. "Once Colquhoun talks Krieger knows the pack will turn on him. The irony is that Krieger will fall without Colquhoun uttering a word."

"Do we make the gesture Major?" Orr asked.

"We have no choice." Mannerling said flatly. "Like it or not our seemingly noble gesture will force Krieger to openly try to kill him."

"What good will that does?" Orr asked.

"Let's hope that London gets this part right." Mannerling said putting his overcoat back on. "If any strangers show up you know what to do."

"Of course I do I'm a professional." Orr hissed. "You just don't get yourself killed."

"Don't plan to." Mannerling said.

[4]
04:30 hrs

Gasthof Gruenling

Schiller lit a cigar as he surveyed the room. "Where is Gerhardt?"

"I sent him to your office." Heinz said.

"Cover Brandt up Otto please." Schiller said. "Who is the woman?"

"Frau Keller." Heinz said. "She was an Army nurse in the last war; she is the only person in the town with enough medical experience."

"Brandt?" Schiller growled.

"This is still a crime scene Kurt." Heinz said.

"Find Muller and take some damn pictures." Schiller snapped. "Then take him to Gruber's." Heinz nodded and left to wake up the photographer.

"We are now into this too deeply to pull out." Kohlberger hissed entering the room. "Even sheep will turn and fight."

"Damn, this is not what I wanted." Schiller said grimly.

"The simple solution is to get rid of them all." Kohlberger said bluntly.

"Only as a last resort my friend." Schiller said flatly. "If it is not done right they will join forces to burn the town to the ground."

"Avalanches happen all the time around here." Kohlberger hissed.

"Fuchs is coming." Schiller said

"He is an unknown quantity." Kohlberger said. "He is not a Party man."

"He will be an honest broker." Schiller said firmly.

"Muller will be here in fifteen minutes." Heinz said flatly, as he reentered the room. "He wants his money up front."

"I'll handle him." Kohlberger said harshly. "Find anything Chief?"

"Across the street in the Rotebahr, my men found two .375 magnum H&H shell cases and a shooting stand." Heinz said.

"That's over 250 meters." Kohlberger said looking out the window with the two bullet holes in it.

"He was a professional shooter." Heinz said.

"Professional hunter Otto that doesn't help." Schiller said icily realizing that he had more unknowns in his town.

"Fingerprint the corpse on the floor." Kohlberger said. "Then fingerprint Skasch. Send both of them to Sipo headquarters in Munich."

"They most likely have the town under surveillance." Heinz rasped.

"Take the school bus and head for Innsbruck." Kohlberger said. "Once there they can get the train to Munich. Tell them to stop for no one or no thing."

"I'll handle it." Heinz said grimly.
"What about Gerhardt?" Kohlberger asked lighting his pipe.
"No." Schiller said. "It's about time that Krieger and I had a little chat."
"He'll lie through his teeth." Kohlberger snapped.
"Every lie has a grain of truth." Schiller said moving up to Frau Keller. "Can we move him without killing him?"
"How far do you plan to move him Herr Schiller?" Frau Keller asked.
"Downstairs." Schiller said. "The manager's room has no windows."
"You'll just have to be careful." Frau Keller said. "I'll need Maria Fessenthal."
"I'll get her." Schiller said.

[5]
04:40 hrs

The Monastery

"How well do you know these monks?" Orr asked pouring Donner a glass of wine.
"They are Trappist monks." Donner hissed removing his snow-covered overcoat. "It makes for a one-sided conversation."
"Did you find out anything?" Orr asked somberly.
"We are facing between 20-30 heavily armed men." Donner said. "The town is surrounded."
"Are they still looking for us?" Orr asked.
"They are patrolling and will eventually reach here." Donner said. "They will come in and search."
"Will the Abbot help?" Orr asked.
"He'll allow them to search." Donner said flatly.
"Ask him for some monk's habits." Orr said. "Tell the Abbot we will not fight."
"I'll speak to him now." Donner said.
"What the bloody hell are we going to do besides play monks?" Carey asked lighting a cigarette in a slow deliberate manner. "That is pretty lam isn't it?"
"We shall do something very simple actually." Orr said flatly. "We go into town and take Colquhoun out."
"You're crazy." Browne said. "Right about now everyone in that damn town is pissed at us and we have our friends too."
"The last thing anyone would expect anyone to do." Orr rasped.
"Just waltz in?" Carey hissed.
"Walk in." Orr said. "The last thing anyone would expect."
"Why not just cut and run?" Browne asked.
"We British don't like leaving people behind." Orr hissed. "Bad for morale I'm afraid."
"This is not exactly healthy for us either when you come down to it." Carey said.

[6]
05:00 hrs

Donner's Farm

"Are you certain that Wassenberg is dead Willi?" Hothman asked in a flat voice.

"Yes." Eidernau said. "I waited as long as possible."

"What about the target?" Hothman hissed.

"The bastard is still alive." Eidernau said. "Sniper got Wassenberg."

"Now what do we do besides freeze?" Hothman asked.

"I'll have to talk to the Countess." Eidernau said.

"You better have Bruno do that." Hothman said bluntly. "You don't have to be a military genius to know what she'll want."

"She is very dangerous." Eidernau rasped.

"You have 32 pissed off men." Hothman said. "Did they find the sniper?"

"No." Eidernau said lighting a cigar. "Does it matter?"

"Of course he does." Hothman said sternly. "That means the bastard is still out there and he ain't on our side Willi."

"He can't run far." Eidernau said.

"We better get on our toes." Hothman said. "We better check that monastery; an excellent place to hide."

"No." Eidernau said bluntly. "Dead citizens is one thing, dead priests are another."

"When did you get religious Willi?" Hothman hissed.

"This is the South Hothman." Eidernau said. "Priests are not Jews; most of the people around here are Catholic."

"We let the sniper go free?" Hothman asked sharply.

"He is protecting Skasch." Eidernau said. "He won't be that far away."

Chapter Eighteen
December 9, 1942
08:00 hrs

RSHA
Berlin

Himmler moved slowly to the desk in the interrogation room and sat down. "Krieger is not in Berlin. Are you certain?"

"Yes Herr Reichsfuhrer." Standartenfuhrer Paulus said. "His wife is not at the estate either."

"What do your contacts say about our erstwhile General?" Himmler asked crisply.

"He had a private meeting with Vochner and disappeared shortly thereafter." Volker said. "He is not alone; Ehrlich and Klugge are with him."

"Has there been any activity over at Abwehr?" Himmler asked.

"Nothing Herr Reichleiter dull as ever." Paulus said.

"Is von Tanz in Berlin?" Himmler asked seriously.

"He was at the OKW meeting yesterday morning." Paulus said. "May I ask what is going on sir?"

"Betrayal Herr Standartenfuhrer." Himmler said flatly.

"I don't understand sir." Paulus said.

"Two days ago a Waffen SS unit near Leningrad disobeyed the Commissar Order and took a NKVD officer prisoner." Himmler said. "I have forgiven the officer in command for this serious breach of conduct."

"May I ask why sir." Volker asked.

"NKVD officer was a senior colonel carrying documents that proved to be very important." Himmler said pressing the intercom button twice. "You speak Estonian and Russian Paulus is that correct?"

"Yes sir." Paulus said. "Why?"

"He is Estonian not a full bloodied Russian." Himmler said as two SS men dragged a man into the room and dropped him into a chair. "His papers say his name is Andres Laaneots."

"Why is he still alive sir?" Paulus asked.

"I need to confirm the information he was carrying Standartenfuhrer." Himmler said flatly removing his glasses to polish them. "He has been resistant, but you are my master interrogator."

"What do you want to know Reichsfuhrer?" Paulus asked.

"Why is Laaneots carrying documents referring to Krieger?" Himmler asked.

"What do I promise him?" Paulus asked somberly.

"You promise him everything he asks for." Himmler said rising to his feet. "You have three hours."

"What if he doesn't talk?" Paulus asked.

"I have Gruber standing by." The Reichsfuhrer said. "His methods are cruder than yours Standartenfuhrer."

"My Estonian will talk Reichsfuhrer." Paulus said. "He will not be expecting the velvet glove."

"There will no notes taken Paulus." Himmler said bluntly. "You are capable of forgetting Standartenfuhrer?"

"I am very capable sir." Paulus said.

[2]
08:00 hrs

OSS GHQ
Washington DC

The Colonel moved to the conference where the guest the Deputy Chief of Staff had palmed off on him. Coffin was used to dealing with politicians but this guest was hardly just any politician. Senator 'Gentlemen' Jim Colquhoun was a legend in his time. He was one of the senators that keep the South solid for the Democratic Party and had his fingerprints all over the New Deal. He was now serving on the Senate Oversight Committee for Military Affairs.

"General, I'm not used to being kept waiting." Colquhoun said testily as he lit his cigar.

"I apologize, Senator for the delay." Coffin said. "Your appointment was not placed on the calendar."

"I'm a United States Senator Colonel." Colquhoun said. "I don't need an appointment. Are you from the public relations office General?"

"I'm from OSS G2 liaison Senator." Coffin said. "How may I help you?"

"You have misplaced my son it seems." The Senator said.

"I can not discuss OSS operations sir." Coffin said. "He is assigned to the ETO and that is all the information I can give."

"I'm afraid that you don't understand Colonel." Colquhoun hissed tartly. "I want to know where my son is."

"I can't tell you." Coffin said. "If I do I'll be breaking the Official Secrets Act."

"Sonny who do you think help write that law." Colquhoun rasped with a smile. "So look at the fine print before you talk again. My advice son is to get on that telephone and call someone with more stars."

"I know who you are." Rear Admiral Amos Coffin said motioning the senator to sit down.

"Good." Colquhoun said. "Saves a lot of time dancing around the bush testing each other."

"Your son volunteered for the OSS Senator." Coffin said. "The last I looked he was free, white and twenty-one."

"I served in the Spanish War Admiral." Colquhoun said flatly. "I understand the concept of volunteering. I want him back in the United States in 48 hours."

"Or what Senator," Coffin said. "There is always and a what?"

"It is extremely hard to run something without money oiling the wheels." Colquhoun said firmly with little emotion.

"That is very irresponsible even for you." Coffin said. "How many men will that kill?"

"No appeals to patriotism?" Colquhoun said.

"Would it do any good?" Coffin asked cynically.

"No." Colquhoun said. "All I want is my son back here and no poor sharecropper's son dies because you played hero."

Admiral Coffin had heard that the elder Colquhoun was an utterly ruthless man, which was hidden under the veneer of Southern gentleman. Coffin had heard the stories of Major Bedford Colquhoun, who rode with General Nathan Bedford Forrest's Calvary, during the Civil

War. His battalion took the fewest prisoners during the war and was a leading figure in the massacre of black Union soldiers at Fort Pillow.

After the war, Major Colquhoun returned home to his law practice in Macon, Georgia. Since he was below the rank of colonel, he was not barred from the practice of law or dabbling in politics under Reconstruction. When the KKK was created by his former commanding officer Colquhoun enthusiastically joined rising to be second-in-command of the State before it was officially disbanded.

Six months later Colquhoun was elected to the state house of representatives thus launching his political career. Four years later Colquhoun was elected to the Federal House of Representatives. Colquhoun pulled enough strings to get his son John appointed to VMI and later to West Point.

The Major arranged for his son, after graduation, to be on the staff of fellow Congressman Joe Wheeler, who was commissioned a major general of volunteers, when war with Spain became unavoidable. The Major found it ironic that a former Confederate general officer had been given a major generalcy in the Yankee Army.

After the war, young Colquhoun was ready to proceed with his Army career when the fates intervene. The Major, basking in the glow of his last reelection, suffered a stroke. The Party official strong-armed the governor to avoid calling an election until John could get home from the Philippines. John won the special election and served in the House three terms before he got himself elected to the US Senate one of the last senators to be elected by the state legislature.

"Your son is in the field Senator and he can not be recalled." Coffin said plainly.

"Make the teletype to Lord Snort's manor house and get him to London Admiral." Colquhoun said bluntly. "I do not bluff Admiral."

"Major Colquhoun is on the continent Senator." Coffin said sternly.

"What the hell is he doing there?" The Senator growled. "After that Dieppe fiasco he was suppose to be on staff."

"He got bored." Coffin said. "So he volunteered."

"Bullshit Admiral." The Senator rasped. "That dog won't hunt as they say where I come from. You forget I know my eldest son, he doesn't volunteer for anything."

"The Army has changed him or perhaps it was Dieppe." Coffin said.

"You can recall him." The Senator said coldly. "You have radios, use them damnit."

"I'm not going to risk hundreds of lives to do that." Coffin rasped. "I doubt that neither General Marshall nor the President will be amused if start fucking with the war effort."

"Your career has just fallen into the cesspool Admiral." Colquhoun hissed.

"How many factories do you have making war goods in your state Senator?" Coffin asked sharply. "You want to explain to your people a 50% reduction?"

"You can't do that." Colquhoun said gruffly.

"I don't but the White House does." Coffin said curtly. "Your friends at home might not like the FBI asking questions."

"Hoover doesn't like you." Colquhoun rasped.

"He likes you less." Coffin said. "Even the rich and powerful have to make sacrifices at times Senator."

"I want him back alive Admiral." Colquhoun said. "I have plans for Jefferson."

"He'll be sent home after the mission." Coffin said. "This conversation never took place."

"You learn quickly for a Yankee." Colquhoun said. "I want him back in one piece."

[3]
13:35 hrs

The Kremlin
Moscow, USSR

"What does Denovich report Comrade General?" The little bespectacled man asked speaking Russian with a Georgian accent. The other officer with him remained in the shadows.

"Laaneots was taken trying to cross into Leningrad Comrade Marshal." The NKVD General said in a flat voice. "Most of his party was killed Colonel Denovich reports."

"Was he convincing?" The Marshal asked.

"For a paper pusher he was quite convincing." The NKVD General said. "Denovich said that there was movement along the German lines a few hours before Laaneots made his attempt."

"Was it regular Army that took him?" The Marshal said.

"Denovich wasn't certain Comrade Marshal." The NKVD General said. "Does it matter sir?"

"The Waffen SS doesn't take prisoners." Lavrenty Beria said flatly.

"Denovich said he was taken alive Comrade Marshal along with two others." The NKVD General said dryly. "Is there anything else sir?"

"Keep me informed General." Beria said.

The NKGB Major General lit an American cigarette. "Why are you going to so much trouble Comrade?"

"I thought you would understand why Comrade Alexisovich Orenstadt." Beria said sitting down.

"Blenkov is not expecting this," Orenstadt said bluntly. "He understood the risks before he accepted the mission."

"That was twenty years ago." Beria said. "There are only three of us left who meet that night."

"We can't help him Comrade." Orenstadt said cynically. "Blenkov is a faded memory, only a shadow."

"I could have had him remain a shadow." Beria said icily. "But he was reminded of him and started to ask questions."

"Who was the fool who did that Comrade Marshal?" Orenstadt asked.

"It was a chance meeting with Eugenia Blenkov." Beria said. "She works as a typist at Party Central."

"Conscience, that is very odd considering the circumstances?" Orenstadt asked.

"Guilt and remorse haunts him." Beria said. "Human feelings are not gone from him."

"Blenkov had a child." Orenstadt quipped.

"A boy," Beria said. "Took his mother's name to avoid the shame of his father's 'treason' and went to live with his grandfather in Odessa."

"Where is he now?" Orenstadt asked.

"London." Beria said. "He is a GRU liaison with our Allies."

"Mikhailov, I'll be damned." Orenstadt said. "Does he know about his father?"

"No."

"He is not to find out I assume." Orenstadt said.

"Correct." Beria said bluntly. "It is bad enough that we have to share this information with our 'friends' Orenstadt. Keep the pressure on Bukharin."

[4]
09:45 hrs

Bergdorf, Switzerland
Haussmann Chalet

Greene lit his pipe and watched the skiers moving down the hill. "Hard to believe there is a war going on Thomas."

"I agree sir." Withgate said. "Looks like a bank holiday out there."

"Have you seen any signs of our friends Captain?" Greene asked.

"None,' Withgate said. "They are following the decoys."

"Americans are always late." Greene said looking at his pocket watch.

"Sherman is near the fireplace sir." Withgate said. "Shall we go over?"

"You watch the store." Greene said standing. "The Germans will come from the entrance not the ski slope."

"May I ask what you did before the war Mr. Sherman?" Greene asked stirring his tea slowly.

"I taught at Harvard." Sherman said. "Why?"

"Meaningful amateurs are dangerous Mr. Sherman." Greene said. "Everyone here knows you are an American."

"They know you are British." Sherman said drably. "The Germans are not here."

"They have friends." Greene said sternly.

"We have also have friends." Sherman said. "I don't see the problem." The American lit a cigarette. "Has something gone wrong?"

"The plan has gone slightly astray." Greene said blandly as he lit his pipe.

"How far astray may I ask?" Sherman asked grimly.

Sherman crushed out the cigarette slowly. "Your Major Mannerling will he stay?"

"His orders have not been changed." Greene said. "I'm afraid London might have underestimate Colquhoun."

"How far is this rendezvous?" Sherman asked.

"It is about 10 kms from the border." Greene said. "This section of the border is not that well patrolled by either side."

"That is the only good news Greene." Sherman said. "Have you been watching the sky?"

"No, what's wrong?" Greene asked.

"Mother Nature is not coming in on the side of the angels." Sherman said.

"How bad will it be?" Greene asked.

"Back in New England we would call it a blizzard." Sherman said. "We won't be able to fly them out."

"Mannerling will have to walk out." Greene said sternly.

[5]
10:10 hrs

Potsdam, Germany
Von Tanz's Home

Frau von Tanz brought the visitor to the General's private study. "Herbert, you remember Oberst Maatz?"

"Yes." Von Tanz said looking up from the easel.

"Will the Colonel be staying for lunch?" Frau von Tanz asked.

"I don't think so my dear." The General said.

"I have to get back to Brandenburg as quickly as possible Frau von Tanz." Maatz said in a polite voice. "Perhaps another time I might Frau von Tanz."

"Lunch is at12:30 Herbert." Frau von Tanz said as she left the room.

"Your wife is a lovely woman Herr General." Maatz said.

"What is the reason for this visit Herr Oberst?" Von Tanz asked removing the painter's smock.

"Have you heard from your Major Gerhardt?" Maatz asked.

"He has no orders to contact me Maatz." Von Tanz said. "Are you certain you were not followed?"

"Oberstgeneral Dietrich is above suspicion." Maatz said flatly. "He is totally apolitical as far as Himmler is concerned unlike certain people in your operation."

"Why are you here?" Von Tanz asked in a blunt voice.

"Oberleutnant Dietrich did not go with Major Gerhardt to Adlerberghof." Maatz said flatly.

Von Tanz motioned Maatz to sit down as he lit his pipe. "Is he with you?"

"No." Maatz said.

"Do you know where he is?" Von Tanz asked. "I don't want the military police picking him up with no travel orders."

"He went to Adlerberghof." Maatz said dully.

"I do not enjoy jokes or riddles." Von Tanz said caustically. "I need an explanation of this Colonel."

"Young Dietrich went to Adlerberghof to stop Gerhardt." Maatz said.

"He is hardly a match for Gerhardt." Von Tanz said grimly.

"Dietrich is not stupid." Maatz said. "He went with Weiss and a few Freikorps comrades. Weiss is more than a match for Gerhardt."

"Why the sudden need to tell me this?" Von Tanz asked.

"Dietrich and Weiss are not back from Adlerberghof." Maatz said. "They have not contacted me."

"Gerhardt wouldn't advertise any difficulty." Von Tanz said firmly. "Who are you worried about?"

"General Dietrich." Maatz said. "He is not that well."

"You believe Carl is dead." Von Tanz stated.

"Yes." Maatz said.

"Death is an occupational hazard of being a soldier." Von Tanz said. "You want a hero for the old man."

"It would help the grieving process if Carl died a hero." Maatz said. "With Carl dead the General would have nothing to live for if his son died in dishonor."

"You are assuming that Carl is dead." Von Tanz said. "He could have run."

"Not with Weiss." Maatz said. "If he had killed him he would have told me."

"You should stay with the General." Von Tanz said firmly. "Himmler's people are not that particular about whom they shoot."

Chapter Nineteen
December 9, 1942
08:00 hrs

Adlerberghof
Gasthof Gruenling

"This isn't Berlin Herr Burgermeister." Ehrlich hissed dourly at Schiller's melodramatic entrance. "You impress no one."

"The SS is all showmanship." Schiller said glibly.

"Where is my sergeant?" Krieger asked.

"Safe." Schiller said. "He is downstairs in momentary protective custody."

"I suppose you are here about the commotion down the hall." Krieger said in a matter-of-fact voice.

"Yes." Schiller said. "By nine o'clock this morning Colonel Jherling will be here with a company of his men from Jaegerfeld." Schiller lit a cigar. "Also the Kripo will be here by then too."

"I understand the Army." Krieger hissed. "The Kripo being here is very odd."

"Murder Herr General." Schiller said. "I have six bodies with no explanations on why."

"I have murdered no one." Krieger said. "Self-defense is not murder."

"Are you making accusations Herr Schiller?" Ehrlich snarled. "You know the penalty for making a false accusation against a government official."

"That is not my job." Schiller said. "The Kripo will determine that. My duty is to make certain that all the facts and witnesses remained intact."

"You are still an arrogant bastard." Ehrlich sneered. "Is this reserved solely for us?"

"If you mean Gerhardt, I'll be speaking to him later." Schiller said curtly. "This floor will be your world until further notice."

"If we should go stray Herr Schiller, what will happen?" Ehrlich rasped.

"Anyone other than Klugge my people will leave you where you fall." Schiller said in a blunt voice. "Colonel Jherling may have further restriction."

"If you are wrong about anything Schiller," Krieger hissed. "I will see you before a Court of Honor."

"Judge Kohlberger has signed the judicial order under the revise provision of the Protection of the Reich statue." Schiller said flatly. "All actions are legal and Kohlberger is a personal friend of the Minister of the Interior and Justice."

"You have learned Schiller." Krieger said.

"Yes." Schiller said. "Is the prisoner Viktor Skasch?"

"Who else would he be?" Ehrlich quipped.

"You'll both swear to that?" Schiller asked bluntly.

"Jung is the one who actually knew him." Krieger said. "He is the one who did business with him."

"I have little confidence in a dead man's word." Schiller said dryly.

"That is a problem." Krieger said. "I sincerely hope that you'll be able to survive this intact- a misstep could make this place look like heaven."

"I have no intentions of rotting here for the rest of my life." Schiller said in a firm voice. "I don't care who I have to step over to get out of here."

"As I said you have learned the game very well." Krieger said.

"Then we understand each other." Schiller said.

[2]
11:00 hrs

Twickem-Hallesy
Red Boar Pub

Colonel Mikhailov could pass for a country squire in his civilian clothes as he moved into the private booth with the two other gentlemen.

"Why here?" Crawford asked.

"I needed to have this conversation private." Mikhailov answered. "Also I enjoy the atmosphere of English pubs."

"You think we wired the manor house?" Crawford growled.

"We would." Mikhailov said. "So would the British. The noise in a pub makes eavesdropping harder."

"Please." Austen-Halton said lighting his cigar. "You called us."

"Moscow has agreed to your idea about *Boris*." Mikhailov said. "They were very reluctant to do so gentlemen"

"Time is running out." Sir Peter said. "This is unraveling slightly."

"How much is it unraveling?" Mikhailov asked bluntly.

"Krieger brought Jung to Adlerberghof." Crawford said. "During the meeting Krieger brought in Jung; all hell broke loose."

"What about Jung?" Mikhailov asked.

"He was killed during the melee." Austen-Halton said dryly. "Colquhoun was wounded and captured."

"That was the intention." Mikhailov said icily. "How is that a problem?"

"We don't know if Jung was able to warn Krieger," Crawford said cynically. "If he did this puts a different slant on this."

"Is the mission continuing?" Mikhailov asked as he removed a cigarette from his gold cigarette case.

"Yes." Sir Peter said. "We need to know how long it will take to get your man in position."

"He is already there." Mikhailov said in a matter-of-fact voice as he lit an American cigarette

"What?" Crawford gulped.

"Moscow has sent his orders." Mikhailov said.

"May I inquire how?" Austen-Halton asked.

"It was via the courtesy of Radio Berlin, very similar to how you pass along instructions to the resistance."" Mikhailov said.

"I'll be damned." Crawford growled. "You are a sonofabitch."

"War is hell." Mikhailov said. "Your General Sherman said that."

"Boris has been there all the time." Crawford said. "Hasn't he Colonel?"

"Perhaps he has been there." Mikhailov said.

"What orders have he received?" Sir Peter asked.

"Keep everyone alive." Mikhailov said. "Complete the mission. Krieger is a very dangerous man to us also."

"Does that include killing Krieger?" Crawford hissed.

"Yes, Krieger has become a problem." Mikhailov said. "Your people have to kill him not Boris."

[3]
13:15 hrs

Adlerberghof
Town Hall

"I really don't give a damn about your problems Schiller." Gerhardt said bluntly. "My prisoner was almost killed."

"Skasch is MY prisoner Major." Schiller snapped. "Heinz has lost two men and two of my citizens."

"Two?" Franz hissed.

"I send two messengers one hasn't made it." Schiller said.

"That does not mean he is dead." Gerhardt said.

"We found him by accident." Schiller said. "Throat cut, the snows should have kept the body hidden until spring."

"This place is becoming unhealthy." Gerhardt said dourly.

"That is why the Army and Kripo are coming here." Schiller said.

Gerhardt lit a cigarette. "The Army I can see, why the criminal police?"

"This is criminal case when you boil this down." Schiller said. "Fuchs is a policeman first, last, always. He will find the murderer, no matter who he is."

"You seem to have great faith in this Fuchs." Gerhardt said.

"I've dealt with him before in the past." Schiller said. "He is anomaly, an honest policeman."

"Krieger isn't going to like either development." Franz said.

"I'm not interested in making him happy." Schiller rasped.

"Where is the prisoner Skasch?" Gerhardt asked. "What about him?"

"He is under heavy guard in the manager's flat." Schiller answered.

"Have you confirmed he is Skasch?" Gerhardt asked.

"His fingerprints were taken and sent to Vienna and Berlin." Schiller said. "Some time today his identity will be confirmed."

"How could you do that if the telephone lines are down?" Gerhardt asked.

"I have my ways Major." Schiller said. "However, it still will take hours to get the information back."

"Have you searched the room?" Franz asked.

"Nothing has been touched." Schiller said. "Krieger was moved to the next room as you well know."

"What is our status?" Franz asked somberly.

"Circumstances force me to accept you as allies." Schiller said flatly.

"That is hardly a ringing endorsement." Gerhardt said.

"You are more acceptable than Krieger." Schiller said.

"An offhanded compliment, but I'll take it." Gerhardt said.

"Avoid contact with Krieger." Schiller said. "Klugge will have the run of the town like you. Heinz's men will not discriminate whom they shoot after any trouble." Schiller paused. "You're missing Lieutenant?"

"He is resting." Gerhardt said.

"You better tell him about the ground rules Herr Major." Schiller said. "I don't any accidents."

"I understand Herr Burgermeister." Gerhardt said. "I will point out that the people in the woods will not know about your rules."

"I don't plan to tell them." Schiller said. "How many are out there?"

"I say perhaps twenty or more men." Franz said dully. "They have to have that many to surround the town."

"Whose friends are they?" Schiller asked.

"Not ours." Gerhardt said. "Right now they are most likely interested in keeping us in town."

"I see no problem at the moment Herr Major." Schiller said. "It will be to our mutual benefit if we have a live prisoner."

"I agree that a live Skasch would be better." Gerhardt said standing. "What about our weapons?"

"One of my men will bring them to you." Schiller said.

[4]
13:40 hrs

Gasthof Gruenling
Gerhardt's Room

"Did you see any major problems out there Franz?" Mannerling asked.

"Good shot by the way." Franz said dryly. "They have the town surrounded tight enough to stop any mass movement to leave. You haven't killed any during your coming and goings?"

"I avoid them." Mannerling said.

"How well armed are they" Gerhardt asked.

"They have at least one MG-34." Mannerling answered "What about Colquhoun?"

"He is still alive." Gerhardt said. "An old Army nurse is keeping him alive since Dr. Brandt was killed."

"That couldn't be helped." Mannerling said. "He killed him before I had a clear shot."

"There is no blame." Gerhardt said. "We need to be flexible now."

"Schiller is no fool." Franz said. "He has the Army and the Kripo coming here sometime today."

"How much scrutiny can our Identity cards take?" Mannerling asked.

"Enough." Gerhardt said. "The others, what is their condition?"

"They are surviving." Mannerling said bluntly. "Orr and the others were forced to kill a few of them. Donner took them to the monastery; the farm house is no longer an option."

"Shit." Gerhardt rasped. "Nothing is going right."

"How much time are we going to give this?" Mannerling asked.

"48 hours." Gerhardt said. "You can't blindly charge into this. If Colquhoun doesn't talk you'll be evacuated to the border."

"I'm not going to leave the poor bastard behind." Mannerling said bluntly.

"Nobility can get you killed." Franz warned. "Along with us Englander and I have no desire to die for him."

"Will make the witnesses more convinced that he is important if we keep trying to rescue him." Mannerling said.

"You better let Schiller's men get a look at you for a while." Gerhardt said flatly. "It would be a grave error to let Schiller get too curious about you, below that cosmopolitan smile is a hard core Nazi with the skill to survive."

"Sounds like a lovely idea." Mannerling said.

[5]
14:30 hrs

Gasthof Gruenling

Mannerling nodded his head slightly tacitly acknowledging Heinz's man in the lobby. The Chief's man was trying to remain unseen, but was failing miserably. Mannerling rose from his chair and headed for the door; he was tired of Heinz's men gawking at him. Mannerling would take a walk around the town then go back to the hotel.

The town had settled down after the incident at the Gruenling and returned to its picture postcard look. Mannerling after a few minutes knew that Heinz's men were primarily watching the Gasthof and town hall. Mannerling went down a side street and halfway down stopped in front of Kristoffer's watch shop and looked in. Mannerling stiffened when he heard the sound of a pistol slide pulling back. Mannerling glared at the reflection in the window seeing Klugge standing behind him.

"Move slowly down the street." Klugge ordered. "Keep your hands by your side at all times. You'll be dead before you could do anything stupid."

"This is hardly smart Klugge." Mannerling said. "I don't care if you want to die today, but Schiller's men are not going to be careful about whom they shoot."

"You worry too much." Klugge said. "Please head towards the lake Herr Oberleutnant."

"If I should refuse this invitation for a stroll Sergeant-Major, what will you do?" Mannerling asked turning to face Klugge.

"We both deal in death and dying is part of the job." Klugge said flatly. "However, I could shoot you so that you will live but never walk again."

"You have a point." Mannerling said.

The journey ended at the boathouse on the lake. Klugge had them go inside the boathouse which was unlocked.

"Sit at the table." Klugge said. "Hands on the table palms down, hook your feet around the chair rails."

"At the present mood of Burgermeister Schiller killing me would be extremely foolish Hauptscharfuhrer." Mannerling said in a plain voice. "You won't live out the day."

"I have no intentions of killing you Herr Major." Klugge said sitting down after lighting the oil lamp.

"Oberleutnant, I'm not a Major." Mannerling said.

"Major." Klugge said laying his pistol on the table and removing his pipe from his overcoat pocket. "Aka Praetorian, is that not correct Herr Major?"

"You have my attention." Mannerling said dryly.

"*Moscow is warm in the summer.*" Klugge said as he lit the pipe. "Major Mannerling."

"Damnit what the hell is going on?" Mannerling hissed. "*London is wet in the spring.*"

"Now we can stop dancing." Klugge said. "You have a wireless?"

"Yes." Mannerling said. "Control says to cooperate in this; do I have to explain this?"

"Your mission is transparent." Klugge hissed. "At least to me, but Krieger has other things on his mind. He suspects that General von Tanz is behind this."

"Von Tanz?" Mannerling quipped.

"Abwehr." Klugge said. "You people are so squeamish at times; killing him outright would have caused me less problems."

"Sorry for the inconvenience." Mannerling said. "My orders are often asinine too."

"This stupid plan could most likely get me killed." Klugge said. "I don't like that idea."

"Your non-cooperation could get me killed." Mannerling said grimly. "Who the hell are you? The SS doesn't make men Hauptscharfuhrer without a deep background check."

"I was with Krieger before the SS was in existence." Klugge said plainly.

"Who are you?" Mannerling asked placing his pistol on the table. "Mine is loaded."

"I was Captain Sergei S. K. Blenkov, Imperial Army of Russia." Klugge said. "I've been Klugge for twenty-eight years and I want to go home in one piece."

"Traitor and spy." Mannerling said. "A unique accomplishment, now you work for the Reds."

"Tsar or Stalin either way you're dead and forgotten." Klugge said flatly.

"I need a drink." Mannerling said. "Hard to kill someone with an empty weapon Sergeant."

"I prefer silent work." Klugge said placing a throwing knife on the table. "Messy, but gets the job done."

"How about a drink Hauptscharfuhrer, I'll pay?" Mannerling asked.

"What will everyone think if we do?" Klugge quipped.

"We will be two lions sizing each other up." Mannerling said. "We'll be observing each other trying to find a weakness in the other as we drink."

"Sounds interesting Herr Oberleutnant, it will draw attention away from our friend." Klugge said

Chapter Twenty
December 9, 1942
11:30 hrs

Jaegerfeld
Battalion HQ

    Major Utlaut brought the two civilians into Jherling's office. The colonel's sojourn to Adlerberghof had been postponed do to an avalanche 10 kms out of town.
    "Herr Oberstleutnant, may I introduce Reichkriminaldirektor Fuchs and Kriminalinspektor Wulff from the Stuttgart Kripo." Utlaut said flatly.
    "Be seated gentlemen." Jherling said. "Stuttgart is a long journey; is this journey for pleasure or business?"
    "Business Herr Oberstleutnant." Fuchs answered. "We are heading for Adlerberghof."
    "That is interesting." Jherling said as he lit a cigarette. "What is in Adlerberghof that could possibly interest two policemen from Stuttgart?"
    "The Burgermeister requested us." Fuchs said. "You know Kurt Schiller?"
    "I know who he is." Jherling said. "Are you here officially?"
    "Not at the moment colonel." Fuchs said honestly. "However, the situation might change once we get there. Schiller hinted that there might be trouble brewing."
    "This trouble Herr Reichkriminaldirektor," Jherling said firmly. "Has it to do with a man called Krieger?"
    "Yes." Fuchs answered. "This shouldn't be common knowledge."
    "We have lost contact with Adlerberghof." Jherling said grimly.
    "That can't be that unusual for this time of year." Wulff said dryly.
    "We lost contact before the storm." Jherling said. "Krieger's wife was at the hotel until an hour ago, they left soon after the word came that the road was cleared much against advice."
    "How long will it take to drive there?" Fuchs asked.
    "I would say in this weather perhaps six/seven hours if you are lucky." Jherling said.
    "The railroad tracks are they blocked?" Wulff inquired.
    "No." Jherling said. "I'm getting a troop train ready to go to Adlerberghof, there is room."
    "What about weather?" Wulff asked.
    "The Bavarian State Railroad for some strange reason spent millions of Reichmarks to make a tunnel through the mountain to Adlerberghof." Jherling said. "The engineers have just put the plow on the engine and caboose."
    "Is it long by train to Adlerberghof?" Fuchs asked.
    "It should take three, four hours." Jherling said.
    "How many men are you bringing?" Wulff asked.
    "Two companies and three armored cars should handle any situation." Jherling said.
    "It should handle any problems." Fuchs said.

[2]
12:30 hrs

Donner's Farm

    "What is she doing here Mundt?" Hothman asked as they stood by the barrel burning wood.

"Lover boy is in the town." Mundt said flatly.

"Looks like the blood is going to flow in the streets sometime today." Hothman said grimly.

"You can bet on that." Mundt said looking at the farmhouse. "She is a bitch."

Eidernau lit his cigar. "It is damn foolish for you to be here Countess; have Mundt drive you back to Berlin."

"You overstep the boundaries Eidernau." The Countess hissed.

"At least in Berlin you'll have protection." Eidernau said. "I can not guarantee your safety if you go into town."

"That is what you're being paid to do Willi." The Countess snapped.

"Suicide is not part of the deal." Eidernau said. "The town still has able-bodied men capable of fighting."

"They are unarmed." The Countess said tersely. "The Party saw to that."

"Why make yourself a gift to them?" Eidernau hissed.

"Schiller knows who I am and my circle of friends." The Countess said. "Harming me in any way would be as if Schiller was cutting his own throat."

"When do you plan to go?" Eidernau asked seeing that further arguing would be useless.

"Thirty minutes." The Countess said. "Find the tunnel entrance and use it when the time comes."

[3]
12:45 hrs

The Monastery

Zoeller picked up the pewter cup and placed it back on the table. "I thought monasteries had silver plate at least Abbot."

"We take a vow of poverty my son." Brother Fritz said.

"You know what will happen if we find someone." Zoeller rasped.

"This place has been vandalized before my son." Brother Fritz said firmly.

"If we find someone who isn't a monk we'll be the only ones leaving this place alive." Zoeller said.

"If that is God's will." Brother Fritz said calmly.

"From your build and the scars on your face you weren't always a monk." Zoeller hissed dourly. "You speak with an upper class accent."

"I am Brother Fritz now." The monk said as one of Zoeller's men entered the room and whispered something to him.

"We found nothing monk." Zoeller said. "Do I need to leave men here?"

"Our doors are always open." Brother Fritz said firmly.

"I'll two men." Zoeller said. "They will be your doorkeepers."

"Do what you must." Brother Fritz said. "They can stay in the gatekeeper's hut; they will be protected from the weather."

"Any trouble Brother Fritz and I will level this place with you and your fellow monks in it." Zoeller said bluntly.

Orr and Donner emerged from their hiding places and watched Zoeller leave.

"We can't have Zoeller's men here." Orr said bluntly.

"I can not allow you to harm them." Brother Fritz said.

"They wouldn't hesitate to kill you." Donner snapped.
"We shall take care of them." Brother Fritz said.
"No doubts with kind words Brother Fritz?" Orr hissed.
"No, with mulled wine Captain," Brother Fritz said. "It will be a special vintage."
"Where can we hide now?" Orr asked.
"We have a cave about 3 kms from here." Brother Fritz said. "We age our wine there. It has heat."
"So, we go into the cold again Donner." Orr said. "I'll tell Browne and Carey."

[4]
13:00 hrs

Adlerberghof
Train Depot

Hronska, the stationmaster, handed Heinz the telegram he had received from Jaegerfeld, the railroad had an emergency telegraph system connecting train stations, which was battery powered.
"Are you still in contact with Jaegerfeld?" Heinz asked.
"No, I was surprised it worked." Hronska said. "The batteries hadn't been tested since the war started."
"How long will it take for Jherling gets here?" Heinz asked somberly.
"If nothing is blocking the tracks I will say two or three hours." Hronska said.
"Emile you keep your big mouth shut about this." Heinz said bluntly. "Word leaks out and you'll find your fat ass in Russia, do you understand?"
"Yes, I understand Otto." Hronska said.
Kohlberger lit his pipe. "Bringing that cop here was not brilliant Kurt, but what we don't need is the fucking army here messing things up."
"The Army will keep us alive." Schiller said.
"Otto's men are not pushovers." Kohlberger snapped.
"Our friends in the woods are not amateurs." Heinz said. "I will be more comfortable with the regular Army here."
"We'll have to make the best of this," Schiller said. "Since we can't stop them we'll have to cooperate with them."
"Their arrival should shake some one up." Heinz hissed tartly.

[5]
13:00 hrs

Berlin
Reich Chancellery

Heinrich Koch stood as Reichleiter and Chief of the Party Chancellery Martin Bormann entered the room and returned the Hitler salute. Bormann went to the desk and sat down.
"What have you found out Heinrich?" Bormann asked.
"The Abwehr and the SD officially deny the existence of *Albatross.*" Koch said. "They consider him a 'Flying Dutchman' from the last war."

"What do they say unofficially Koch?" Bormann asked stiffly.

"They consider him very dangerous." Koch said. "My sources have told me that Himmler has assigned Krieger to track him down at all costs."

"The Abwehr has not counter moved?" Bormann inquired.

"Von Tanz is looking for him too." Koch said.

Bormann rose from behind the desk and went to the window. "Are either of them close to finding him?"

"The answer is no." Koch said.

"Are you being polite Koch?" Bormann rasped. "You have my protection Heinrich."

"There is a rampant rumor that Krieger is very close to identifying *Albatross*." Koch said in a firm voice.

"Enlighten me Heinrich." Bormann said. "Is he chasing a phantom?"

"I do not wish to sully the reputation of a serving officer sir." Koch said.

"I will tell you then Koch." Bormann said flatly. "He believes that *Albatross* is a Wehrmacht officer; more particularly one certain Wehrmacht officer."

"Krieger is being vindictive for personal reasons Herr Reichleiter." Koch said. "They have clashed in the past sir."

"Does von Tanz have similar feelings?" Bormann asked.

"No." Koch said. "There is nothing to prove von Tanz is *Albatross*."

Bormann turned from the window. "The Reichsfuhrer doesn't feel that way and Krieger is the leading contender to succeed Heydrich as Chief of the RSHA."

"Why isn't von Tanz under arrest sir?" Koch said.

"The answer I thought was obvious Heinrich." Bormann said. "Von Tanz isn't our 'Flying Dutchman'."

"May I ask who is sir?" Koch asked.

"Stay here Heinrich." Bormann said. "The Reichsfuhrer will be arriving shortly to discuss the phantom. Keeping the lid on scandal is what my office does best."

Chapter Twenty-One
December 9, 1942
15:30 hrs

Adlerberghof

    The train arrived in the town with little fanfare. The Colonel's men quickly and quietly secured the train station. Schiller, Kohlberger, and Heinz met Jherling and the two civilians fifteen minutes after the train arrived. They moved to Schiller's office in town hall.
    "Who belongs to the Wehrmacht vehicle?" Jherling asked crisply stepping away from the window. "I don't recognize the unit."
    "It belongs to a major from the Abwehrpolizei." Schiller said. "His name is Gerhardt."
    "Is he alone?" Wulff asked.
    "He has two other officers with him." Heinz said hollowly.
    "Is there a reason why they are not here Herr Schiller?" Fuchs asked lighting his battered pipe.
    "I thought that we should talk first." Schiller said flatly. "Establish the ground rules so to speak."
    "As of this moment I'm in charge." Fuchs said hollowly. "This will be kept very simple."
    "No objections Herr Oberstleutnant?" Schiller asked.
    "I have none at the moment." Jherling said.
    "I see no problem with that from a legal point of view." Kohlberger said.
    "Are you certain you have Krieger?" Wulff asked bluntly.
    "I know him personally." Schiller rasped. "The identification cards are real."
    "Tell me what happened." Fuchs said. "Leave out nothing."
    "That will take time." Heinz said.
    "All I have is time." Fuchs said relighting his pipe.

[2]
17:30 hrs

Gasthof Gruenling

    Jherling and Fuchs entered the dining room where Heinz's men had brought Krieger, Ehrlich, and Klugge. Fuchs immediately sat at the head of the long table without waiting for Krieger to make the gesture for him to sit.
    "Gentlemen, no formality please." Fuchs said with a slight smile. "No doubt you are anxious to have this matter settled quickly. I hope to have this finished by tomorrow so all of us, except the guilty, may go home."
    "Who the hell are you?" Ehrlich asked.
    "I am Reichkriminaldirektor Fuchs Stuttgart Kripo." Fuchs answered softly
    "You have no authority to hold or even question me Herr Reichkriminaldirektor." Krieger said bluntly, as he sat down at the table. "I am traveling under orders from the Reichsfuhrer himself." Krieger lit a cigarette. "I am immune to your petty authority."
    "Do you have a signed document confirming that?" Fuchs asked nonchalantly.
    "No." Krieger said. "It was verbal."

"Then what you say is useless." Fuchs said sternly. "This is a criminal investigation Herr General involving murder."

"They tried to kill me Herr Reichkriminaldirektor." Krieger hissed. "I am the victim Herr Fuchs."

"Who killed Heinz's men and Dr. Brandt?" Fuchs said icily. "Who tried to kill Skasch?"

"You should be protecting me." Krieger said hollowly. "Not worrying about trivial matters. I'm here on orders."

Fuchs shook his head slowly. "My authority is clearly defined by Reich Law and Interior Ministry regulations." Fuchs said. "I'm certain that Colonel Jherling will allow you to radio Berlin to have the Reichsfuhrer confirm your orders."

"Secret orders." Ehrlich said. "Berlin will not confirm this."

"Then we have a problem Herr Gruppenfuhrer." Fuchs said. "You have gone from victim to suspect."

"I hold military rank in the Waffen SS." Krieger said. "I fall under Colonel Jherling's military jurisdiction."

"This is a civilian matter." Jherling said flatly. "I'm here to protect the nation."

"I will just leave." Krieger said. "No little tin god is going to stop me."

"My men will shoot to kill." Jherling said bluntly.

"Anyone trying to leave the town without authorization will tantamount to an admission of guilt." Fuchs said firmly.

"I will formally protest to the Reichsfuhrer." Krieger snarled. "Your career is finished."

"Protest all you want." Fuchs said blandly unaffected by Krieger's threat. "All communication with the outside world is prohibited."

"You are pushing too hard Herr Direktor." Krieger said stiffly. "State Security is the responsibility of Sipo not Kripo."

"Kripo is part of Sipo." Fuchs said.

"Only a small part though." Krieger said.

"Remain upstairs." Fuchs said. "I will have further questions."

[3]

The Braunfuch

Franz lit a cigarette, Lang slowly shook his head, and Gerhardt crushed out his cigarette.

"Christ, I don't like this." Lang hissed.

"Out of the blue is very suspect." Franz said crisply.

"Hell, it happened." Mannerling said. "He could have killed me, but he didn't."

"I didn't like Klugge when he was a Nazi." Franz said dourly. "Being a Red doesn't help either."

"Why pick you?" Lang asked.

"I was available." Mannerling said.

"No." Gerhardt said flatly. "It was more than that I'm afraid. Klugge was looking for you Major."

"Why?" Mannerling asked.

"London told him who you are." Gerhardt said.

"Who is this Klugge?" Lang hissed.

"He is a legend Lang." Franz said bluntly.

"You better explain that." Mannerling said.

"Klugge is Sergei Blenkov." Franz said. "Towards the end of the first war he was driving our counter intelligence people crazy until the Reds signed an armistice ending the war in the East and Blenkov disappeared."

"How can you be certain Klugge is this Blenkov?" Lang asked. "Why would the Reds plant a spy with an unknown officer in a defeated Army?"

"That would be classic Communist revolutionary tactics." Franz said. "Destroy from within. Krieger wasn't chosen by chance."

"Twenty-eight years is a long time to be with one man and loyalties to Moscow could be blurred." Lang said, "Blenkov had to submerge himself into Klugge in order to have survived this long."

"The Reds were underground in those days." Gerhardt said. "He was planted before the end of the war, before the Communist controlled Russia."

"Since we are still breathing Blenkov is still loyal to Mother Russia." Mannerling said dully.

"How much do we trust him?" Lang asked.

"We have no options." Mannerling said lighting a cigarette. "We are outnumbered now."

"Why have the Ivans decided that Krieger is better off dead?" Lang asked.

"They are almost impossible to understand." Gerhardt said. "It has to benefit them some how."

"Forget Klugge for the moment." Mannerling said. "Sooner or later that cop will get to us and we better have the right answers."

"We point him towards Colquhoun." Gerhardt said coldly.

"He'll want answers." Franz said. "Can we afford that?"

"The evidence will bring the police to him eventually." Mannerling said. "The first order of business is to get our stories straight."

"What if Colquhoun toughs it out or just dies on us?" Lang asked.

"Our orders are to see that Krieger never leaves this place." Mannerling said bluntly.

"That could be messy." Franz said.

"London wants him gone no matter the cost." Mannerling said. "Then every man for himself."

[4]
20:00 hrs

Gruenling Gasthof

"Does your medical officer know how to perform autopsies?" Fuchs asked the Colonel.

"Captain Lederer was the chief pathologist in Hesse before he was called up." Jherling said. "I decided to bring him at the last minute."

"Good decision." Fuchs said. "I want a basic autopsy nothing fancy."

"You're not assuming the extraordinary?" Jherling asked.

"Not here." Fuchs said as Wulff entered the dining room. "I want this town sewed up tight."

"It will be." Jherling said leaving the room.

Wulff poured himself a cup of coffee and sat down at the table. "Was there anything of interest from Krieger sir?"

"He won't talk now." Fuchs said.
"Major Gerhardt?" Wulff asked.
"Later." Fuchs said. "Did Heinz recover any weapons?"
"Heinz found a rifle." Wulff said. "English made Harrison & Harrison .375 magnum."
"That is a sporting rifle." Fuchs said. "It is a non military weapon sir."
"It had a very expensive Zweiss telescopic sight." Wulff said. "Two expended cartridge cases were found in the building across from the Gasthof, 203 meters from the Gasthof."
"The shooter is a professional." Fuchs said. "Our friend, who ever he is, has a guardian angel."
"Very dangerous guardian angel though." Wulff said.
Fuchs lit his pipe. "You know who the dead man is?"
"Felix Wassenberg." Wulff rasped. "No great lost to the world; but why would someone do us the favor of killing him?"
"It wasn't done for humanity." Fuchs said flatly. "Wassenberg was brought in to kill the fake Skasch."
"You have proof sir?" Wulff asked.
"Forty years of experience." Fuchs said. "Skasch is a man in his mid-fifties, ours is in his thirties."
"How could Krieger make such a mistake?" Wulff asked somberly.
"Skasch always used middle men before." Fuchs said. "Where has Wassenberg been hiding?"
"Munich." Wulff answered. "He was reportedly a friend of Willi Eidernau, who keeps on avoiding preventive arrest as a habitual criminal."
Fuchs tampered his pipe. "A picture is beginning to develop in my mind my young friend. This is more than just homicide." Fuchs relit his pipe. "The key is the man in the manager's suite."
"The sergeant is quite good at getting answers sir." Wulff said flatly.
"This is delicate." Fuchs said. "Schiller fears that he might be dealing with possible treason, which even a whiff reaching Berlin could ruin what's left of his career."
"Treason is very strong word sir." Wulff said. "We are out of our league if it is- this would rightly belong to the Gestapo."
"This is homicide Wulff, treason is incidental." Fuchs said standing on seeing Heinz enter the room. "Find out where Eidernau is."
"I'll have that in a few hours." Wulff said dully.

[5]
20:30 hrs

The Crime Scene

Chief Heinz cut the seal on the door and the three men entered the room.
"I left the room as we found it." Heinz said flatly.
"Good." Fuchs said seeing that Heinz was not playing at being a police officer. "Who belongs to the two attaché cases?"
"One belongs to Krieger, the other Skasch." Heinz said pointing to them. "I dusted for fingerprints."

"Are they locked Herr Heinz?" Wulff asked.
"Yes." Heinz said. "I have the keys."
"Are their any useable prints from the cases Chief?" Fuchs asked.
"The grain is too rough for prints." Heinz said. "They are expensive cases, Moroccan leather, both imported."
"Please handover the keys Herr Heinz?" Fuchs asked.
Fuchs checked the cases carefully because a police inspector in Konigsberg died, blown to shreds by a booby-trapped case six weeks ago. Not finding any telltale signs of tampering Fuchs slowly opened both of them.
"Christ." Fuchs hissed on seeing the contents of both cases. Wulff and Heinz moved up beside Fuchs.
"I'll be damned." Wulff gasped.
"Shit." Heinz rasped on seeing both cases filled with American and British bank notes. Fuchs picked up one of the bundles.
"What dreams are made of?" Fuchs hissed. "We better count this."
"We need a witness." Wulff said coldly.
"I'll get Jherling." Heinz said.
"Do it quietly." Fuchs hissed.
"This settles the matter for me." Jherling said after they had finished counting the money twice. "We have a traitor on our hands."
"Let's not jump to any conclusions Colonel." Fuchs said. "One case would make this so simple, but two doesn't."
"A deal of some sort was going on." Heinz said firmly.
"Or a double-cross that didn't take the path desired." Wulff hissed. "Some one was selling something to someone."
"We've missed something." Fuchs said flatly.
"How could someone like Krieger get his hands on this amount of foreign currency?" Heinz asked.
"The Bitch is the answer." Jherling said caustically.
"Who is The Bitch?" Fuchs asked.
"The Countess vom Rodelbach is Krieger's wife." Jherling said harshly. "Her family is Old Prussian Junker family with money and influence."
"The bands from one case say Rothmann Bank." Heinz said. "The other says Reichbank-Berlin."
"Rothmann is a private bank in Zurich." Fuchs said firmly. "Also branches in Lisbon, Stockholm and London."
"Jewish?" Wulff quipped.
"I would say that." Fuchs said.
"This works either way for me." Jherling said bluntly. "Krieger is guilty of receiving a bribe or trying to take money out of the country." The colonel paused. "You know the currency laws better than I. Homicide with either crime carries the death penalty even for an SS General."
"The General might be greedy." Fuchs said lighting his pipe seeing that Jherling would not need much prodding to kill Krieger. "But you can't call him stupid."
"Set up." Heinz muttered.

"Not beyond the pale." Fuchs conceded. "Then ask the question- why is Gerhardt here? The SD and the Abwehr wouldn't agree that the sun rises in the East."

"It adds to the interest." Jherling hissed.

"The connecting thread is Skasch." Heinz said.

"This is made more connecting by the fact that our Skasch is a fake." Fuchs said in a flat voice.

"How do you know that?" Heinz asked grimly.

"I met the doctor once, years ago." Fuchs said wryly.

"Then who the hell is in the room?" Heinz asked in a bewildered voice.

"No idea." Fuchs said hollowly.

"Could he be an Allied agent?" Jherling hissed.

"That could be a possibility or he is some poor bastard of a clerk delivery the package." Fuchs said dryly.

"Now what do we do?" Jherling asked.

"Someone went to a lot of trouble to arrange all this and bring all the players here." Fuchs said. "After we talk to our Skasch we will know why."

"I suggest you arrest Krieger now." Jherling said. "Why give the bastard a chance to slip away?"

"I want everyone involved in this." Fuchs said. "Krieger is at the center of this."

"Anyone runs we'll kill them." Heinz said.

"That will prove guilt." Fuchs answered. "I'll mention the money to both of them."

"All you might get is a bullet." Jherling warned.

"That is a calculated risk." Fuchs said. "I need to keep everyone alive until I can sort this out."

"You could do this the easy way." Heinz suggested.

"No." Fuchs said icily. "I'm too old fashion."

"What about the people watching us?" Jherling asked.

"Once I have sorted this out Colonel you can go on maneuvers to your heart's content." Fuchs said.

[6]
21:45 hrs

Manager's Office

Wulff lit a cigarette as he sat down on the sofa. Fuchs lowered himself slowly into the chair rubbing his eyes slowly.

"If you want my humble opinion sir," Wulff said. "We climb aboard the train and go back to Stuttgart."

"We can't do that Arthur." Fuchs said tiredly.

"This is a one way street." Wulff said harshly.

"Like it or not we are stuck with it." Fuchs said flatly lighting his pipe.

"They are not going to let us just leave sir." Wulff said. "The SD, Abwehr tossed together with the likes of Eidernau mixed lightly with the OSS equals one thing: somebody is going to die." Wulff paused taking a deep breath. "I don't want to join him."

"The fall guy was already chosen." Fuchs said.

"Could it be our friend next door?" Wulff quipped in a low voice.

"He is more the Judas goat I think." Fuchs said. "My gut feeling is that the poor bastard wasn't suppose to live."

"This is a job is for the Gestapo." Wulff said firmly. "We are over our heads."

"It is too late." Fuchs sighed. "The Gestapo turns a blind eye when it comes close too home Arthur."

"Christ, we'll be groping in a minefield blindfolded." Wulff said.

"That's what makes life interesting." Fuchs said. "We'll talk to him after breakfast."

Chapter Twenty-Two
December 10, 1942
07:00 hrs

Adlerberghof
Mayor's Office

"Do you have a theory about what is going on Herr Oberstleutnant?" Schiller asked stepping onto the balcony that overlooked the Town Square. "Are you allowed to have an opinion?"

"Being a soldier doesn't mean you can't think." Jherling said relighting his cigar. "I have figured this out."

"Enlighten me." Schiller said. "Being a Party member doesn't mean you are brain dead."

"The SD, Abwehr tossed together will the likes of Wassenberg and Eidernau." Jherling said flatly. "Sprinkle lightly with OSS or SOE and you get the recipe for death."

"Then our friend in the Gasthof," Schiller asked. "Is he the bait?"

"He is the stalking horse." Jherling said.

"That implies a trap either way." Schiller said. "I need to know a trap for whom?"

"I have a friend at OKW." Jherling said. "The Intelligence people have been going crazy trying to find a ghost called *Albatross*."

"I heard of him." Schiller said. "The bogeyman of every mistake made at OKW. Are you saying he is real?"

"They think he is." Jherling said. "That is what counts."

"Where does our friend fit in?" Schiller asked.

"*Albatross* is here or will be here." Jherling said. "This is coming to a head."

"Then we better be careful." Schiller said. "There is a lot of lead poisoning around her."

[2]
08:00 hrs

Gruenling Gasthof

Dr. Lederer quietly left the room leaving Fuchs and Wulff alone with the prisoner. Fuchs locked the door passing the key to Wulff. Without Lederer to keep him drugged, the prisoner was wide-awake.

"I am Direktor Fuchs." Fuchs said. "This is my associate Inspektor Wulff. We are from the Kripo."

"Go to hell." The prisoner muttered in German. "I see no difference, you are both bastards."

"We are the police." Wulff rasped. "We are CID Detectives damnit."

"Drop dead." The prisoner rasped.

Fuchs lit his pipe. "What was your mission Major Colquhoun?" Fuchs spoke in English instead of German. "We know your military identification Herr Major."

"My name is Dr. Viktor Franz Skasch of Bern Switzerland." The prisoner said bluntly.

"The OSS does not select idiots." Fuchs said. "Your companion has talked Major."

"That would be a neat trick since I saw him die." The prisoner said.

"He was only wounded." Wulff said grimly.

"Half his head was blown off." The prisoner said. "I did serve in the Hungarian Army."

"The real Skasch did serve in the Hungarian Army for six weeks." Fuchs said. "Family influence got him out and he fled to Switzerland."

"I'm here Direktor." The prisoner said.

"What your control in London couldn't possibly control is the fact you would meet a police officer who knew the real Skasch." Fuchs said as he lit his pipe. "Skasch was a suspect in a jewel robbery ten years ago. I was one of the police officers who went to Bern to talk to him."

"People change Herr Direktor." The prisoner said bluntly.

"You are twenty-years too young." Fuchs said. "Also Swiss Radio reported that Dr. Viktor Franz Skasch was killed in a car accident three days ago. Swiss Radio has no reason to lie about this."

"They are wrong." The prisoner said.

"We found the money." Wulff said.

"What money?" The prisoner quipped.

"Be a fool." Fuchs said bluntly standing up. "I take you back to Stuttgart and you will be executed for the murder of Hermann Jung. The Reich will bury you in an unmarked grave end of story."

"Once we get you back to Stuttgart how long will do you think it will take before we establish you are not Skasch." Wulff said coldly.

Fuchs and Wulff left the room to let the prisoners absorb what was said to him. Dr. Lederer met them outside the room.

"Are you finished?" The Doctor asked.

"No." Fuchs said relighting his pipe. "We are just giving him time to reconsider his position before we go back in."

"He is badly injured." Lederer said firmly. "He really needs a hospital, we have one at Jaegerfeld."

"We shall not linger long Herr Doktor." Fuchs said.

"Did you check him for an L-pill?" Wulff asked.

"Yes." Lederer said. "I had many Jewish patients before 1935; the Gestapo disliked them dying in their offices."

"Did he have one?" Fuchs asked.

"He had a pill sewn in his shirt collar." Lederer said. "I removed it and tested it."

"Was it Cyanide?" Wulff asked.

"No it was aspirin." Lederer said blandly. "I put it back where I found it."

"That is an interesting revelation Herr Doktor, very." Fuchs said. "Use your best bedside manner with him. We'll give you fifteen minutes."

[3]
07:45 hrs

Braunfuch

"Sergeant Schimdt let it slip that Fuchs was going to question Skasch this morning." Franz said as he stirred his chocolate.

"Thus begins the down fall of Krieger." Lang said.

"Just hope that we don't get caught in the maelstrom." Gerhardt said plainly. "The Eastern Front would be a holiday."

"These are uncharted waters." Mannerling said. "We should be prepared to run like hell at any moment."

"Have you seen our forest dwellers?" Lang asked Mannerling.

"Glimpse here and there." Mannerling said. "They seem to know what they are doing."

"Can Jherling fight his way out?" Gerhardt asked.

"Unless our friends have heavy explosives all Jherling has to do is get back on the train and go home." Franz said. "He can fight his way out if he has to."

"You don't need explosives to disable a train track." Mannerling said. "Loosen some rails and the train slides off the track."

"Jherling has ten man patrols guarding the tracks to the tunnel." Lang said.

"I suggest Major that you wander over to the town hall to see how our 'friends' are doing." Mannerling said as he lit his cigarette.

"What shall you be doing?" Gerhardt asked.

"I'll be snooping around the hotel." Mannerling said.

"Hell, I might as well take a stroll through the woods." Franz said.

[4]
08:50 hrs

Donner's Farm

"Where is her majesty?" Brosch asked somberly.

"She is making her grand entrance into the town." Eidernau said removing one of Donner's cigars from the humidor. "Why?"

"Does she know about the train in the town?" Brosch asked.

"What the hell are you talking about?" Eidernau asked.

"The Army decided to show up in Adlerberghof with a train." Brosch said. "200 men from a Jaeger battalion are in the town."

"I thought the goddamn trains had stopped?" Eidernau hissed.

"They did before the war." Brosch said. "We are dealing with the regular army Willi not Schiller's bully boys." Brosch lit a cigar. "Herschell is a good alpine skier."

"Herschell isn't going anywhere." Eidernau rasped tossing his cigarette into the fireplace.

"You're not going to warn here?" Brosch said bitterly.

"I'm not married to the bitch." Eidernau said coldly. "I really don't like her."

Brosch hunched his shoulders. "Our men work for money Willi and she is the bitch who is paying us."

"Unless she gets real stupid Brosch and gets herself killed we have nothing to worry about." Eidernau said.

"Ah, the tunnel I forgot." Brosch said knowingly.

"Yes, the tunnel." Eidernau said. "Send men to check the railroad tracks to see if the regulars are on their toes."

"If they are not guarding the tracks Willi, then what old friend," Brosch asked.

"You tear up the tracks." Eidernau said.

An Honorable Betrayal

[5]
09:00 hrs

Gruenling Gasthof
Lobby

"I assume you are the man in charge?" The well-dressed woman asked in a crisp voice. "That idiot desk clerk told me to stay here."

"Yes Madame." Fuchs said. "Reichkriminaldirektor Fuchs, Kripo. Who may you be?"

"Countess Vom Rodelbach." She said firmly. "I was expecting my husband to greet me not the Army or the police."

"You have arrived at an inconvenient moment Madame." Fuchs said.

"Inconvenient?" The Countess asked in a surly tone.

"Is your husband expecting you?" Fuchs asked.

"Of course he is." The Countess said tartly.

"Why are you here?" Fuchs asked.

"On holiday if you must know." The Countess said in the same surly manner. "What in hell is going on? Do you know Herr Oberstleutnant?"

"This is a civilian matter." Jherling said.

"I am conducting a murder investigation Madame." Fuchs said flatly.

"What does my husband have to do with murder?" The Countess asked.

"He is a material witness Madame." Fuchs said. "Inspektor Wulff, please inform the General that his wife is here."

Wulff walked up the stairs as Schiller and Heinz entered the Gasthof. The Countess looked over at them for a moment not indicating if she recognized them. After a few minutes, Krieger came down the stairs with Wulff.

"Elsa?" Helmuth asked. "What are you doing here?"

"I got tired of waiting." The Countess said. "Have Klugge pack your clothes and we'll leave within the hour."

"I'm afraid that will be impossible Madame." Schiller said. "We are under martial law and no one leaves." Schiller looked at Fuchs. "You have things to do, I'll handle this."

"Who are you?" The Countess hissed.

"I am the Burgermeister." Schiller said. "Bad weather is moving in fast and you'll never get through the pass. You'll have to stay."

"I see, very well then." The Countess said looking at her husband's blank expression.

"You'll stay with your husband." Schiller said.

"Is it true about the storm Herr Heinz?" Fuchs asked lighting his pipe as they headed for the manager's office

"Yes, quite true." Heinz said.

"This is becoming interesting." Fuchs said stoically. "Who is she?"

"She belongs to the Old Prussian nobility." Heinz said. "She is as ruthless as her husband, perhaps more so."

"This is becoming very interesting." Fuchs said.

"What are you doing here?" Helmuth growled. "This was not the plan."

"I am protecting our interests." Elsa said sharply. "Since you have apparently bungled this dearest badly from the onset."

"There are always unforeseen problems." Helmuth snapped angrily. "I have the situation under my complete control."

"It doesn't look that way." Elsa said. "Where in the hell did the train come?"

"One of the unforeseen problems I have encountered." Helmuth said wryly.

"Then you haven't anticipated the storm either." Elsa hissed.

"I'm not a meteorologist, neither is Ehrlich." Helmuth said icily. "We are not trapped here as they are Elsa."

An Honorable Betrayal

Chapter Twenty-Three
December 10, 1942
09:10 hrs

Gruenling Gasthof
Manager's Office

Fuchs settled in his chair and Wulff took out his notebook and pencil. "Have you had enough time to think over your situation Herr Major?"

"Go to hell." The prisoner said. "Leave me in peace damnit."

"You know that is impossible." Fuchs said. "If you don't talk to us you'll talk to the Gestapo."

"Either way I'm a dead man." The prisoner said coldly. "Honor dictates resistance."

"Honor doesn't demand that you commit suicide." Wulff said. "If you are an enemy agent we can protect you."

"Right up to the gallows when they pull the trap door out from under me." The prisoner said sourly.

"In your case it will be the guillotine." Fuchs said flatly.

"I'll be damned." The prisoner said cynically.

"You can't be as stupid as you are acting." Fuchs said bluntly. "You must realize that you have been a pawn in all this. Skasch is dead and we know it. Jung was brought here solely to sabotage your plan." Fuchs lit his pipe. "The only person who could possibly recognize the real Skasch, within 1,000 kms, strolls into the room. I don't believe in consequences."

"There is no question of honor now." Wulff said. "It is a matter of survival."

The prisoner sat silent for ten minutes before he spoke again. "What do need?"

"Who are you?" Fuchs asked firmly.

"Colquhoun, Jefferson Davis." Colquhoun said. "I am a Major in the United States Army."

"Why are you here?" Fuchs asked.

"You got all you are going to get." Colquhoun said angrily. "I'm a prisoner of war."

"You are out of uniform Major, thus you could be considered a spy and liable to be turned over to our Security people." Wulff said crisply.

"I have my dog tags sewn in my coat." Colquhoun said.

"That is a technicality." Fuchs said flatly. "The SD doesn't believe in technicalities."

"My name and rank is all you bastards get." Colquhoun hissed. "So fuck off!"

Fuchs and Wulff heard the loud crunch as Colquhoun jaw tightened as he glared at them defiantly. The defiant glare slowly dissolved as Colquhoun realized that he was not dead after a few seconds.

Fuchs lit his pipe. "Your side didn't want you to die."

"Impossible." Colquhoun quipped disbelievingly.

"No my poor friend London has betrayed you for some reason." Fuchs said coldly

"They are bastards." Colquhoun hissed. "Those lousy bastards, sonofabitches they sold me down the river."

"This has all the earmarks Herr Major." Fuchs rasped.

"But you people are just cops?" Colquhoun quipped. "Just plain ordinary cops, why are the police interested in me?"

"You are a principal in a homicide investigation." Wulff said.

"You're joking." Colquhoun hissed.

"I never have found murder to be a joking matter Herr Major." Fuchs said in a deadly serious voice. "The mayor has an aversion to corpses in his town."

"This is hardly my problem." Colquhoun said sourly. "I have nothing to do with murder; it was a clear case of self-defense anyway."

"Sorry son." Fuchs said. "Like it or not you are right in the middle. I do not have the time or inclination to explain the ins and outs of German Law to you. The question you have to answer is simple: Are you here to help kill Krieger?"

"I walked into a room and some sonofabitch shoots me." Colquhoun hissed.

"You are alone major." Fuchs said seriously. "You are far from home with one foot in the grave. Hermann Jung wasn't here by accident."

"Who the hell is Hermann Jung?" Colquhoun asked. "I have no idea what you're talking about."

"Jung knew the real Skasch in Bern." Wulff said.

"Make some sense." Colquhoun hissed.

"Radio Bern has reported that Dr. Viktor Skasch was killed in Switzerland days ago." Fuchs said. "We found the attaché cases with the money Herr Major. Krieger was going to double-cross you." Fuchs paused. "You were never supposed to leave that room alive. I can't help you unless you tell me the truth."

Colquhoun closed his eyes remaining silent. It suddenly became clear to him why control told him so much about Krieger. Fuchs was only partially right- he was never to succeed in the first place. Jung's unexpected arrival is what caused this to fall apart so rapidly.

"Truth has a price." Colquhoun rasped.

"I'll guarantee your safety." Fuchs said.

"How can you do that?" Colquhoun asked. "Gestapo trumps cops, right?"

"That will be my problem Herr Major." Fuchs said. "You don't want to be the guest of the Gestapo. They are expert at obtaining information unpleasantly. They enjoy getting it that way."

"You'll never believe me." Colquhoun said. "I don't believe it myself... Telling you would be a waste of breath."

"Allow us the opportunity to be the judge Herr Major." Fuchs said. "I'm investigating a murder and only a murder."

"Christ, I'm not naive." Colquhoun said. "I know how your system works; the good ole boy network. Never bite the hand that feeds you."

"I never heard it described that way." Fuchs mused. "Even in your ole boy network the truly guilty are punished?"

"The top dog is always protected." Colquhoun rasped. "The poor slob on the bottom of the totem pole gets the hemp neck tie."

"No guilty man has ever escaped me in over thirty years of police work." Fuchs said in a blunt voice. "Murder is still a crime even under this regime."

"Does that go for everyone?" Colquhoun asked.

"We try to." Wulff said coldly. "The guilty are punished not necessarily for the crime they actually commit, but sometimes perception of a crime is enough."

"That is hardly comforting." Colquhoun said.

"Embarrassing the Party leadership is very unhealthy." Fuchs said.

"What is the penalty for a Party man for murder and treason?" Colquhoun asked.

"I won't lie to you Herr Major." Fuchs said grimly. "He could get away with murder, but not treason. He would die for that if Berlin believed it true."

Colquhoun turned his head away from Fuchs for a few minutes. "Are there any guarantees on the table?"

"The best I can offer is your life." Fuchs said bluntly. "That isn't guaranteed either."

"Is it the best you can offer?" Colquhoun asked somberly.

"I would be lying if I told you more." Fuchs said. "Do we have a deal?"

"I'm going to make your day." Colquhoun said. "Prepare the death warrant."

"Whose name shall I put on it?" Wulff asked wryly.

"Obergruppenfuhrer Helmuth Krieger." Colquhoun said hollowly.

"Why should I select him?" Fuchs asked showing no visible surprise.

"Ever hear of *Albatross*?" Colquhoun asked.

"Vaguely, mention in some reports I've read." Fuchs said remembering the incredibly boring meetings about security and spies.

"Krieger is *Albatross*." Colquhoun said.

"Can you prove it Herr Major?" Fuchs asked as he relit his pipe.

"I have the proof." Colquhoun said firmly.

"Will you make a written affidavit to that affect?" Wulff asked blandly.

"You do not seem very interested." Colquhoun hissed. "I'm giving you him on a silver platter."

"I'll need time to do some checking." Fuchs said. "Are you willing to go to the end with this Herr Major?"

"Yes." Colquhoun said coldly. "The bastard did shoot me after all."

[4]

Fuchs slowly lit his battered pipe as he read the notes Wulff had taken in his own shorthand. Colquhoun had given them clear precise information that had the ring of truth to it. Fuchs removed his glasses and rubbed his eyes knowing that Colquhoun would have to go to Berlin for detailed questioning.

Fuchs put his glasses back on. "You have been very cooperative Herr Major, perhaps too cooperative."

"You think I'm lying." Colquhoun quipped dourly. "Understandable."

"Field agents aren't usually briefed with so much detail." Wulff said bluntly. "Need to know maxim."

"What would cops know about that?" Colquhoun asked.

"The Kripo is part of the security police." Fuchs said. "My assistant is an Oberleutnant in the Abwehr reserves. We are not gifted amateurs Herr Major." Fuchs paused for a long moment. "I don't want to turn you over to the SD."

"I had to know the details about him." Colquhoun said. "We were taking him out and I had to know if I was dealing with the right man."

Fuchs removed his glasses again and started to twirl them around by one bow in his left hand. "Is *Albatross* SIS or SOE?"

"They never said." Colquhoun said wryly. "Does it matter?"

"Not really." Fuchs said. "Is he English or German?"

"I get the impression that he is a South African Boer." Colquhoun answered. "That is the impression I got."

"How did they recruit him?" Wulff asked.

"The legend says by accident." Colquhoun said. "During the First War some bright light saw that a South African officer was a dead-ringer for Krieger. You know he was captured in late 1917 and made a spectacular escape in 1918."

"The rest is history as they say." Fuchs said with a slight smile putting his glasses back on.

"I'm only the guide." Colquhoun said.

"All of this has to be typed up and you must sign it." Fuchs said. "Then all has to be verified. That will take time and one lie will sink you."

"What do I have to gain by lying?" Colquhoun asked.

"Some will question your motive in this matter." Wulff said briskly.

"Question what?" Colquhoun asked.

"You have betrayed your country." Wulff hissed. "Solely to stay alive you betrayed a fellow agent."

"I'll worry about that after the war ends." Colquhoun said. "Besides he is British."

"Revenge is not part of this?" Fuchs asked.

"All I have against him is that he shot me." Colquhoun said curtly. "I never heard of him until a few days ago."

"It doesn't matter." Fuchs said. "My sergeant will keep you company at all times. You understand that there is no turning back."

"What are you going to do about him?" Colquhoun asked.

"I have murders to investigate." Fuchs said. "Some criminals to arrest I hope."

"Do a good job." Colquhoun said.

"That is my intention Herr Major." Fuchs said. "We'll be back for you to sign your statement."

[5]

Gasthof Dinning room

Jherling read Oldenburg's rough draft of the statement with positive glee in his eyes. In his hands, he held the paper that would allow him to put Krieger and Ehrlich in front of a wall.

"When are you going to arrest him?" Jherling asked pointedly.

"When I have this verified." Fuchs said. "I'm not going to Berlin until I have this carved in stone."

"What?" Jherling hissed.

"I need to talk to Gerhardt." Fuchs said.

"Arrest him on suspicion." Jherling said. "If you hesitate he could wiggle free."

"I want all the pieces of the puzzle to fit together before I arrest him." Fuchs said firmly.

"He isn't going anywhere." Jherling said bluntly.

Fuchs lit his pipe. "Someone might try to take him out of the town."

"You mean this Eidernau?" Jherling hissed. "He isn't that stupid to go against regular troops."

"I understand that the Countess can be very persuasive." Fuchs said firmly. "Eidernau is not an amateur Herr Oberst. He served on the Western Front for 4 years rising to the rank of Oberleutnant. He served in the Freikorps and the Black Reichwehr after the war."

"Is she that dangerous?" Jherling asked.

"From what I understand from Schiller she is very dangerous." Fuchs said coldly relighting his pipe. "They both are not fools and have survived this long by not being stupid."

"How can he deny the facts?" Jherling asked.

"He will scream conspiracy as loud as he can." Fuchs said.

"We have Colquhoun, Gerhardt and the money." Jherling said bluntly. "Berlin can't ignore that."

"They could if it suited them." Fuchs said firmly. "This after all could be an elaborate rouse by the Allies to get us to kill Krieger for them."

"Where the hell did you get this from?" Jherling asked. "Is this out of the blue?"

"Krieger is a danger to them." Fuchs said. "It makes sense if you think about it."

"This is a dangerous game Fuchs." Jherling said flatly. "Do you have the guts to ride this out to the end?"

"Do I have a choice?" Fuchs asked somberly.

"You can leave." Jherling said flatly. "Then pray that Krieger doesn't decide you known too much and have to be eliminated at a later date."

Fuchs tapped his pipe gently on the side of the ashtray. "War brings out the worse in people."

"Krieger had a head start." Jherling said. "He is a bastard plain and simple. He will run once you tell him what he has to face."

"Why run at all Herr Oberst?" Wulff asked. "Berlin will need proof of guilt."

"Facing the truth would be something rare for him." Fuchs said. "Catch him off guard with that rare commodity."

An Honorable Betrayal

Chapter Twenty-Four
December 9, 1942
10:30 hrs

Gasthof Gruenling
Gerhardt's Room

"Why is the Abwehr in this dreary little corner of the Reich Herr Major?" Kriminalinspektor Wulff asked in his matter-of-fact voice. "I thought the Admiral would have better things for you to do?"

"It is call orders Herr Inspektor." Gerhardt said firmly. Wulff had the face of an innocent but he was an experienced interrogator.

"Yes orders from whom did the orders come Herr Major?" Fuchs asked not looking up from the newspaper. "The Admiral no doubts Herr Major?"

"No." Gerhardt said. "Generalmajor von Tanz. I have travel orders."

"Undoubtedly you will have your papers." Fuchs said lowering the paper. "Lying would be stupid."

"The General will confirm the orders." Lang said.

"Where are Franz and Thiel?" Wulff asked.

"They are trying to find out if we can communicate with the outside world Herr Direktor." Gerhardt said.

"That is fine." Fuchs said putting the newspaper away. "Why are you in Adlerberghof in the first place? Patrolling the border is the job of the Grenzpolizei not the Abwehrpolizei."

"I'll give you that answer." Gerhardt said lighting a cigarette. "Once you have been cleared by Berlin sir."

"I have all the necessary security clearances Herr Major." Fuchs said lighting his pipe slowly. "You're not here on a ski holiday Herr Major Gerhardt."

"I'm sorry sir, but I can't." Gerhardt said stiffly. "I take my orders from the military."

"Herr Major." Fuchs said. "I don't have the time to play polite games with you. Schiller has an enormous problem on his hands and he might solve his problem a simpler way- kill everyone."

"That would be murder sir." Lang said firmly.

"State security allows many things." Fuchs said. "That covers a multitude of sins Herr Major and Schiller wants to leave this place. The only way he can is if he absolutely knows the murderer is dead."

Gerhardt crushed out the cigarette seeing that Fuchs wanted justice served regardless of the method employed. Gerhardt saw if killing all of them accomplished this Fuchs will not stand in the way. "Would you allow him to do that?"

"I would, of course, object." Fuchs said coldly. "However, Schiller would still kill you."

"What do you want then?" Lang asked.

"Truth Herr Leutnant." Fuchs said. "That would be refreshing."

"I see you even have to be pragmatic even in the Kripo." Gerhardt said. "Since an official inquiry would reveal it there is no harm in telling you."

"Then be pragmatic Herr Major." Fuchs said. "Dying here is not such a good idea."

"I'll assume that you have guessed that the real Viktor Skasch is dead." Gerhardt said crisply. "What you might not know is that he was assassinated by Smersh in Bern."

"Why would the Ivans kill him?" Wulff asked drolly.

"Skasch tried one too many double-cross." Lang said. "The Ivans don't like to be double-crossed."

"Can this be confirmed?" Wulff asked.

"Contact the Swiss Federal police." Gerhardt said. "Or our people in Bern should know that."

"Okay." Wulff said. "We'll confirm that."

Fuchs tampered his pipe slowly. "Then you know who the man in the manager's flat is?"

"If I had to hazard a guess I would say OSS agent." Gerhardt said flatly.

"How do you know that?" Wulff asked.

"He is an American." Gerhardt said.

"He was also photographed in Lisbon last year." Lang said. "Our people sneaked into his room and took his fingerprints." Lang lit a cigarette. "He used his real name in Lisbon Thomas J. Colquhoun."

"Why is he in Adlerberghof?" Fuchs asked.

"Our counterintelligence people in Switzerland learned through informers that Skasch was working for Allied intelligence." Gerhardt said. "Skasch was hired to deliver money to a deep agent code named *Albatross*. We were sent here to make the arrest."

"Something went wrong." Wulff said.

"Hermann Jung." Gerhardt said. "We really don't know why he was here."

"Who is this *Albatross*?" Fuchs asked.

"Obergruppenfuhrer Helmuth Krieger." Gerhardt answered without hesitation.

Fuchs's face remained impassive as well as Oldenburg's choirboy face. Fuchs removed his glasses and twirled them slowly in his right hand by the left bow. "That is a very serious charge on what proof?"

"The man killed last night was named Wassenberg." Gerhardt said sternly. "Wassenberg was associated with a known professional criminal named Willi Eidernau."

"They are both known to us." Wulff said. "That is hardly proof Herr Major."

"Eidernau and Ehrlich served together in the Free Corps." Gerhardt said. "During the early '30s Ehrlich used Eidernau boys for street fighting."

"Everyone's hands are not clean from that time." Fuchs said. "What you have is very tenuous evidence so far. You have to have more."

"Jung was working for us as well as his cousin." Gerhardt said.

"Don't leave town." Fuchs said. "Jherling's men have orders to shoot-to-kill anyone trying to leave."

"I assumed that." Gerhardt said. "What about *Albatross*?"

"My investigation is hardly over Major." Fuchs said standing. "I may need clarification on some areas and I will contact you."

"What about weapons?" Lang asked.

"Keep them." Fuchs said flatly.
"Why?" Gerhardt asked.
"Accidents happen." Fuchs said. "I like my witnesses to be alive at trial."

[2]
11:30 hrs

Krieger's room

Fuchs knew that questioning Krieger would be difficult as well as delicate because the Kripo was part of the RSHA, but supposedly independent of the SD. The Kripo was to deal with criminal matters of a nonpolitical nature. The only official function they shared was the Security Police, which combined personnel from the Kripo, SD and Gestapo. In addition, Krieger's wife being present would just make it harder.

"Sir, I am only a policeman trying to find the truth." Fuchs said firmly not backing down even after Krieger's tirade after learning, what Fuchs wanted.

"You have MY written statement Herr Oberst." Krieger said taking umbrage that an inferior officer was arguing with him. "That is all that should be required."

"The General is allowing this as a courtesy." The Countess said hollowly. "As a policeman you do understand the law because of your rank."

"I understand the law and I have read your statement Herr General." Fuchs said looking at the single sheet of paper. "Legally this is worthless sir. You were not under oath; Ehrlich and Klugge are hardly unbiased witnesses."

"Are you an idiot or just a damn fool?" Krieger hissed.

"I am neither sir." Fuchs said. "You have the option of talking to me now or General Freyling in Stuttgart." Fuchs paused. "You denied Freyling's son a commission in the Waffen SS."

"What does that have to do with this?" The Countess asked bluntly.

"General Freyling is the senior SS officer in the area." Fuchs said. "He would convene a Court of Honor."

"Ask your damnable questions." Krieger grumbled not wanting to talk to Freyling for any reason. Freyling had to cash in every favor he had to get his son into the Waffen SS.

"Why was Jung here?" Fuchs asked. "I've checked with our embassy in Bern before I left Stuttgart. Ausbruk, the third secretary, told me that they didn't know Jung was in Germany."

"Ausbruk is from the Foreign Ministry, no authority over Jung." Krieger said. "I asked him to come here."

"Why?" Fuchs asked.

"Jung knew Skasch in Bern." Krieger said.

"Then you expected trouble?" Fuchs asked.

"Skasch was not known for his scruples." Krieger answered.

Fuchs lit his pipe. "When did you realize something was wrong?"

"Immediately after they shot Hermann as he walked into the room." Krieger said flatly. "Then I realized it was an assassination attempt."

"Assassination Herr General?" Wulff asked. "Why would Skasch want to assassinate you?"

"Skasch was a freelance killer among other things." Krieger said coldly. "He hired out to the Allies to kill me. I am not unknown to the Allies."

Fuchs removed his glasses and rubbed his eyes. "The question is why you were dealing with a known criminal?"

"State Security prohibits me from answering." Krieger said smugly.

"Inspektor Wulff, arrest the General, Colonel Ehrlich and the Sergeant-Major." Fuchs ordered harshly. "If they resist kill them."

"What?" Krieger gasped.

"That would be murder to kill unarmed men." The Countess said cynically.

"There is nothing to stop me." Fuchs said. "Cooperation is needed."

"I'm under orders." Krieger said. "Arrest is the road to judicial murder and you damn well know it."

"You give me no choice Herr General." Fuchs said. "Berlin will turn you over to the Gestapo." Fuchs paused. "You and General Mueller are friends."

"Damn you." Krieger hissed. "You are pushing the limit of survivability. Call off your hound Fuchs I'll answer your questions." Krieger angrily lit a cigarette. "This meeting was supposed to be secret because Skasch was working for me. He was bringing me a list of allied agents in Germany and the name of the spymaster. In this I was betrayed Fuchs."

"Betrayed by whom?" Fuchs asked relighting his pipe.

"*Albatross*" Krieger hissed.

"Who is this *Albatross*?" Fuchs asked in a firm voice.

"He is von Tanz." Krieger hissed. "*Albatross* is Generalmajor Herbert von Tanz of the Abwehr."

"You accuse the Abwehr?" Fuchs quipped. "Saying that is a crime Herr General. You are accusing a Wehrmacht general officer of espionage and treason."

"That is what I said." Krieger said.

"You have proof?" Wulff asked bluntly.

"Of course I have the proof." Krieger said bluntly.

Fuchs put his glasses back on. "This is an interesting fairy tale Herr General if the other prisoner was Skasch but the prisoner is not Skasch, as you well know Herr General."

"Yes." Krieger said. "Skasch has used proxies in the past."

"The real Skasch is dead." Fuchs said.

"He is dead, since when?" Krieger asked.

"He died a few days ago." Wulff said. "The Russians killed him in Switzerland."

"The Swiss Security police believe the Russians were responsible?" Krieger hissed. "How do you know that?"

"The prisoner told us." Fuchs said.

"He is awake." The Countess muttered. "Did he give you a name?"

"He says his name is Colquhoun." Fuchs answered. "He is a Major with the American OSS."

"Interesting but they are taught to lie." Krieger said wryly.

"Was Skasch supposed to bring anything else besides this missing list?" Fuchs asked. Krieger lit a cigarette. "You have not found the list?"

"Sorry no." Fuchs said. "That list could be anywhere, microdots are easy to hide."

"You know about them." Krieger grunted. "Have you bothered to search?"

"Yes." Fuchs said. "The total sum found in both attaché cases is 1.5 million Reich marks."

"I brought no money." Krieger said. "Skasch had been paid."

"The currency is American dollars," Fuchs said "With Reichbank wrappers and Rothmann's Bank wrappers." Fuchs paused. "The Rothmann's Banks are in Zurich and London they are owned by Jews."

"All part of the plot to discredit me." Krieger said coldly.

"Arrest Gerhardt and his men." Ehrlich growled breaking his long stony silence as he stood. "Start being this country policeman."

"Arrest him on what evidence?" Fuchs hissed.

"Are you blind?" Ehrlich snarled. "Only the Abwehr would have access to large amount of foreign currency."

"Arresting Gerhardt prematurely could get us all killed." Fuchs said.

"You are a sonofabitch Fuchs." Krieger rasped. "You need us for bait damnit."

"You are very quick." Fuchs said.

"I'll play along with your game for awhile Herr Reichkriminaldirektor." Krieger said tartly.

"Then we'll have a chance to survive." Fuchs said.

[3]
12:00 hrs

Schiller's Office

Schiller motioned Fuchs to sit down seeing that the police officer was clearly agitated. Fuchs sat down and lit his pipe.

"You have something to say." Schiller said. "Say it."

"Why in hell after all these years did you send for me?" Fuchs snapped. "I was quite content not knowing where you were."

"I needed an honest man." Schiller said.

"I'm not getting in the middle with the Abwehr and SD." Fuchs said bluntly. "I say the hell with them and you Herr Schiller."

"I needed someone I could trust to sort this mess out quickly and quietly." Schiller said sharply. "With all the bodies lying around I didn't want to be next to them."

"Dead bodies never bothered you before." Fuchs said tersely.

"They don't belong to me." Schiller said. "I've been exiled here since 1940 and Adlerberghof is hardly Berlin."

"Damn you to hell." Fuchs hissed. "You are not stupid Kurt. Damnit, you knew the killings intertwined before you called. With this cast of characters, you knew you were in deep shit. You didn't need me to tidy up."

"So far they have killed only two of my own people." Schiller said. "I've grown to love these people and I don't want them used as cannon fodder. Your reputation is beyond reproach."

"You are ass-deep in espionage and treason." Fuchs hissed. "I'm just a tired goddamn cop hoping for retirement."

"Is it that bad?" Schiller hissed.

"Calling Berlin may be the only way to save your life." Fuchs said. "You must have one friend left there. I can't help you."

"None that would take risk with this shitstorm swirling" Schiller said frankly.

"You fall back to the old street solution Kurt?" Fuchs hissed. "I'm not your personal executioner. If I decide to help I only want the guilty."

"You are still the same old fart, Janus." Schiller said lighting a cigarette. "Handle this anyway you see fit. Now what in hell is going on?"

"You haven't guessed?" Fuchs asked.

"No." Schiller said.

"The prisoner is an allied agent." Fuchs said.

"Great." Schiller hissed. "What is Krieger's reason for being here?"

"His story is he was buying something from Skasch." Fuchs said. "Gerhardt's is that he was following a traitor."

"What is the prisoner's story?" Schiller asked.

"Krieger is an enemy agent." Fuchs said. "Code named *Albatross*."

"Is that what Gerhardt believes?" Schiller quipped.

"I would say yes." Fuchs said. "But, Krieger's candidate is an Abwehr general named von Tanz."

"Do you have anything worthwhile?" Schiller asked.

"I have the money." Fuchs said. "Does this place have a bank?"

"No." Schiller said. "Why do you need a bank?"

"Check the money." Fuchs said flatly. "I had a chilling thought that it could be counterfeit."

"That is a comforting thought." Schiller said. "Heinz might know somebody, but with the weather he can't get to him."

"With a heavy army escort the man could be brought here." Fuchs suggested.

"Jherling might not wish to weaken himself." Schiller said. "The snow is getting heavier even if he did agree."

Fuchs put his pipe away. "Our colonel seems to dislike Krieger; does he have an ax to grind?"

"He has a big one." Schiller said. "Jherling was an officer in the Waffen SS but was denied a promotion because of Krieger's intervention, but the bad blood stems from the old days in the Reichwehr."

"Wonderful." Fuchs hissed. "Will he obey orders? I don't want a loose cannon running amuck."

"He will." Schiller said. "He wants more than Jaegerfeld."

"Ambition is good." Fuchs said. "I'll need him and his men."

"You need him for three men?" Schiller asked.

"Wassenberg ran with the psychopath Eidernau." Fuchs said. "That bastard is still hovering around because Krieger is still here."

"Christ, one helluva mess." Schiller said wryly.

"It will not get any better in the near future." Fuchs sighed.

"Can we get out alive?" Schiller asked.

"How religious are you Kurt?" Fuchs asked solemnly.

"I was thinking of becoming a minister when I was a teenager." Schiller said. "You are talking about praying?"

"I found it never hurts to pray." Fuchs said.

[4]
13:00 hrs

Krieger's room

"You took your time getting here." Krieger said as Eidernau emerged into the room from the hidden entrance. The former owner, an émigré Jew, had honeycombed the Gasthof with secret passages in case of trouble.

"I dislike getting shot." Eidernau said.

"Wassenberg won't need my help getting his medical license back." Krieger said in a flat voice. "He failed."

"Who got him?" Eidernau rasped.

"The police are saying person or persons unknown." Krieger said. "Bring in your men at 03:00 hrs."

"Attack this place?" Eidernau gulped. "Are you god-damn crazy? Use the damn tunnel."

"My husband says attack." The Countess said. "That is why you are getting paid."

"You can be out of this shit-pile; hours before they miss you." Eidernau said. "No fireworks."

"I can't." Krieger hissed. "It is a matter of honor."

"You are insane the hell with honor General." Eidernau snapped. "I dislike getting shot."

"Jherling can't keep all these men here forever." The Countess said. "You don't have to fight fair."

Eidernau looked at the Countess shaking his head. "I've lived this long by avoiding fire fights with professional soldiers."

"They are not bulletproof." Krieger said.

"This will cost you." Eidernau hissed.

"Two attaché cases filled with American money." The General said. "They are yours."

"How much money are we talking about?" Eidernau asked.

"1.5 million Reichmarks plus travel permits." The Countess said.

"I think you have a deal." Eidernau said. "Spain is warm this time of year, but there has to be a catch."

"It is only a small catch." Krieger said offhandedly.

"No such thing." Eidernau said bluntly.

Krieger lit a cigar. "Kill Gerhardt and his companions."

"I see no problem with that." Willi said dully.

"Then kill this cop Fuchs." Krieger said. "Then the ersatz Skasch before you leave for sunny Spain."

"Killing the cop is bad." Willi said anxiously. "Senor Franco doesn't like visitors who kill cops; he likes law and order."

"Then say good-bye to that villa on Minorca." Krieger said.

"The hell with Franco's notions I'll kill them." Eidernau rasped. "I'll be back this morning."

"Bags are already packed." Krieger said with a slight smile.

Ehrlich poured three cups of coffee bracing it with cognac after Eidernau left by the secret passage. "Willi really doesn't trust you Helmuth."

"Good instincts." Krieger said contemptuously. "He shouldn't trust us."

"What if the prisoner starts to talk before Willi gets back?" The Countess asked.

"He already spilled his guts to Fuchs." Krieger said. "Fuchs is good, but not that good."

"He is the only witness." Ehrlich said.

"Only if he is alive to talk in court could he be a witness." Krieger said. "Also dead men can't use information."

"We're not leaving." Ehrlich said.

"Correct Albrecht, we are not leaving." Krieger said plainly. "Every story needs a hero and an epic battle."

"Willi will provide that for you." The Countess said. "He will burn this place down to the ground."

"He'll try." Krieger said. "Did Jherling bring anyone ambitious with him?"

"Oberleutnant Dolenz." Ehrlich said. "I spoke with him, he is the warrior type."

"Speak to him again." Krieger said. "They like to be heroes."

"Do you object Countess?" Ehrlich said. "Eidernau is a friend."

"Bullets don't care who they hit Albrecht." The Countess said.

[5]
14:00 hrs

Twickem-Hallesy
Halton Manor

Air Vice-Marshal Daulton was with Bomber Command staff. He had flown with Austen-Halton during the First War. After the war, Daulton moved from station to station mostly in staff positions moving to Bomber Command on the outbreak of the war.

"The Air Ministry will not sanction this Peter." Daulton said in a dry voice. "We do not have the aircraft to waste."

"You do have targets in the general area Maxwell." Austen-Halton said.

"Your target is too near the Swiss border for a night time attack." Daulton said. "The Foreign Office dislikes apologizing to the Swiss for accidental violations of their airspace and the occasional stray bomb." Daulton lit a cigarette. "Have you talked to the Americans?"

"I prefer to keep this in house." Sir Peter said.

"Adlerberghof is not a military target." Daulton said. "How many civilians will be in the town Peter?"

"300." Sir Peter said.

"A squadron of Lancasters will level the town." Daulton said. "There will be no survivors."

"It is a last resort Maxwell." Austen-Halton said. "Will the Air Ministry release the bombers?"

"If Downing Street goes along with your plan." Daulton said crushing out the cigarette. "Will you get Downing Street's approval?"

"Crosland is working on that." Austen-Halton said.

Crawford undid his tie and sat down in the leather chair near the fireplace. "Did the old school tie work?"

"Not in the least." Austen-Halton said as he lit a cigar. "They are not interested in risking valuable bombers on a shadowy mission."

"You can scratch the 8th Air Force from the list." Crawford grunted. "They aren't the least bit interested." Crawford relit his cigar. "Does Witcombe have anything?"

"Tweedmuir is too far away for what he has." Peter said.

"You must have more ferry stations." Crawford stated.

"Witcombe could ferry down his Mosquitos to Kent." Austen-Halton said wryly. "We have a lovely place on Lord Chesterton's farm."

"Will your Air Ministry object?" Crawford asked.

"Our aircraft do not appear on any RAF inventory." Sir Peter said. "Who shall be blame?"

"The blame goes to the goddamn krauts of course." Crawford hissed. "Does Witcombe have anyone who is an artist?"

"He has Leading Airman Humphries." Sir Peter said. "Why may I ask?"

"I want Luftwaffe markings painted on your planes." Crawford said. "Do the Swiss have an airbase near by?"

"Yes." Sir Peter answered. "They will fire on intruders."

"Have they shot at German aircraft?" Crawford asked.

"They have several times over the past few months." Sir Peter said. "Confusion is our ally in this mess."

Chapter Twenty-Five
December 9, 1942
17:30 hrs

Gruenling Gasthof
Dining Room

    Wulff poured the coffee into the cups and handed one to the pensive Fuchs. "I could get use to this place sir, real coffee sir."
    "Smuggling is illegal Arthur." Fuchs said taking the coffee. "It only counts if you get caught though."
    "What is our next move sir?" Wulff asked.
    "It will be nothing dramatic." Fuchs said. "We have set the stage and someone has to make a move. Nobody has told the whole truth to us yet." Fuchs lit his pipe. "The closest has been Colquhoun, but he hasn't yet realized that he was sold out from the beginning."
    "Sold out sir?" Wulff asked.
    Fuchs tapped the stem of his pipe on the table. "If the Allies simply wanted Krieger dead why bother with this whole charade?"
    "Skasch was a paid assassin." Wulff said. "He could have killed Krieger any where and any time."
    "Thus bringing an OSS man to pull the trigger makes no sense." Fuchs said.
    "Why employ a Byzantine plan for no reason?" Wulff asked in a frustrated voice.
    "*Albatross* is not a myth." Fuchs said. "This is all being done to protect him."
    "Which one is this myth?" Wulff asked. "Is it Krieger or von Tanz?"
    "It could either one." Fuchs said. "Please ask Major Gerhardt to come here. I might as well light the fuse."

[2]
18:00 hrs

Twickem-Hallesy
Halton Manor

    Group Captain Witcombe pinned the meteorological map to the board after giving his verbal report.
    "How long will this weather last Group Captain?" Austen-Halton asked lighting his cigar.
    "I estimate at least 72 hours sir." Witcombe said. "It will be very heavy snow here and on the continent."
    "Is there any chance that you are wrong Group Captain?" Crawford asked blandly.
    "This is not an exact science sir." Witcombe said. "This is a major system moving in from the arctic bringing the snow."

"What about a clearing long enough for us to get something into the air?" Crawford asked.

"Sorry sir." Witcombe said. "No flying for at least 72 hours."

"Switzerland?" Crawford asked.

"Sorry." Witcombe said.

"Thank you Group Captain." Austen-Halton said. "If there is a change contact Colonel Tremayne."

Crawford moved to the map and looked at the lines and notations. "They go to college for this?"

"Witcombe is not a doomsayer usually." Sir Peter said.

"An aircraft can fly above the storm." Crawford said.

"Neither Bomber Command nor the Air Ministry allow anything up." Sir Peter said. "This weather won't change your people's mind?"

"We aren't crazy either." Crawford said. "Greene?"

"The Swiss are not insane either." Austen-Halton said. "Witcombe still has time to move his planes to Kent."

Crawford lit a cigarette. "If Witcombe is right they'll be trapped in Adlerberghof."

"Along with everyone else I'm afraid." Sir Peter said.

"We'll have to contact Donner." Crawford said. "He'll have to guide them out."

"15 kilometers in a snowstorm would be dangerous." Austen-Halton said.

"They have to escape." Crawford said. "Time is running out for them."

"Greene will contact Donner." Sir Peter said. "Portlander will be here from London late tonight."

"They might get out before the weather breaks." Crawford said.

"Let's hope so." Sir Peter said.

[3]
18:00 hrs

Gruenling Gasthof
Dining Room

Gerhardt found Fuchs alone in the dining room smoking pipe at one of the tables. Gerhardt pulled out a chair and sat down.

"You asked to see me?" Gerhardt asked.

"Try the tea." Fuchs said. "It is quite excellent considering the war."

"The Swiss most likely invented the black market." Gerhardt said. "But, you didn't ask me here to talk about tea Herr Direktor."

"You are right." Fuchs said handing Gerhardt Calhoun's confession. "Wulff is an excellent typist."

"It is very professional." Gerhardt said as he glanced through the document.

"Please Herr Major." Fuchs said. "I need your opinion."

Gerhardt lit a cigarette after reading the statement, handed it back to Fuchs, and leaned back in his chair. "Congratulations."

"That is a bit premature Major." Fuchs said flatly. "He weaves an interesting tale, but it all has to verify. When it all boils down all I have is a very strong circumstantial case."

"When does that cause a problem nowadays?" Gerhardt rasped.

"There has to a sliver of proof even for the current Ministry of Justice." Fuchs said in a firm voice. "Do you believe him?"

"He gains nothing by lying." Gerhardt said dryly.

"Allied intelligence does." Fuchs said. "You don't find his confession too detailed?"

"Ready made to impress us." Gerhardt said. "Why?"

Fuchs relit his pipe. "Yes why? Colquhoun must have known by then that his wounds were not fatal, but he talked." Fuchs paused. "Why then entrust such a mission to a man with no moral fiber?"

"I have no idea." Gerhardt said. "What is your opinion?"

"In my opinion they would send him only if they knew he would talk under pressure." Fuchs said.

"Was pressure applied Herr Direktor?" Gerhardt asked plainly.

"I did not use Gestapo methods." Fuchs said.

"Set up." Gerhardt said. "Then you must be implying that *Albatross* could be someone else."

"That is what we are supposed to believe." Fuchs said cynically. "Or the Allies want us to find him."

"Either way someone gets caught in the cross hairs." Gerhardt said. "All you have to do is pick one."

"The stage has been for that." Fuchs said. "You have preference?"

"Mine would be bias." Gerhardt said.

"Krieger is an ambitious man." Fuchs said.

Gerhardt crushed out his cigarette. "If given the opportunity he'll deny it."

"I would." Fuchs said flatly. "He would demand to confront his accuser."

"You are going to allow that." Gerhardt said wryly.

"That of course should be considered." Fuchs said. "That is one way to find the truth. When you solve a crime you usually find the truth along with the guilty."

"Are you asking for my moral support in this endeavor?" Gerhardt asked.

"What morality in the Third Reich?" Fuchs said bitterly. "Don't be absurd Major."

"That is dangerous point of view for a police official representing the Reich." Gerhardt said cautiously.

"This is all a game Gerhardt." Fuchs said. "I prefer that the Abwehr to win a minor victory here."

"Then you imply that von Tanz is *Albatross*." Gerhardt rasped.

"I hardly said that." Fuchs said firmly. "Even if Krieger can wiggle off this hook Himmler couldn't possibly appoint him Heydrich's successor. Savior your victory Gerhardt, but you still have a long war to fight, so do not linger for too long." Fuchs said. "Our days are numbered my friend."

"If you feel this way, why bother to continue?" Gerhardt asked seriously.

"I have my duty to perform." Fuchs said in a soft faraway voice.

"For whom do you perform your duty?" Gerhardt asked.

"Myself." Fuchs said flatly.

"Is justice involved in any of this?" Gerhardt asked.

"Nowadays that is an abstract notion." Fuchs said.

"Abstract or not you know what price Berlin will ask." Gerhardt said.
"Yes." Fuchs said. "He is the cog for all of this."
"They'll want him dead." Gerhardt said.
"Herr Colquhoun is my prisoner and I deliver live prisoners." Fuchs said. "I am not his judge or executioner."
"That is a dangerous road my friend." Gerhardt said.
"It is the only road I know." Fuchs said.

[4]
18:00 hrs
Donner's Farm

"This ain't going to work Willi." Hothman said taking a big gulp from the cognac bottle handing Eidernau the bottle. "We are now out numbered."
"Vogel got a weather report on the wireless." Eidernau said. "By the time we launch this suicide attack we won't be able to see our hands in front of our faces."
"We go in early." Brosch said.
"No." Eidernau said. "I don't want to get caught in the town before the storm."
"When do we go in?" Hothman asked.
"The early morning is the best time when the storm is in full force." Eidernau said.
"We better find a better place to wait out the storm." Brosch said.
"Where do you suggest?" Willi asked.
"Sonderbirge spotted a monastery about five kilometers from here." Hothman said.
"Then we have to deal with monks." Brosch said coldly.
"They shouldn't cause any trouble." Willi said. "Pass the word for the men to change into the Grenzpolizei uniforms and head for the monastery."
"All 60 of us go?" Hothman lamented. "Monks are religious not stupid."
"We are tracking down a gang of smugglers." Willi said.
"Do we still guard the roads?" Hothman asked.
"No." Eidernau said. "Check out any buildings on the way to the monastery."
"Who is going to have the honor of telling Krieger?" Hothman asked.
"He likes you." Eidernau said. "You better bring a lamp and a portable stove for heat."
"I'll deliver the message fast." Hothman said. "Monks make very good wine and beer."

Chapter Twenty-Six
December 9, 1942
15:00 hrs

Berlin
Fischer House

    Generalmajor Herbert von Tanz always felt out of place wearing civilian clothes in particular more so in the private home of a retired Generalleutnant. The only thing he wore that said he was a soldier was the miniature Iron Cross his wife had bought him ten years ago. Von Tanz had been enjoying a rare day away from the office when Oberst Stahl arrived at his home in Potsdam. Stahl was one of those glorified messenger-boys from the Chief of the Oberkommandowehrmacht (OKW), Feldmarschalgeneral Keital. The colonel delivered the invitation to be at Fischer's at three PM in civilian attire.
    Politically Fischer was an archconservative monarchist who loathed the Socialists, Communists, and the Nazis equally. After Hitler, came to power Fischer retired from the regular Army in 1934. Four years later Fischer found himself recalled to the Home Amy as the commander of a Wehrkries.
    On his arrival, von Tanz noticed that several of the cars had SS number plates as well as Wehrmacht. When von Tanz entered the living room, he now knew why Carnaris had declined the invitation and sent Stahl to him instead. The party guests slowly dwindled until only three men left in the living room.
    Himmler hardly looked sinister in his dark business suit. He had the appearance of a schoolteacher that the Chief of the dreaded SS. The man sitting on the sofa was Henrik Koch. He was assigned to the Chancellery from the Party and was thought to be one of Bormann's shadowy assistants. His job was cleaning up embarrassments left by Party and government officials.
    "Our host has disappeared it seems." Von Tanz said.
    "Fischer always had impeccable timing." Koch said. "That's what made him a good officer."
    "I assume this meeting was arranged from a reason." Von Tanz said looking at each man. "Why Fischer's home if I may ask?"
    "The general is a man of impeccable honor." Koch said. "Anyone watching us would hardly pick this place for this meeting."
    "That is a wise precaution." Von Tanz said.
    "We had hoped that the Admiral would be here." Himmler said flatly. "I assume that he gave you complete authority."
    "Yes Reichsfuhrer." Von Tanz said. "Is this your meeting sir?"
    "No." Himmler said. "Herr Koch is running this."
    "Cloak and dagger isn't the field you run in Henrik." Von Tanz said. "Where is Schellenberg?"

Koch smiled briefly as he lit a long thin Dutch cigar. "The Chancellery has heard rumors about an enemy spy code named *Albatross* operating freely in Germany."

"You mean Bormann has." Himmler said icily. "He is a state security problem."

"He is also an Abwehr problem Herr Koch." Von Tanz added.

"Then the rumors are true that he has been active for over 20 years?" Koch hissed.

"Why the sudden interest in *Albatross*?" Himmler asked coolly.

"Let's say that it has come to the Chancellery's attention." Koch said.

"Every few years this fairy tale emerges." Von Tanz said. "There was once an agent called *Albatross* during the last war, but we believe he was more than one man using the same code name. The last confirmed interception was in 1918."

Koch lighted a cigarette. "He is not a fairy tale as you both know."

"We know nothing of the sort." Himmler hissed. "What is Bormann's interest?"

"As Party Secretary Bormann has the complete and total confidence of the Fuehrer in all matters." Koch said smugly. "What concerns Bormann is that the Fuehrer might hear about this problem. The Fuehrer has to concentrate on winning the war not worrying about this extraordinary *Albatross*."

"He doesn't exist." Himmler said bluntly. "I do not have the resources to chase shadows based on vague rumors. Who told Bormann that he exists?"

Koch crushed out the cigar. "*Albatross* is real gentlemen not an illusion. The damage he has done thus far is hardly imaginary. He has been slashing us with surgically precise razor cuts having us hemorrhage slowly."

"Then Herr Koch you know more than us." Von Tanz hissed.

"He could be more than one man as I said." Himmler said. "It is a very clever tactic to perpetuate this myth."

"We have discounted that approach." Koch said coldly.

"Just what in hell do you have?" Von Tanz snarled angrily glancing over at Himmler, who seemed upset over what Koch was doing. "Blind man's bluff is for children."

Koch lit another cigar with no visible sign that he had heard either of them. Koch smiled to himself knowing that under normal circumstances either man would gladly cut the other's throat for the sheer pleasure of it.

"This is no children's game." Koch said stiffly. "I know who this *Albatross* is."

"How could you possibly know that?" Himmler hissed. "Who gave you this startling tidbit which seemingly has eluded us?"

"We received it from the Spanish consulate in Cape Town." Koch said.

"They are hardly a reliable source the Spanish." Von Tanz sneered. "The British know we use them at time."

"This came to our attention via a request for information by the Special Branch of Scotland Yard and MI5." Koch said.

"They work together?" Von Tanz said.

"The request was funneled through the High Commissioner Office." Koch said. "We have friends in the Irish Commission and they passed it to the Spanish."

"What was this request?" Himmler asked coldly.

"They wanted to know of the travels of a certain German officer before the First war." Koch said.

"Why are they asking questions?" Von Tanz asked.

"They no longer feel that he is working for them." Koch said.

"Who could he be working for?" Himmler asked.

"The Communists are at the top of the list." Koch said.

"Tell us the name of this officer Herr Koch if you please?" Von Tanz asked. "or do we guess all night long?"

"The name will come as a surprise." Koch said with a dramatic pause at the right moment "Obergruppenfuhrer Helmuth Krieger." Koch said dully with little enthusiasm.

"Are you insane?" Himmler asked icily. "Krieger is a senior officer of the SS."

"I find that hard to swallow." Von Tanz snapped. "He served as an Imperial General Staff officer at the latter stages of the war."

"We have that information." Koch said matter-of-factly. "However, he is the officer the British were inquiring about. He was a frequent visitor to England it seems."

"That is not all that unusual Herr Koch." Von Tanz said. "I visited Sandhurst many times before 1914 and they visited us."

Krieger wasn't moved to the Imperial General Staff until mid-1917." Koch said flatly. "Two months after his escape from a British POW camp."

"I was a POW too Herr Koch." Von Tanz hissed.

"We use rumors and innuendos now Herr Koch?" Himmler hissed. "We don't commission officers in the SS without a thorough investigation."

"Naturally this has to be confirmed either way." Koch said. "Bormann has suggested that an investigation be conducted jointly."."

"We are being asked?" Himmler hissed. "Why are we being asked?"

"Investigation in this case would be a waste of time." Von Tanz said dryly. "He has a large estate a few kilometers from here drive over and ask him if he is this *Albatross*."

Koch smiled as if von Tanz had said something amusing. "We would, but no one seems to know where he went."

"I talked with him a few days ago." Himmler said flatly. "Nothing seemed out of place."

"I've had no contact with him for months Herr Koch." Von Tanz said wryly.

"Our preliminary inquiries have established that." Koch said. "However, there has been an unusual amount of interest in a small town near the Swiss border." Koch said. "It called Adlerberghof."

"I never heard of it of the place." Himmler said. "Who has expressed interest in this place?"

"We understand a variety of people." Koch said. "Both Military and civilian seem interested."

"Anyone of importance live in Adlerberghof?" Von Tanz asked.

"Kurt Schiller." Koch answered.

"What does he have to do with this Adlerberghof?" Himmler asked.

"He is the Burgermeister of the town." Koch said.

"You better tie everything up Herr Koch or this meeting will have one less participate." Von Tanz said in a blunt voice. "You have information we need to know in order to be useful."

Koch quickly sketched out a thin outline of what Bormann knew. "Schiller apparently brought in a police colonel from Stuttgart to investigate some murders. One of the victims is a Viktor Skasch."

"The name means nothing to me." Himmler said drolly.

"Skasch was a professional go-between." Koch said.

"He was a fence." Von Tanz said. "He would sell out his mother for 5 pfennig. He was a university professor many years ago until he found out that crime paid more." The General lit a cigarette. "We have used him for minor jobs in the past. He was destined to die violently."

"So why should he be of interest to us?" Himmler asked.

"Because the Allies were so interested they sent in a team." Koch said.

"Why?" Von Tanz asked.

"*Albatross,* we believe that he is being sold out." Koch said flatly. "Krieger is in Adlerberghof along with an Abwehr major named Gerhardt."

"With *Albatross* being Krieger I assume?" Himmler hissed. "Why is the Abwehr there Herr General?"

"I'm not in personnel Herr Reichsfuhrer." Von Tanz said. "There could be a thousand reasons for Gerhardt being in Adlerberghof unrelated to Krieger or *Albatross*."

"That is the question that has to be answered." Koch hissed.

"You have a solution on how we get the answers?" Himmler asked.

Koch restrained himself from giving a sarcastic answer, working for Bormann had certain immunities, but insulting a man like Himmler was not one of them. "Herr Bormann suggests that you send a three man an investigating team to Adlerberghof immediately."

"I assume which the Reichleiter took upon himself the responsibility to select the team already?" Von Tanz hissed.

"He has selected Oberfuhrer Sepp Clausborg and Generalmajor Klaus Blausen." Koch said. "They are familiar to you gentlemen?"

"Yes." Von Tanz said. "Blausen is recovering from wounds received on the Eastern Front currently assigned to the Adjutant General."

"Clausborg is from my Inspector General office." Himmler said. "Who is the third man?"

"He has selected you Herr General." Koch said. "Admiral Carnaris has agreed."

"By what authority does he commandeer people?" Himmler asked coldly.

"He obtained a Fuhrer commission." Koch said. "They ascertain if *Albatross* is real and what is going on in Adlerberghof."

"When do we leave?" Von Tanz asked somberly.

"The Luftwaffe has a winterized JU-52 waiting for you at Tempfehof to leave at 6 AM tomorrow morning." Koch said. "Land at Jaegerfeld then drive to Adlerberghof."

"Fly in this weather Herr Koch?" Von Tanz asked tartly.

"I am told that the pilots flew as volunteers in the Finnish Air Force during the Winter War in 1939." Koch said.

"Who will command?" Himmler asked.

"Von Tanz is the senior officer." Koch said. "Admiral Carnaris has agreed to this and General Jodl."

"When and if they find *Albatross,* then what Herr Koch?" Himmler asked.

"Kill him and any accomplices." Koch said bluntly.

"No questioning?" Von Tanz asked.

"I doubt he'll be taken alive." Koch said.

"Will there be a time limit?" Von Tanz asked.

"Accomplish the mission." Koch said. "Once you leave Jaegerfeld you'll be on your own."

"This sounds plausible.' Himmler said standing. "However, I will give no official sanction to this venture."

"You'll have part of the glory if we succeed though." Koch said bitterly.

"We understand each other." Himmler said looking at von Tanz then back at Koch. "You will find that the Admiral shares my opinion about this."

"General von Tanz?" Koch quipped.

"The Reichsfuhrer is correct." Von Tanz said flatly.

[2]
15:30 hrs

Twickem-Hallesy

The communications room was located in the East wing of the mansion on the third floor next to the old servants' quarters.

"The bait has been taken sir." Commander Richards, Communications Officer, said dryly. "The Spanish contacted the Irish High Commission in Cape Town."

"Griswald's contacts come through?" Sir Peter asked.

"Flying colors sir." Richards said. "The Cape Town police were cooperative and gave Dublin everything they asked for."

"That is very obliging of the Micks." Crawford said.

"Chief Superintendent Griswald knows his people." Austen-Halton said. "O'Harady has been known to the Irish Section and the Garde for years as an IRA sympathizer. He hates us more than Hitler hates the Jews."

"Colonel Tremayne informs that Colonel Mikhailov is your office Air Vice-Marshal Sir." Richards said to Sir Peter.

Colonel Mikhailov was standing by the fireplace when Sir Peter and Crawford entered the office admiring the life size portrait of General Lord Hallesy.

"Things are starting to buzz in Berlin." Crawford said after explaining to the Russian what had happened. "If Colquhoun can continue to play his part to the end we'll win."

"You selected him." Mikhailov said. "Your operation is proceeding on course?"

"More or less it seems so." Crawford said wryly.

"No plan is perfect Colonel." Sir Peter said. "You understand that."

"I do." Mikhailov said. "Moscow doesn't reason that way. They are uneasy despite my assurances."

"Washington is full of armchair heroes these days." Crawford grumbled. "We are under great pressure here."

"Special pressure, I know what you mean General." Mikhailov said. "An OSS major is hardly a problem to involve special pressure?"

"You can't be immune to pressure." Crawford hissed. "You don't offend a powerful U.S. Senator by making his son a hero by getting him killed."

"Is there a problem?" Mikhailov asked.

Crawford lit a cigarette. "No, just a touch of the illness you can't afford in this business."

"You are human." Sir Peter said.

"Are you having doubts about your Major Colquhoun?" Mikhailov asked bluntly.

"I have blood instead of ice-water." Crawford said. "The initial reports are telling us that Colquhoun isn't acting right."

"That was expected." Sir Peter said.

"He will fall apart?" Mikhailov asked.

"He is suppose to crumble." Crawford said. "Colquhoun, however, might want to play the hero instead."

"The Major knew the risks." Austen-Halton said.

"Does Albatross know the risks?" Mikhailov asked coldly.

"He has known the risks for over twenty years." Austen-Halton said as he lit his cigar. "He doesn't need a Russian colonel doubting his resolve."

Mikhailov lit an American Camel cigarette. "How much does Colquhoun know about him?"

"Only what we told him." Crawford said.

"Self-preservation will kick in soon." Mikhailov hissed. "It is automatic."

"It is necessary for his survival." Sir Peter said. "His talking is what is keeping him alive."

"The cop from Stuttgart is what is bothering me." Crawford said. "He only has to be competent to smell out a phony story."

"Unforeseen events must be adapted to." Sir Peter said.

Mikhailov crushed out the cigarette and lit another. "What is your prime mission?"

"Protecting *Albatross* is our prime mission." Austen-Halton said bluntly relighting his cigar.

"Is Krieger an after thought?" Mikhailov asked.

"Killing him will protect *Albatross*." Austen-Halton said. "He is too ambitious for all our good."

"Killing him is Mannerling's primary mission." Crawford said sternly.

"I know we don't deal in sentimentality gentlemen." Mikhailov said wryly. "Has any thought been given to how you bring Colquhoun out? It is insanity to leave him to the mercy of the enemy" Mikhailov paused. "They all fall under the Commando order."

"That is Mannerling's decision." Sir Peter said. "The worse that could happen is that they die."

"The shitty end of the stick again." Crawford hissed standing.

"Thousands are dying every day General." Mikhailov said bluntly. "I never have understood this concern for the individual."

"In the end that is why we'll win you bastard." Crawford said coldly leaving the room.

"Stress affects all of us." Sir Peter said. "Tired men say and do strange things Colonel."

"I understand this stress." Mikhailov said. "We live with it all the time."

"Greene and Withgate will move to the border and wait for them." Sir Peter said firmly as he relit his cigar.

"They have to get there first." Mikhailov said dryly. "The weather will not help and you know Krieger will not die easily."

"As I see it so long as he dies Colonel. That is what counts at the end of the day." Sir Peter said blandly.

"Pray that everything works out." Mikhailov said in a sincere voice. "God should know which side to help."

"Pray and God Mikhailov?" Sir Peter mused cynically "Communists are atheists."

"My great-uncle was a priest." Mikhailov said. "My father was a Tsarist Army officer and I sang in the choir."

"Small world" Sir Peter quipped.

[3]
15:30 hrs

Donner's Farm

Orr and Browne were in the barn gathering up some equipment that they had left when they left for the monastery. Donner had come with them to check his house. The visitors had apparently left for the monastery.

They heard the noise and Orr turned off his flashlight and they both drew their weapons ducking behind some bales of hay. The small man-door rattled as if something slammed into it with a heavy thud. The door sprung open and Donner staggered in. He stumbled around as if he was drunk until he collapsed to the ground with a knife sticking out of his back. They remained silent and motionless as two men wearing Army style great coats entered.

"Eidernau said no trouble Albrecht." The taller man said. "Not to play games with an old man. This is going to be hard to explain to Willi."

"The hell it is Felix." Albrecht hissed. "This old bastard was spying on us."

"He is a god-damn thief." Felix said as Donner groaned. "Losing your touch Albrecht, the old bastard is still alive."

"Not for long." Albrecht said removing the pistol from the holster.

"Christ, cut his throat." Felix said. "Gunshots carry."

"The monastery is far away." Albrecht rasped. "It won't carry that far."

"I wouldn't if I were you." Orr said stepping out from behind the hay bales with his hands behind his back. Both men turned and faced him with weapons drawn.

"Who the hell are you?" Felix growled.

"It doesn't matter." Orr said. "What are you doing here? What did Eidernau tell you?"

"He is alone." Albrecht hissed.

"Move again Albrecht and I'll kill you." Orr said.

"Kill him!" Albrecht snarled.

"Not right yet Albrecht." Felix said icily. "This bastard has balls."

"I'll cut them off for you." Albrecht said.

"You are bungling this." Orr snapped. "Eidernau is not known for tolerating fools."

"Just who the hell are you?" Felix asked damningly. "You ain't with us"

"You are stupid bastards." Orr snarled.

"What are you doing here?" Felix asked stiffly.

"We had a rendezvous here." Orr rasped. "Eidernau change his plans?"

"He had to with the storm coming." Albrecht said. "We're moving to the monastery until the storm blows over."

"Then you changed the assault time?" Orr hissed.
"Willi doesn't tell us a damn thing." Felix answered.
"You better leave then." Orr said.
"Not yet." Albrecht grunted pointing at Donner. "I have unfinished business."
"No." Mannerling said thumbing pack the hammer of the P-38. "I'll handle it."
"Kill him Albrecht!" Felix shouted bringing his pistol up, but his face exploded into a bloody mass as he lifted off his feet collapsing into a heap. Albrecht crumpled to the ground with three bullets in the chest. Brown came out from hiding breaking open Donner's shotgun.
"Good." Boyden said. "Not good enough though."
"They are dead Donner." Mannerling said sharply.
"It's about time." Donner said cynically. "I thought you were waiting for him to cut my throat before you did something. Take the god-damn knife out of my goddamn back."
"The knife hardly stuck in." Brown said examining the small wound.
"I use this coat for my smuggling because it is heavily insulated and I'm just a good actor." Donner rasped. "But it still hurts damnit."
"You have a place to dump them?" Orr asked.
"Manure pile outback." Donner said getting up. "Nobody will look for them there."
"What about the monastery?" Orr rasped.
"I'll get the wireless." Brown said.
"Donner you bring them into town." Orr said.
"What?" Donner hissed.
"Schiller is nervous enough now." Orr said. "This might force someone's hand."
"Or get everyone killed." Brown said.
"Do they have any identification on them?" Orr asked.
"No." Donner said. "Grenzpolizei would have identity cards."
"That should be enough to start the dancing." Orr said lighting a cigarette. "You have a sled?"
"Ja." Donner hissed. "I'm the jackass that will pull it."

[4]
15:45 hrs

The Monastery

"Has everyone come in?" Eidernau asked Hothman lighting a cigarette by the great fireplace in the great hall. The monastery was once a castle given to the monks two hundred years ago.
"Everyone is in except Albrecht and Felix." Hothman said.
"When did you see them last Hothman?" Willie asked.
"I think they went to loot that farmhouse most likely." Hothman said. "You want me to send someone to get them?"
"No." Eidernau said. "We are supposed to be the border police."
"That damn Abbot wants to talk to you." Hothman said entering the room. "He is waiting outside."
"That is fine." Eidernau said. "Remember I am Major Eidernau not boss or Willi."

Brother Fritz was slightly over six feet tall and his beard was snow white. He had been Abbot for ten years.

"Brother Fritz." Eidernau said politely. "What may I do for you?"

"How long are you planning to be with us Herr Major?" Brother Fritz asked.

"Two maybe three days." Eidernau said. "I know it will be awkward for that time span."

"You are very heavily armed Herr Major for border police." Brother Fritz said. "This is the first time since the Thirty Years War that armed soldiers have been inside this monastery Herr Major."

"We are chasing a vicious gang of smugglers." Eidernau said. "Berlin understands the need of a black-market, but they are smuggling in drugs and smuggling out Jews."

"Jews, really?" Brother Fritz said dryly.

"It is vicious circle." Eidernau said flatly. "You are very observant for a monk."

"I was not always a monk Herr Major." Brother Fritz said. "I served four years on the Western Front and 10 years in the colonial army in Africa."

"I will keep my men in the great hall area Brother Fritz." Eidernau said.

"Breakfast is at 5 o'clock in the morning." Brother Fritz said. "Simple, but hardy fare Herr Major."

"Thank you." Eidernau said. "I however, insist on supplying the coffee."

"Thank you." Brother Fritz said. "5 o'clock."

[6]
16:00 hrs

The Cavern

Brother Hugo walked into the cavern using one of the great wooden doors at the end of the cavern.

"You people are full of surprises." Carey said as the monk walked through the door.

"You are comfortable?" Brother Hugo asked as he closed the door.

"Warm here." Carey said.

"The bakery funnels heat right below you." Brother Fritz said.

"How many of them are in the monastery?" Carey asked.

"50-60." Brother Hugo said.

"Are they the police?" Carey asked.

"They try to look like the Grenzpolizei." Brother Hugo said. "I believe they are ones who chased you away from Donner's. They have the feel of mercenaries."

Carey lit a cigarette. "How could you know that?"

"Twelve years in the French Foreign Legion." Hugo said. "I spent the last four years on the Western Front as a sous-officer."

"French Foreign Legion?" Carey quipped.

"I was born in Alsace." Brother Hugo said. "Unfortunately it was after the Germans came in 1870."

""How long does he plan to stay?" Carey asked.

"He says two or three days." Brother Hugo said.

"Wonderful." Carey said hollowly

An Honorable Betrayal

16:35 hrs

Adlerberghof
Police Station

    Heinz lifted up the old piece of canvas and looked at the two bodies on the wood-sled then dropped it. He then looked at Donner puffing away on his pipe in side Lanzt's barn.
    "They are wearing uniforms Donner." Heinz grunted.
    "I know that Herr Heinz." Donner said gruffly.
    "You shoot them Donner?" Heinz asked somberly.
    "If I didn't kill the bastards in self defense you would never find them." Donner said dryly. "I didn't want one of your hotshots spotting the bodies in my barn and jumping to the wrong conclusions."
    "Damnit, they are wearing Grenzpolizei uniforms." Heinz growled.
    "The one without a face stuck me with this knife." Donner said tossing it on the canvas with no expression on his face. "Look at them Otto, they ain't no border police. I shot them with this." Donner tossed the old Mauser 98 broom handle on the canvas. "This is from the last war."
    Heinz flipped the canvas over again, turned on his flashlight, and checked out the bodies. "You're right Donner, let's go to my office."
    "I want to get home before the heavy snow starts." Donner rasped.
    "It's not snowing that bad Donner" Heinz quipped.
    "You are arresting me?" Donner rasped indignantly.
    "No." Heinz said. "I have coffee on the stove but I have to confiscate the Mauser."
    "Damn." Donner grunted.
    Donner walked over to the wood stove and he poured himself a cup of coffee then sat down. In front of Heinz's desk
    "You know how to write." Heinz said handing Donner a pad of paper and a paper. "It should be short and to the point, no colorful language."
    "I'll print so you can read it." Donner grunted as the door opened and Inspector Wulff entered the office.
    "Anything wrong Chief?" Wulff asked removing his gloves. "I heard something about bodies." Donner got up and went into the other room with his pad and pencil.
    "Old Donner bagged two deserters." Heinz said flatly.
    "Where did this happen?" Wulff asked.
    "Donner's farm outside of town." Heinz said. "The coffee is free."
    Wulff sat down. "I glanced at the bodies before coming here. Good shooting for a farmer."
    "Not really Inspector." Heinz quipped unbuttoning his uniform collar. "This old bastard was a professional tracker in Southwest Africa before the First War. He then became one of the best snipers on the Western Front. The Kaiser himself presented him a gold-plated Mauser along with his Pour Le Merit; they made him a Lieutenant after that."
    "One of them had his face blown off by a shotgun." Wulff said.
    "I'm good with one of them too." Donner said from the other room.
    "I saw a specimen of your skill?" Wulff said flatly. "Did you suffer any injuries to yourself Herr Donner?"
    "One of the bastards stuck me with a blade." Donner said in a matter-of-fact voice.

"Jherling's doctor is at the Gasthof." Wulff said.

"Free medical treatment." Heinz said. "Go with the Inspector Kurt."

"Wait one damn minute Otto." Donner rasped. "You check through the bulletins see if those two had a reward on them."

Gruenling Gasthof

"What is all the excitement about Arthur?" Fuchs asked emerging from the dining room.

"Some farmer killed two men wearing Grenzpolizei uniforms." Wulff said. "They seemingly attacked him…self-defense."

"Is there any reason to doubt his story?" Fuchs asked.

"No." Wulff said. "They have them listed as unknowns and I saw no reason to change their minds."

"You know something so out with it Arthur." Fuchs said.

"I recognized one of them." Wulff said. "Albrecht Fassbinder, he usually runs with Felix Nurheim, two sacks of shit, but very good at killing people."

"Aren't you certain about Felix?" Fuchs asked somberly.

"One body didn't have a face sir." Wulff said.

"Are they independents?" Fuchs asked.

"They were guns-for-hire for a price sir." Wulff said. "They have worked for Eidernau in the past."

"Damn." Fuchs said. "The time has come to strengthen our position."

"How do we do that sir?" Wulff asked.

"Find Colonel Jherling." Fuchs said flatly. "Have him quietly surround the Gasthof."

"Krieger is dangerous." Wulff said.

"So am I Arthur." Fuchs said firmly. "After you find Jherling I want Schiller in on this."

Chapter Twenty-Seven
December 9, 1942
17:00 hrs

Berlin
Abwehr HQ

Von Tanz looked up from his desk as the familiar shape entered his office. "Good evening Herr Admiral."

"How sharp are the knives?" The Admiral asked.

"They are very sharp sir." Von Tanz said. "I dislike Bormann's interest in this matter."

"He is going after Himmler." The Admiral said. "How is Himmler handling this?"

"I find him unreadable." Von Tanz said. "He has agreed to participate but I feel that he knows more than he is saying." Von Tanz lit a cigarette "They both believe that *Albatross* is involved in this."

"*Albatross* is a convenience for the both of them." The Admiral said. "Has Himmler broken with Krieger?"

"I couldn't tell sir." Von Tanz said. "Even a slight scandal would destroy Krieger's chances of succeeding Heydrich sir."

"Yes it would but the alternative could be far worse than Herbert." The Admiral said sitting down.

"Ernest Kaltenbrunner." Von Tanz hissed. "He is not that bright."

"He is more brutish than Heydrich." The Admiral said flatly. "But he has one virtue that would please Himmler; no ambition to succeed Himmler."

"There is still time to avoid this sir." Von Tanz said. "Going to Adlerberghof may not be in our best interest sir"

"We can't afford not to be there." The Admiral said. "It will be to our advantage to see that Krieger not be taken alive."

"You believe that Krieger could be a traitor?" Von Tanz asked.

"I would rather have the witch hunt that would follow destroy them not us." The Admiral said flatly. "Be careful Herbert on this journey."

"As always sir, I'm very careful." Von Tanz said.

[2]
17:30 hrs

RSHA

Himmler removed his glasses and began to polish them while the officer sitting in front of his desk read the dossier. The officer would have been a poster boy for SS recruitment except for the scar that ran from his left temple to cheek and the black eye patch.

"What is your opinion Obersturmbannfuhrer of what you have read?" Himmler asked putting his glasses back on.

"The Russians are quite good at inventing this sir." The Obersturmbannfuhrer said. "They wiped out most of their senior officer corps with a fairy tale."

"Do you Krieger Colonel?" Himmler asked.

"No sir." The Obersturmbannfuhrer said. "I have heard of him."

"What if this information came from any other source but the Russians, what would then be your opinion Colonel?" Himmler asked seriously.

"I would be concerned sir." The Obersturmbannfuhrer said. "However, the British and Americans are quite capable of producing this too sir?"

Himmler smiled for a moment. "Do you fear Martin Bormann Obersturmbannfuhrer Danzig?"

"Only a fool doesn't fear him sir." Danzig said plainly. "Is he involved with this sir?"

"Have you recovered fully from your injuries?" Himmler asked ignoring Danzig's question.

"I could pass the physical for the Waffen SS if the doctors would allow it sir." Danzig said. "I've been working with the SIPO for the last eighteen months."

"Has it been satisfying work Danzig?" Himmler asked plainly.

"To be honest Herr Reichsfuhrer no it hasn't been. I am not a glorified policeman." Danzig said. "I said nothing because I assumed that it was punishment duty."

"Your actions in the United States were never in question." Himmler said. "Are you interested in using your old skills?"

"How may I do that sir?" Danzig asked.

"Cleaning up this mess Krieger has made for us." Himmler said matter-of-factly. "I will give you a free hand." Himmler paused. "Do you need assistance?"

"Hauptsturmfuhrer Stoessel and three men will do sir." Danzig said. "When do I start?"

"You begin tonight Colonel." Himmler said handing him a sheet of paper. "I have prepared a list, memorize the list and destroy it."

"Do you know what happened to the British sir?" Danzig asked.

"They all unfortunately survived." Himmler said. "I want this started by tonight Danzig. Do what you have to do and you answer to no one."

[3]

Adlerberghof
Schiller's Office

"We already know that they are out there." Schiller said flatly. "I don't see the need to get all excited Fuchs."

"Grenzpolizei uniforms tell me that this is not a last minute venture." Fuchs said.

"There is no way that anyone could have anticipated this kind of trouble." Jherling said.

"We are facing a deepening problem." Schiller said firmly. "You'll have to tell your men not to trust anyone wearing a Grenzpolizei uniform."

"I'll pull my men into a tighter circle around the hotel and the train station." Jherling said in a flat voice. "The overall visibility will decrease as the storm heightens."

"I would suggest men inside the hotel." Fuchs said. "As the weather worsens everyone will become concerned with finding shelter."

"What about Gerhardt?" Schiller asked.

"The major is intelligent and will figure something is going on without us telling him." Fuchs said.

"He'll start to ask questions." Jherling said.

"Let him." Schiller said. "It will keep him occupied."

"Let's hope that this storm ends quickly." Fuchs said in a hopeful voice. "Then we can get the prisoners to Jaegerfeld."

[4]

Swiss-German Border
Kaufman's Chalet

"Below that mountain Thomas is Adlerberghof." Greene said pointing to the mountains in the distance.

"Which makes it about 30 kilometers from here sir?" Withgate said sipping his hot chocolate.

"Actually it is closer to 40 kilometers Captain." Greene said. "This weather will make it impossible to fly them out."

"Driving out doesn't seem viable either." Withgate said dryly. "Mannerling might know how to Alpine ski."

"Being Canadian doesn't automatically make you a skier." Greene said deftly. "They might just have to walk out."

Withgate lighted a cigarette. "Has Mannerling been ordered to take Colquhoun out sir?"

"I really don't know Thomas." Greene said as he relit his pipe. "The major has an independence streak which no one has been able to contain. He is just as apt to leave him there as take him."

"Colquhoun is not just anybody." Withgate said. "His family is quite powerful in the United States."

"That will hardly impress Mannerling." Greene said. "When the weather lifts you'll make your way to a hunting cabin about 2 kilometers from the border. There you'll wait for Mannerling."

"The German side could be mined sir." Withgate said.

"They haven't done that yet." Greene said. "Too many Swiss cows wander around in the Spring/Summer and the border is not clearly defined."

"Do I give them assistance?" Withgate asked.

"That is up to you." Greene said. "The Germans will shoot back."

[5]

London
Soviet Embassy

General Sergeyev poured the Irish whiskey into two large glasses and sat down undoing his collar. "Sit down Sergei."

"I prefer to stand Comrade General." Mikhailov said politely.

"At least take the drink Colonel." Sergeyev said. "It is a gift from the Lord Mayor of London."

"Thank you Comrade General." Mikhailov said taking the drink. "Is there a reason that you ordered me back to London sir?"

"Moscow contacted us a few hours ago." Sergeyev said grimly.

"What have they done?" Mikhailov asked.

"They have made Krieger the fall guy." Sergeyev said plainly. Mikhailov downed his drink and poured another.

"Where does that place *Boris* in the scheme of things sir?" Mikhailov asked bluntly.

"He is an expert in survival." Sergeyev said.

"Who arranged this?" Mikhailov asked bluntly.

"Someone you can ill afford to have as an enemy Sergei." Sergeyev said. "Krieger will fall."

"The Nazis have a great tendency to kill everyone attached to an embarrassment." Mikhailov said firmly.

"This was meant to help *Boris*." Sergeyev said gruffly. "The idiot who arranged this help knows the connection between *Boris* and Stalin. He would not jeopardize his life for petty gain."

"Is there any reason why I can't return to Twickem-Hallesy sir?" Mikhailov asked.

"Our Allies will expect you to be there." Sergeyev said. "Why feed their natural skepticism about us?"

"Is there any plan to help *Boris*?" Mikhailov asked bluntly.

"Sorry my friend" Sergeyev said hollowly. "He is on his own."

An Honorable Betrayal

Chapter Twenty-Eight
December 9, 1942
20:00hrs

Berlin
Vochner Home

    The clearly frightened maid ushered the three men into the first floor library. The Hauptsturmfuhrer told the maid to gather up all the household help and leave the house immediately.
    "What in hell are you doing Captain?" Vochner snapped.
    "Remain seated sir." The Captain said briskly. "Frau Vochner?"
    "She and the children have gone to Mainz." Vochner answered opening the middle draw of his desk slightly. "What is going on?"
    "That will be explained to you sir." The Captain said.
    "Who gave you the right to burst into my home and order people about?" Vochner said coldly. "I'll need your name and organization."
    "Hauptsturmfuhrer Stoessel was following my orders Herr Vochner." The fourth man said entering the room. The man was tall blond and the Aryan look was marred by the black eye patch over the left eye. "Our business should be conducted in private."
    "I have no business with you." Vochner rasped. "Who the hell are you anyway?"
    "The name is Obersturmbannfuhrer Erich Danzig." The Colonel said. "RSHA"
    "You are one of Himmler's lapdogs." Vochner sneered. "I'll assume you know whose house you have broken into?"
    "I am quite aware Herr Vochner." Danzig said. "You should have expected a visit sooner or later."
    Vochner lit a cigarette. "I have no idea what you are talking about or why you have decided to ruin my evening?"
    "This letter will explain." Danzig said placing the letter on the desk.
    Vochner open the envelope and read the letter. "You've out done yourselves Colonel. This fiction is amazing."
    "I didn't write it." Danzig said. "Are you saying the content is in error?"
    "Did Herr Goebbels write this tripe?" Vochner said. "I would expect this from smut peddler Streicher."
    "The Gauleiter of Franconia is a respected member of the Party Herr Vochner." Danzig said.
    "You said private business." Vochner said bluntly.
    "My men will step outside." Danzig said.
    "They have ears." Vochner said bluntly.
    "You speak English." Danzig said "My people don't."
    "I want them outside the house." Vochner said in English watching Stoessel's face for any hint that he understood English.
    "Stoessel take the men outside and wait in the car." Danzig ordered. "I doubt will try anything stupid."
    Vochner lit a cigarette. "How many letters are you delivering tonight?"

"Yours is the only one." Danzig said.
"You have the block secure." Vochner said.
"Blockleiter Roemer has been cooperative." Danzig said.
"Roemer has always been a fool." Vochner said.
"Do you have any comments about the letter?" Danzig asked flatly.
Vochner leaned back in his chair. "You understand that once I pick up the telephone I can not help you."
"I don't need help." Danzig said grimly.
"Reichleiter Bormann will not be pleased." Vochner said bluntly placing his hand on the telephone.
"Call the Reich Chancellery I have no objections." Danzig said. "However, you'll learn that he is not there."
"I'm to meet him later tonight." Vochner said bluntly.
"Make your call." Danzig said. "I have plenty of time."

[2]

Danzig lit a cigarette while Vochner talked to someone at the Reich Chancellery. Danzig watched Vochner as the Chancellery explained to him that Bormann was not there and they had no idea where he had gone.
"These are all lies in that letter." Vochner said.
"You are acquainted with Gruppenfuhrer Krieger and his wife Countess Rodelbach." Danzig said flatly. "The letter is quite clear about the charges."
"I don't give a damn what the letter says." Vochner said bluntly. "I have known the Countess' family since we were children. I just can't believe the lies."
"Krieger has been a traitor since the last war," Danzig said. "More importantly he continues to be a traitor."
"Neither of them are Communists, that is impossible." Vochner said. "Krieger killed Reds in the twenties."
"The Reds value nothing." Danzig said plainly. "Killing their own is not new to them."
"The Countess' family has been part of the aristocracy since Frederick the Great." Vochner said. "She would not dishonor the family for a mere husband."
"We are not interested in that Herr Vochner." Danzig said. "Where are Krieger and the Countess?"
"Try the estate." Vochner hissed.
"We are not stupid Vochner." Danzig said sharply. "I've been to the estate and the estate keeper said he had no idea where they went. In fact he kept on insisting right up to the moment he jumped out of the car bringing him to Berlin."
"You killed him?" Vochner hissed.
"It was a suicide." Danzig said. "There was no need for him to do that."
"Christssake you were taking the poor bastard to Berlin." Vochner said. "What the hell do you want?"
Danzig crushed out the cigarette. "We want *Albatross*."
"Who or what is *Albatross?*" Vochner grumbled.
"Krieger is *Albatross.*" Danzig said firmly. "Tell us where he is and I just leave."

"I don't know where they are." Vochner said. "You people are wrong about them."

Danzig shook his head. "Why are you protecting them? Is it out of friendship or family loyalty?"

"You people have botched this." Vochner rasped. "Krieger is incapable of friendship."

"Then help the Countess." Danzig rasped.

"She hardly needs by protection." Vochner said firmly. "Why are you here?"

"I thought that would be obvious." Danzig said. "The government can't appear to look foolish or incompetent."

"You better leave Herr Danzig." Vochner said bluntly. "I'm not some scared office clerk who is frightened at his own shadow. I have many powerful friends in the Party."

"Your friends will melt away once you are charged with treason." Danzig said. "You'll be tried in the Volksgerichtshof in Berlin with Freisler as the presiding judge."

"The people's court for a senior party official is a very dangerous gambit." Vochner said icily "You can't control the foreign press."

"The trial will be the last resort." Danzig said. "It will be carefully scripted with your confession being the highlight."

"Now we copy the Reds by having a show trial?" Vochner hissed. "The confession will be false because the signature will be a forgery."

Danzig lit a cigarette. "The trial would be unnecessary if you handwrite your confession. You would save the State much expense and time." Danzig paused for a moment. "For your cooperation the State would be merciful."

"The noose instead of the guillotine quite merciful on the State's part I see the compassion Danzig." Vochner sneered.

"No cooperation will result in your wife and mother-in-law being sent to Buchenwald." Danzig said flatly. "Your 75 year old father-in-law will be sent to Dachau. The children would be taken by the state."

"What does cooperation buy?" Vochner asked.

"I can offer your family's safety and security as guaranteed by the Reichsfuhrer in writing." Danzig said. "No hint of scandal would be attached to your name."

"You're asking for more than just a confession." Vochner hissed.

"It will be tragic news." Danzig said watching Vochner reach into his desk draw. "Killing me will only extend your family's existence for a few hours."

Vochner laid the Luger on the desktop. "How many others are going to pay to protect your master?"

"Very few will die." Danzig said. "This is not Operation Kolibri Vochner. Where are they?"

"They are in Adlerberghof." Vochner said pointing the Luger at Danzig. "They'll not die easy."

"It makes little difference to me." Danzig said ignoring the Luger pointing at him as he stood. "I'm not going after him."

"What if you are wrong about Krieger?" Vochner hissed.

"Mistakes happen." Danzig said coldly. "I'll give you fifteen minutes to write a letter to your wife explaining the why."

"I'm supposed to take you at your word?" Vochner asked.

"Yes." Danzig said flatly. "My way there is the chance of hope."

[3]
21:30 hours

RSHA

"This is very good work Colonel." Himmler said after reading Vochner's confession. "Have someone from the ordinal police find the body before Frau Vochner returns."

"Inspektor Gottleib has been given a tip." Danzig said. "I can be in Adlerberghof by tomorrow afternoon despite the weather sir."

"There are others on the lists that have to be talked to Colonel." Himmler said. "Krieger will be dealt with by someone else."

"I am capable of doing this sir." Danzig said.

"I know that you are quite capable Danzig." Himmler said. "Adlerberghof will be settled by someone else. There are three more names on the list."

"I understand sir." Danzig said not showing his disappointment.

"Finish up in the morning Colonel." Himmler ordered.

[4]
21:45 hrs

Dietrich Estate

Von Tanz could tell from Weiss' expression that he was not pleased that he was there at this hour.

"The General is a very ill man Herr Generalmajor." Weiss said seriously. "The doctors give him six weeks at the most."

"I fully understand Herr Oberst." Von Tanz said. "However, I must talk to him."

"Perhaps tomorrow morning will do?" Weiss hissed.

"It has to be tonight Colonel." Von Tanz said bluntly.

"What is this about sir?" Weiss asked. "What is so damn important it can't wait until tomorrow?"

"Adlerberghof." Von Tanz said plainly.

"I won't bother him about Carl Herr General." Weiss said coldly.

"Tell him I'm here colonel." Von Tanz ordered. "You are still on active duty and can be shipped off to the Eastern Front in command of a penal battalion."

"Give me five minutes sir." Weiss said.

Dietrich was seated by the fireplace the only source of light in the room. The blackout curtains had transformed the room into a mausoleum. The flickering reddish orange light von Tanz made out the family portraits on the walls.

"This is not a social call Herbert." Dietrich coughed. "Not at this hour and weather."

"I have come about Adlerberghof Herr General." Von Tanz said flatly.

"Is it over Herbert?" Dietrich asked.

"It will be over shortly sir." Von Tanz said.

"Then why are you here?" Dietrich asked weakly.

"Gerhardt has sent a report." Von Tanz said. "Your son Carl has been killed."

Dietrich leaned back in his chair his chin resting on his chest for a few moments. "Who killed him us or them?"

"Does it matter sir?" Von Tanz asked.

"No." Dietrich said. "The line ends with me regardless of the out come in Adlerberghof. Will Krieger outlive me?"

"His fate is sealed." Von Tanz said. "However questions may arise which could jeopardize you."

"Let them ask their damn questions." Dietrich said flatly. "There is very little they could do to me now. If they shot me immediately they would be doing me a favor."

"I see your point." Von Tanz said.

"If you can recover Carl's body I wish it brought back here." Dietrich said. "I want him buried in the family crypt."

"I'll try to accomplish that." Von Tanz said. "Anything I can do for you?"

"Put Krieger into the ground before I die." Dietrich coughed. "Send in Weiss."

[5]

Washington DC
War Department

"Have we calmed down Senator Colquhoun?" The Assistant Secretary of War asked. Rear Admiral Coffin.

"It is only for the moment sir." Coffin said. "The shit will hit the fan if he dies."

"That was not the original intent." The ASW hissed. "You people said you had this under control."

"The Major is more resilient than we thought sir." Coffin said. "Those unexpected factors will not interfer with the main objective."

"Is killing this one SS officer that important to the British?" The ASW asked coldly.

"The British have made it abundantly clear that is necessary to eliminate him." Coffin said bluntly, as he lit a cigarette. "They want that asset protected, but that is why they asked us to do the operations."

"The White House gave us very little choice in the matter." The ASW said.

"Is the White House able to keep Senator Colquhoun under control if his son dies?" Coffin asked coldly.

"We will award his son the Distinguish Service Cross either way." The ASW said. "The Senator will have a war hero no matter what happens. The Secretary will have the brother transferred to Washington to be out of harm's way."

"This is one helluva way to run a war sir." Coffin said cynically.

"I agree Admiral." The ASW said. "Look at it this way, how many lives do we save by not having the Senator as an enemy?" The Admiral remained silent as he crushed out the cigarette knowing the ASW was right.

Chapter Twenty-Nine
December 10, 1942
05:00 hrs

Berlin
Tempfehof Airport

    Gruppenfuhrer Sepp Clausborg stood by the window of the VIP lounge at the airport watching the snowfall at a steady rate drinking a whiskey. Clausborg was a veteran of the street wars with the enemies of the Fuehrer and his face bore the scars. Unlike his other street fighting colleagues, Clausborg was a college graduate with a degree in law, which he used to secure a niche in the newly created Secret State Police, the Gestapo in 1932 by Goering.
    Generalmajor Klaus Blausen puffed steadily on his cigar. He had been an enlisted man during most of the First War finally to the rank of Lieutenant in the last week of October 1918. Blausen was one of the lucky ones and remained in the Reichwehr, but being the son of a baker did not help his career. His Army rank one month before Hitler came to power was captain, one-month later lieutenant colonel. Blausen had secretly joined the Nazi Party in 1927 to avoid conflicts with the Army.
    "We are not going out today." Clausborg said turning away from the window and sitting down. "Luftwaffe pilots are not stupid."
    "We are only delayed a half hour." Blausen said gruffly as he relit his cigar. "The pilots were volunteers in the Winter War back in '39. They flew in much worse weather."
    "Aren't we missing someone?" Clausborg hissed.
    "Do you understand what I said?" Von Tanz asked lighting a cigarette.
    "Everything." Clausborg said flatly.
    "Where are the Luftwaffe and Kriegsmarine?" Blausen asked.
    "It's not their concern." Von Tanz said. "The Reichsmarschal would want to run the show and Raeder couldn't care less."
    "Why not let the damn Inspector-General do his job?" Clausborg asked dully.
    "This is supposed to be impartial inquiry or at least appear to be one." Von Tanz said crisply. "Krieger is SD and they have their own ideas of what is right."
    "The Gestapo works closely with the SD." Blausen said blandly. "Hardly independent."
    "We are independent." Clausborg said firmly.
    "Mueller is no friend of Krieger's." Von Tanz said.
    "I understand you two, but me?" Blausen asked.
    "You are considered loyal and incorruptible." Von Tanz said.
    "Berlin is playing this too close to the vest." Blausen said bluntly, being subtle was not one of Blausen's better social graces.
    "They want no mistakes." Von Tanz said. "We will have total freedom of action- we are judge, jury and executioner."
    "You have this in writing Herbert?" Clausborg asked coldly. "Berlin often gets faint-hearted; why don't they order this Jherling just to shoot them."
    "Berlin wants *Albatross* alive." Von Tanz said.
    "Court of Honor?" Blausen grunted.
    "No such nonsense." Von Tanz said. "We'll all be wearing regular Army uniforms without any unit identifications."

"Will this work?" Clausborg asked.

"Damn well better." Von Tanz said as a Luftwaffe Colonel entered the lounge.

"Sorry Herr General." The Colonel said. "The Luftwaffe Area commander has shut down operations for at least 24 hours."

"Does he understand our priority Colonel?" Clausborg asked coldly.

"All air operations are shut down throughout Germany." The Colonel said. "OKL has issued directive. You could appeal the decision to the Air Ministry sir."

"Is land transportation shut down?" Blausen asked.

"The weather is making life difficult sir." The Colonel said.

"Inform the area commander to contact this number." Von Tanz said. "He has thirty minutes to clear our flight or I make the telephone call."

"Yes sir." The Colonel said taking the telephone number.

[2]
06:00 hrs

Adlerberghof
Gasthof Gruenling

"Have you gone mad Jherling?" Krieger shouted at Colonel Jherling. Without warning, the colonel and six men burst into the room. Klugge, who had tried to stop them, lay sprawled on the floor bleeding profusely from a large gash on his forehead. Ehrlich moved in front of the Countess wondering if the colonel had gone stark raving mad. Dasche the driver remained silent and seated.

"In the name of the Fuehrer I place you under arrest Herr General." Jherling said in a stone cold voice. "Corporal Rauscher, escort the Sergeant-Major to the surgeon."

"You are arresting the General on what charge?" Ehrlich snarled.

"Sergeant Fromm." Jherling said sharply. Fromm moved over to Ehrlich and rammed the butt of his rifle into Ehrlich's stomach doubling him up into a ball on the floor.

"The charges Jherling!" Krieger snarled. "I want to hear them now!"

"The charges are treason, murder and espionage." Jherling said plainly.

"What?" Krieger gulped.

"This can't be your idea." The Countess hissed breaking her silence. "Whose orders are you so stupidly carrying out Colonel? One call to Berlin and you might be lucky enough shoveling shit as a private on the Eastern Front. Leave now and we might forget this happened Pieter."

"You and Colonel Ehrlich are under arrest for being accessories before and after the fact of espionage and murder; conspiracy to commit treason." Jherling said bluntly. "I have orders to use deadly force if you resist."

"Don't be a damn fool Jherling." Ehrlich groaned dragging himself to a chair holding his midsection. "You are arresting an SS General who is an aide to the Reichsfuhrer."

"Who talked you into this insanity?" The Countess asked sharply. "Gerhardt? Schiller?"

"Neither Countess." Fuchs said entering the room with Wulff. "I' m solely responsible, the colonel is only following my orders."

"Treason and Espionage Fuchs?" Von Krieger quipped. "I would have expected something more original from you." The General lit a cigar. "You know you are way over your head in all this."

"I can swim." Fuchs said.

"Never in a thousand years will you be able to make this hold up even in a People's Court." Krieger hissed. "A place where everyone is guilty."

"State security charges." Fuchs said. "Murder is different from them."

"Murder?" Krieger hissed. "The State never commits murder and I represent the State. You are finished Fuchs."

"You are not required to make any statement." Fuchs said dully.

"Have you been bitten by a rabid dog?" Krieger asked savagely. "I reject all these ridiculous charges."

"A confession will greatly aid your case." Fuchs said lighting his pipe. "Clemency would likely be extended to you because of your past services to the Reich."

"Himmler will have your balls on a silver platter for this." Ehrlich threatened.

"I doubt that Himmler will come to the aid of a traitor and spy." Fuchs said.

"I demand you call Berlin." The Countess said bluntly.

"Prisoners have no rights." Wulff snapped. "They don't make demands."

"False charges are not forgotten." The Countess said.

Fuchs reached into his suit coat pocket and handed the General a folded bundle of paper. "I don't work like you-I usually have proof before I arrest someone."

"My confession already typed?" Krieger hissed. "How convenient."

"Read." Fuchs said. "You might find this enlightening enough to decide that a confession might be the best road to take."

"You are a dreamer." Krieger rasped. "This will be one lie after and another."

"A child could see through this." The Countess said icily. "We are adults."

"Read." Fuchs said plainly. "Then decide if it is fabrication and denial would be an act of futility."

They read the papers and handed them back to Fuchs. "Enough to persuade you to make it easy?"

"You haven't told Berlin about this." The Countess said wryly lighting a cigarette.

"I plan to do it in person." Fuchs said.

"Be a foolish policeman." Krieger said calmly.

"You are the prisoners." Fuchs said. "The weather has given you only a temporary reprieve."

"We demand to see Colquhoun." Krieger said.

"That could be arranged." Fuchs said. "Overt acts will hasten your demise Jherling's men will have no compulsions about killing you."

"I will not give you that pleasure Herr Fuchs." Krieger said. "I want to be around when I take everything away from you."

"This is my duty Herr General." Fuchs said. "I derive no joy in this, but the law is the law even for the high and mighty."

"There are always fools like you around." The Countess said icily. "Pity you can't or won't see the truth."

"That is not my job countess "Fuchs said. "I do not judge."

[3]
08:00 hrs

Twickem-Hallesy
Red Boar Pub

"Colonel Taggart, is your room comfortable?" Austen-Halton asked pouring the coffee.
"Quite comfortable sir." Taggart said. "However, you didn't invite me down here for a cup of coffee."
"Right colonel." Crawford said. "The coffee isn't worth the trip."
"Where would be a good posting for Major Colquhoun?" Sir Peter asked wryly.
"You expect Colquhoun to survive?" Taggart said coldly.
"Why shouldn't he?" Crawford asked stiffly.
"I was laboring under the impression that this was a one-way trip for Colquhoun." Taggart said his voice still cold. "Am I wrong?"
"Yes." Crawford said. "Sir Peter asked a question Colonel."
"Home." Taggart said bluntly. "He'll be of little use to us when he gets back sir."
"Home being Georgia." Crawford said.
"You would make the Senator very grateful." Taggart said. "He could find him a nice job with the National Guard office in Atlanta. The Governor owes the Senator many favors."
"That might be unwise Colonel." Sir Peter said. "Medically the major might find it hard to be a local hero."
"Hawaii." Taggart said. "Warm and far away from unpleasant memories and his father."
"Hawaii is an excellent choice." Crawford said. "The Army can afford another Lieutenant Colonel on the books."
"I am afraid that good Colonel Taggart didn't believe you." Sir Peter said in a wry voice lighting his cigar. "I thought you did at excellent job Henry."
"Taggart is no fool." Crawford said. "He knows how the Army really works."
"Promotion and a change of scenery for the good colonel?" Sir Peter quipped.
"Training command in Canada." Crawford said. "The promotion should take the stink out of transfer."
"China would be better." Sir Peter said. "The record must show that an effort was made to bring him out."
"Getting a Senator's son killed is not the best way to continue your career." Crawford said flatly.
"You go back to being a police official." Sir Peter said. "You have that option."

[4]
08:00 hrs

Adlerberghof
Rotekeller Hofbrau

Lang picked up the coffee cup and walked over to the table where Mannerling sat drinking his coffee.

"You took your sweet time getting here." Lang said sitting down. "Donner brought in two bodies." Lang said flatly.

"Who the hell are they?" Mannerling asked as he lit a cigarette.

"They are Eidernau's men." Lang said lighting a cigarette.

"No surprise about that." Mannerling said flatly. "The rest are in the monastery about 60 men."

"Shit, that doesn't sound good." Lang said. "Will they come down in this weather?"

Mannerling took a long deep drag on his cigarette. "I wouldn't, but I don't know about Eidernau."

"He works for profit." Lang said. "Fighting a pitch battle in a blizzard is stupid and unprofitable."

"Pray for continuous bad weather." Mannerling said. "What's going on here?"

"Fuchs arrested Krieger this morning." Lang said flatly.

"Whose bright idea is this?" Mannerling asked.

"Fuchs thought this up himself." Lang said. "Colquhoun is going to cooperate apparently."

Mannerling leaned against the back of the chair suddenly feeling extremely tired and longing for ten years of sleep. "How tightly does Fuchs have Krieger?"

"No guaranteed coffin." Lang said. "He could squirm freely if Colquhoun and a few others turned up conveniently dead."

"Now we know why Eidernau is hanging around." Mannerling said. "As lopsided as the odds are we had to make certain that Colquhoun survives and Krieger goes to Valhalla. If we can't kill him outright we'll have to force him to run."

"Run where?" Lang hissed. "His best chance of living is going to Berlin where his friends are."

"Any where but Berlin." Mannerling said. "As long as he runs it will make him look guilty. Perception can be very deadly especially in Berlin."

"What are you going to do?" Lang asked.

"Sleep." Mannerling said. "You?"

"I'll tell Gerhardt your wonderful news." Lang said grimly.

"Life is sometimes one great big pile of shit Lang." Mannerling said with a dark smile lighting a cigarette. "Sometimes you have to dive into it face first."

[5]

Gasthof Gruenling
Gerhardt's Room

"This Fuchs must be living in a dream world Gerhardt." Franz said flatly after Gerhardt told him about the meeting he just had with Fuchs. "He is a dinosaur."

"He has this illusion he clings to." Gerhardt said lighting a cigarette. "He truly believes in law and justice."

"His precious law was discarded years ago by those bastards in Berlin." Franz hissed dourly. "People like Krieger lie, cheat, maim and murder with impunity as long as they don't embarrass the Party."

"Still takes balls to go after someone like Krieger." Lang said.

"We should tell him about Eidernau's men in the monastery." Franz said. "That is slightly more important."

"Fuchs isn't stupid." Lang said. "If he does ask how we known, Jherling certainly will."

"The weather will stop him for now." Gerhardt said. "Our immediate problem is Krieger's trial."

"Schiller is not objecting to this confrontation." Lang said.

"He wants Krieger dead to rights." Franz said. "Then the old man has to get him to Berlin."

"Unfortunately, we can't allow that." Gerhardt said.

Franz took a deep breath then lit a cigarette. "This is a real pisser when you start to think about it. Are you really prepared to kill your dinosaur?"

"Neither Krieger nor his wife are going to let themselves be packed off to Berlin by some damn cop to be shot." Gerhardt said bluntly. "They'll run and our British friends will kill them."

"Innocent people don't run." Lang said.

"Who says he is innocent?" Gerhardt quipped.

"We couldn't get that lucky." Franz said cynically. "Too outlandish to be true."

"Why is it?" Gerhardt asked.

Lang went to the window looking at the snow coming down. "Why would the Allies be so damn eager to kill him if he is this *Albatross*?"

"Perhaps he has gone rogue?" Gerhardt hissed.

"More likely he went Red." Franz said.

"That's good enough for me." Gerhardt said.

"What if our English friends miss their chance?" Lang asked seriously. "Krieger getting to Berlin will mean we better start learning Russian at best."

"We are not passive observers." Gerhardt said coldly. "We kill them."

"Then what do we do?" Franz asked dourly. "Cut our throats."

"Lie like hell." Gerhardt said firmly.

Chapter Thirty
December 10, 1942
15:00 hrs

Gasthof Gruenling
Calhoun's Room

The Army doctor propped Colquhoun up in the bed as the audience assembled in the manager's office. Fuchs had dressed the stage expertly and the smallness of the room worked in his advantage. Fuchs sat in a chair at the side of the bed with Wulff standing next to him. Krieger, his wife, Ehrlich, and Klugge sat in chairs at the foot of the bed. Schiller, Kohlberger, Heinz, stood on one side of the room, Gerhardt, Lang and Franz on the other side. Missing from this group were Jherling and Mannerling.

"What is your name?" Fuchs asked firmly.

"Jefferson Davis Colquhoun, Major, United States Army." Colquhoun said plainly in German.

"Many people speak German." Krieger hissed. "What about English?"

"I speak fluent English." Colquhoun said coldly. "However, most of you don't so we'll speak German."

"What is your present assignment?" Fuchs asked.

"OSS." Colquhoun answered flatly.

"Do you know that man?" Fuchs asking flatly pointing at the poker faced Krieger.

"Helmuth Krieger." Colquhoun said.

"Do you train dogs as a hobby Herr Fuchs?" The Countess asked coldly. "You have trained him well."

"Get to the point Fuchs." Krieger hissed.

Fuchs lit his pipe. "Do you know Krieger by another name Herr Major?"

"*Albatross*" Colquhoun answered crisply.

"He is trying to save his miserable life by lying." Krieger said. "It is so clearly obvious that he is a desperate man."

"What was the object of your mission Herr Major?" Fuchs asked.

"My orders were to help him incriminate an Abwehr officer falsely." Colquhoun said sourly.

"Incriminate?" Schiller asked. "For what purpose would that accomplish?"

"Make it appear that the Abwehr officer is *Albatross*." Colquhoun said dully.

"You know his identity?" Kohlberger asked.

"I do not." Colquhoun said.

"Why go after this officer in the first place?" Fuchs asked plainly.

"He is most likely getting too close to *Albatross*'s true identity." Colquhoun said. "The reason why is not an operational necessity for me."

"Why pick this place?" Schiller asked.

"Krieger choice this place to meet." Colquhoun answered. "It is remote and near the Swiss border."

"Why did he shoot you?" Wulff asked.

"I thought that would be obvious." Colquhoun hissed.

"Consider us country bumpkins." Schiller rasped.

"Krieger is *Albatross*." Colquhoun said.

"If he is *Albatross*, why did he try to kill you?" Heinz asked bluntly. Colquhoun turned his head looking directly at Krieger.

"He has gone rogue." Colquhoun hissed.

"Too thin Colquhoun." Schiller said.

"He has become a turncoat." Colquhoun said firmly. "He sold out to the Reds."

"THIS ALL LIES! All damnable LIES DAMNIT!" Krieger shouted.

"If he is lying Krieger," Fuchs said in a cold dispassionate voice. "Why are you in Adlerberghof?"

"I can't say." Krieger said bluntly.

"Your life is in the balance." Fuchs said bluntly.

"Go to hell." Krieger said bluntly. "This involves State Security."

"Wrapping yourself in the flag will not save you." Fuchs said. "The law is very clear about that."

Krieger remained silent as he pondered over the limited options he had for staying alive.

"Tell them Helmuth." The Countess said bluntly. "Let them know the truth before they kill you."

"The real Skasch was in possession of a list of allied agents in Europe." Krieger said in a flat voice. "This also reveals the identity of *Albatross*."

"Who is *Albatross*?" Fuchs asked.

"Generalmajor Herbert von Tanz." Krieger answered.

"Impossible." Gerhardt rasped. "He is just throwing out names."

"Why do you find that so hard to believe?" The Countess asked coldly. "You readily believe this enemy agent."

"If your husband had not tried to assassinate Colquhoun this might have the ring of truth." Fuchs said wearily. The million Reich marks worth of American dollars also taints your story."

"Why aren't you suspicious about Gerhardt being here?" Ehrlich asked. "This shit hill of a town is off the beaten track for them."

"That is a point well taken." Fuchs said. "Why are you here Major Gerhardt?"

Gerhardt lit a cigarette. "I was ordered here by Berlin."

"I doubt that only a handful of people could tell you where Adlerberghof is." Schiller said in a flat voice. "Why would Berlin order you here Herr Major?"

"Our people in Switzerland picked up information that Skasch was involved in something." Gerhardt said.

"Skasch was a criminal Major." Kohlberger said. "What could he do that would be of interest to the Abwehr?"

"In a two month period preceding the events here Allied Intelligence couriers had a series of accidents." Gerhardt said.

"Then this list does exist." Schiller said.

"Skasch had put out the word that he was selling this list to the highest bidder." Gerhardt said.

"What happened?" Heinz asked.

"He wasn't as careful as he thought." Gerhardt said. "We believe that he ran afoul of the Russians. The British and Americans took advantage of this and substituted Colquhoun in his place."

"What makes Krieger *Albatross*?" Schiller asked.

"Colquhoun was sent to warn Krieger about the list." Gerhardt said. "Jung's unexpected arrival set off this chain of events."

"Can you prove Krieger is *Albatross*?" Schiller asked.

"No." Gerhardt said.

"The Major spins a fanciful tale." Krieger said coldly. "He is here to protect the Abwehr. How would it look to Berlin if a senior Abwehr officer was a British spy?"

"Can you prove that von Tanz is *Albatross*?" Kohlberger asked.

"Find the list." Krieger said.

"Can you prove it?" Heinz asked bluntly. "Without the list?"

"No." Krieger hissed. "Let me question the prisoner and the truth will flow out."

"Then all you'll have is a corpse on your hands." Gerhardt said bluntly.

"You have reached a dead end Fuchs." Schiller hissed. "Colquhoun has provided little light and no heat."

"Counterespionage is not my job." Fuchs said. "You have dead citizens."

"Murder is more important than treason?" Heinz asked.

"To me it is." Fuchs said.

"What now?" Schiller asked.

"The truth is worth finding." Fuchs said.

"That is a luxury I can't afford." Schiller said. "I need the guilty."

"You really want the truth Fuchs?" Colquhoun asked seriously. "Or are you paying out lip service to protect your butt?"

"He will lie through his teeth." The Countess said harshly.

"Give him to me." Ehrlich said. "I will give you the truth."

"What do you want for this 'truth' Herr Major?" Schiller asked.

"I want nothing." Colquhoun said.

"Truth should be rewarded." Kohlberger said. "Berlin distrusts people who want nothing. We could arrange for POW status with no possibility of exchange. It is better than being dead."

"Being a live POW," Colquhoun said. "Acceptable."

"What is the truth Herr Major?" Fuchs asked.

Colquhoun gestured for a cigarette, which Wulff supplied. Colquhoun took a long deep drag as his eyes glanced across the room at the faces of his audience.

"Everyone has told part of the truth." Colquhoun said. "Everyone has lied."

"Meaning what?" Krieger said. "With your sudden change of status from corpse to prisoner-of-war you decided to tell the whole truth, how convenient."

"The truth often sounds convenient." Colquhoun said. "Protecting you is a mistake; you are just as bad as them. You have become infected."

"Explain." Schiller said bluntly.

"Krieger was defecting." Colquhoun said. "He knew that the Abwehr was getting close to arresting him for High Treason. My job was to bring him over."

"Then he is *Albatross*?" Schiller asked.

"He could be." Colquhoun hissed, "I don't know."

"What about the money?" Kohlberger asked.

"The price of defection comes high." Colquhoun said coldly. "This was supposed to be simple and straight forward, but Krieger got greedy and decided to take the money, but not to defect."

"You don't believe him Schiller?" Krieger asked tersely. "He spins a tale only a child would believe."

"Kill all of them." Kohlberger said. "With them dead our story will be believed by Berlin."

"Berlin won't believe that." Krieger hissed. "Himmler won't believe it."

"Fuchs?" Schiller asked.

"They are my prisoners." Fuchs said bluntly. "When this weather clears I will transport them to Berlin."

"If we object to that?" Heinz asked.

"Colonel Jherling is on my side." Fuchs said. "The good mayor might have little qualms about killing my prisoners along with me, but I don't think he'll kill thirty-five soldiers."

"Don't be a damn fool." The Countess said. "A blind man can see that this is a set up."

"Then you'll have nothing to fear Countess." Fuchs said. "You'll be confined to your rooms from now on. Klugge can bring you your meals."

"You understand what will happen to you if you are wrong Fuchs?" Krieger asked.

"Yes." Fuchs said. "Regardless of what lies ahead I'll deliver you to Berlin."

"I told you I will cooperate." Schiller said. "What if they attempt to leave without escort?"

"Kill them." Fuchs said. "Fleeing would be proof of guilt."

[2]
15:30 hrs

The Monastery

"Are you certain?" Eidernau asked somberly lighting a cigarette. "The weather is bad."

"Yes." Brosch said. "Hagel got in real close. Felix was wearing those officer's boots he took off that dead officer we found."

"What about his hearing?" Eidernau asked.

"That damn farmer Donner again." Brosch said.

"Who told them to go after that damn farmer?" Eidernau asked angrily.

"They were checking the farm out as a matter of course." Brosch said. "Donner must have gone back to the place and found them."

"What about this farmer?" Eidernau asked. "He is making a habit of killing my men."

"From what I can gather he is a local character." Brosch said. "He likes his privacy."

"What does a farmer know about killing people?" Eidernau rasped.

"Was a hero during the last war." Brosch said. "Iron Cross First Class and they made him a damn officer so they could give him the Pour Le Merit."

"Leave him alone." Eidernau said. "What else did Hagel find on his recon?"

"The soldier boys are dug in." Brosch said. "The Gasthof is surrounded and they have two armored cars with 12 mm machine-guns."

"Are we going in?" Zoeller asked.

"That is what we are being paid to do." Willi said.

"Those tin soldiers are not going to let us in or out without a fight." Brosch said.

"Khittsmueller brought ten more men." Eidernau said. "We out number them right now."

"We are facing people who kill for a living." Zoeller said bluntly. "There is no incentive for our people to die for."

Eidernau lit a cigarette. "Spread the word that there is £ 10,000 in the town for them to split up."

"Not enough." Brosch said.

"Pillage the town." Eidernau said knowing that he would have to kill everyone in the town.

"The money will do." Brosch said.

"Do we have to rescue Krieger?" Zoeller asked.

"That is our deal." Willi said. "The people I want walking out of the Gasthof are ours."

"What about the two armored cars?" Zoeller asked.

"Khittsmueller has brought two panzerfausts." Eidernau said. "When he takes out the cars we move in."

"When do we go in?" Brosch asked.

"Soon." Eidernau said. "Send someone to check the route to Switzerland."

"At night I hope?" Zoeller asked sourly.

"Of course Zoeller at night, I want all the advantage." Eidernau said.

[3]
15:30 hrs

Berlin
Tempfehof Airport

Oberleutnant Dentz, their pilot entered the VIP lounge at the airport.

"You bring us more bad news Dentz?" Blausen asked dourly.

"Actually I have good news sir." Dentz said unfolding a weather map.

"You don't have to be technical Herr Oberleutnant." Von Tanz said.

"This weather will clear for two or three hours." Dentz said.

"Meaning what?" Clausborg asked.

"The planes can take off sir." Dentz said.

"This clearing front is moving south?" Blausen inquired.

"You'll be able to get to Jaegerfeld." Dentz said. "From there you'll have to find your own transportation to Adlerberghof."

"Can't you get us closer?" Clausborg asked lighting a cigarette. "They said you were good."

"Jaegerfeld has an airstrip sir." Dentz said.

"Fit the planes with skies." Clausborg said. "You did that in Finland didn't you?"

"Luftwaffe pilots are skillful, not stupid and suicidal." Dentz said bluntly.

"This is not a joy ride Herr Oberleutnant." Clausborg growled.

"Adlerberghof sits in a valley surrounded by the Alps." Dentz said. "Even in excellent weather landing a plane there would be difficult."

"Get the plane ready." Von Tanz said.

"It is being readied as we speak." Dentz said. "OKL will provide us with two escorts."

"Awful nice of them" Blausen said.

"They just want to know where we crash sir." Dentz said with a half smile.

[4]

Adlerberghof
Gasthof Gruenling
Colquhoun's Room

Major Colquhoun feint sleep in order to keep the guards from talking to him while they guarded him. The last few hours had made it clear to him that it had not been chance that brought him here. Crawford and that Limey Austen- Halton must have shifted vigorously through the Army to find the perfect patsy.

They had found the fall guy, a surrogate Judas, to betray Krieger to his masters. It was clear to him that Krieger was not this *Albatross*, but everything pointed to him. Krieger must now realize that he was a walking dead man no matter what he said or did. The pieces of this jigsaw puzzle had fallen into place and Krieger did not need a gypsy fortuneteller to tell him that the only way he could save his life was to run. What the poor bastard did not know was that this is what Crawford and Austen-Halton wanted.

The rap on the door brought the guard to his feet. He slowly opened the door with his pistol drawn, words exchanged and Major Gerhardt replaced him. The Major pulled up a chair and sat next to the bed.

"The guard told me you were faking Herr Colquhoun." Gerhardt said in English. "I have come to say good-bye."

"Damn decent of you." Colquhoun said.

"There are Honors of war Herr Colquhoun." Gerhardt said. "The last remnant of civilized behavior in this uncivilized action we are engaged in."

"There is no honor in war Major or is it civilized." Colquhoun said. "You don't have to pretend to me."

"Do you have any questions?" Gerhardt asked lighting two cigarettes and handing one to Colquhoun.

Colquhoun took a short drag on the cigarette. "What are the odds?"

"No odds being offered." Gerhardt said. "Dead even at best."

"Better than I hoped." Colquhoun said. "Now what will happen?"

"Fuchs will take you to Berlin." Gerhardt said.

"All of us?" Colquhoun asked.

"That is his intention." Gerhardt said. "Getting to Berlin is the only way Fuchs can keep you alive."

"That's simply wonderful." Colquhoun mused. "That old man doesn't have a snowball's chance in hell of getting me out of here alive."

"That won't stop him from trying." Gerhardt said crisply.

Colquhoun nodded and took an extra long deep drag on his cigarette and exhaled the smoke slowly. "That could be extremely unhealthy for me"

"War is an unhealthy business." Gerhardt said.

You aren't *Albatross* by chance?" Colquhoun hissed.

"Hell no, some other bastard has that honor." Gerhardt said.

"Why?" Colquhoun asked. "Can you tell me at least that?"

"We have a mutual problem." Gerhardt said dryly. "This was a solution that benefited both sides."

"That is really great for you Mack." Colquhoun sneered. "Where does it put me?"

"You better take this." Gerhardt said handing Colquhoun a Walther PPK. "It's the best I can do; use it if you have to."

"Rather limited Herr Major." Colquhoun hissed. "An L-pill would be better."

"Survival is the name of the game." Gerhardt said. "Your friends will try to get you out of here. The Walther is for self-defense. Unfortunately Krieger's friends will be doing the same thing, but they will kill you before they leave."

"I can't run far." Colquhoun said plainly.

"We'll try to stop them." Gerhardt said fatalistically. "Save the last bullet for yourself."

"I'll vote for that." Colquhoun said.

[5]
17:00 hrs

Gasthof Gruenling
Dining Room

Fuchs lit his pipe and put down the month-old newspaper as Krieger entered the dining room with Wulff as his escort. Fuchs had expected Krieger to ask for a private meeting; this was the standard operational procedure of a Party insider when caught. This meeting is solely for making the deal. Fuchs motioned for Wulff to leave and gestured for Krieger to take a seat.

"I'm pleased that you agreed to see me," Krieger said. "without your shadow."

"You said alone." Fuchs said. "Your friends in high places don't impress me Herr General. Threats against my family or me will end the conversion quickly. Do I make myself clear?"

"I have no need to resort to those crude methods." Krieger said lighting a cigarette calmly. "You are a reasonable man."

Fuchs removed his glasses and rubbed his eyes slowly. "What do you want, I'm tired."

"You asked me earlier why I am here." Krieger said in a serious tone. "Are you interested in a further explanation or have you closed your mind Herr Direktor?"

"Only a fool closes his mind." Fuchs said. "What do you want to modify?"

"The truth sometimes has the opposite effect of what you want." Krieger said dryly.

"Stop talking in circles." Fuchs said. "Say what you mean Herr General."

"The real Skasch was to bring me a list of names of all the allied agents operating in Europe." Krieger said.

Fuchs tampered his pipe. "You have this list? We searched everyone and found no such list."

"The list does exist." Krieger said.

"It was awful careless of the Allies to lose such a list?" Fuchs asked cynically. "What would possess them to create such a list in the first place?"

"Skasch was a master theft." Krieger said. "It took him months to piece together the list quietly. The Allies have no idea that they have been compromised."

"This *Albatross* on the list I take it?" Fuchs asked.

"He is at the top of the list." Krieger said.

"Who is he?" Fuchs asked bluntly.

"I told you General Von Tanz of the Abwehr." Krieger said. "He must have got wind of this and sent Gerhardt here to stop me."

Fuchs relit his pipe. "Quite interesting Herr General, but General von Tanz could make the same charge against you. Do you have any tangible proof besides this list?"

"What about the attaché cases?" Krieger asked.

"Both have American money." Fuchs said. "You know that transporting foreign currency is illegal."

"This is for the greater good." Krieger said.

"The other case had money from the Rothmann bank." Fuchs said. "Jewish banking house I believe."

"Counterfeit?" Krieger hissed.

"The money is quite real." Fuchs said. "The Rothmann money violates the Nuremberg Laws."

"The money is a plant." Krieger said coldly. "The British are controlled by the Jews."

"That rings a little hollow." Fuchs said flatly. "You were convincing until the last few moments."

"They want me dead." Krieger said bluntly. "That is the bottom line."

"The missing list is a good idea." Fuchs said. "Even if it does exist it would have little bearing on the final outcome of your case."

"What?" Krieger hissed. "If I'm not *Albatross* you have no case."

"On that point I agree." Krieger said. "You are not *Albatross* and exonerate you on the charges of treason and espionage, but not murder."

"What murder?" Krieger's face flushed with rage as he glared at Fuchs. "You still intend to continue with that goddamned insanity?"

"It is hardly insanity." Fuchs said. "You ordered Eidernau to kill Colquhoun. During the commission of that crime, his agent Wassenberg killed Dr. Brandt and a police officer. Since Wassenberg was acting on Eidernau's orders and Eidernau yours makes you guilty of conspiracy to murder, accessory to murder." Fuchs paused. "The Party espouses law and order."

"You have no proof." Krieger said icily. "No witnesses."

"The web you spun to engulf von Tanz will hang you for murder." Fuchs said damningly. "Berlin has executed people on far less circumstantial evidence."

"You are pitiful Fuchs." Krieger said in a haughtily cold voice. "You have nothing and you damn well know it."

"You have committed a crime worse than murder in Berlin's eyes." Fuchs said. "You have caused embarrassment to the Party."

"You are an idealist." Krieger said. "That means you are a relic of the past."

"I'm not the one meeting with a known criminal who had ties to British Intelligence." Fuchs said. "It is common knowledge in police circles that you know Willi Eidernau and have used him in the past. We know that Eidernau works only for you. Wassenberg was a known associate of Eidernau. That would be enough to cause suspicion."

"You are living in a dream world." Krieger said. "There are men in the highest positions of the Party and Government who know slimmer scum than Eidernau."

"You gave the orders." Fuchs said firmly. "Berlin has no idea what you are doing here do they?"

"You are a fool." Krieger said sternly. "A damn fool, you can't be that naive."

"I may be that Herr General." Fuchs said lighting his pipe again. "However, I'm not the one going to Berlin in handcuffs."

Wulff handed Fuchs a cup of coffee. "Did the General offer anything new sir?"

"This list apparently does exist." Fuchs said tiredly. "We better find it Arthur."

"We searched everyone." Wulff said. "No list was found."

"You were looking for paper." Fuchs said. "Skasch was up on the new methods. He mostly reduced the list to microfilm or micro-dot."

"That makes it harder." Wulff said. "You can hide that stuff almost anywhere sir."

"Quite." Fuchs said flatly. "Skasch was the master of the double-cross Arthur. This list could be sitting in a safety deposit box in Switzerland."

"Meaning what sir?" Wulff asked.

"The list might not be here." Fuchs said. "However, Krieger believes it is and that makes him dangerous."

"Shot while attempting to escape will solve many problems sir." Wulff said. "You could use his methods sir as a last resort."

"I haven't sunk to his level yet Arthur." Fuchs said laconically. "I am not an executioner."

"You have killed before sir." Wulff said.

"During the last war because I had to in order to survive." Fuchs said placing his Walther PPK on the table. "I have never fired this in my thirty years with the police."

"Krieger is a mad dog sir." Wulff said. "Killing him would be justified even by Berlin in this case."

"I'll not play by his rules Arthur." Fuchs said. "There is a chessboard in the lobby Arthur, please bring it in here."

[6]

Schiller's Office

Schiller looked out the window and surveyed his deceptively peaceful town. When he first arrived here, Schiller told himself that he was not going to make the mistake of caring for this town. The townspeople, however, treated him with genuine kindness and respect.

"Fuchs did what you wanted Kurt." Heinz said. "You should be happy instead of looking like somebody just pissed on your leg."

"They are still here." Schiller said. "This damn storm has kept them here. The longer they stay here the danger to the town increases."

"Then you believe that Eidernau will come in." Heinz rasped.

"As the day follows night." Schiller said. "We have something he wants Otto. How many men do we have to defend this place?"

"Counting Jherling's men we have about 100." Heinz said. "It will cost Eidernau a heavy price when he shows up. He is figuring on fighting only the professionals not the townspeople. That will be a nasty surprise for him."

"Old men, women and children are a surprise." Kurt said hollowly.

"They are the ones who held off the freebooters during the Thirty Year's War." Heinz said bluntly.

"My job is not to get any more of them killed." Schiller said.

"The weather is helping us at the moment." Otto said. "Why would he come in at all?"

"Eidernau is many things, but he is loyal." Kurt said in a sharp voice. "However, the incentive is the cash- he'll do anything for money. He would burn down the town to make a point."

"You think Fuchs could be talked into killing them?" Heinz asked.

"Doubtful." Kurt said. "It wouldn't bother Gerhardt or Jherling."

"That money would make an excellent bonfire." Heinz said. "Killing them would get rid of a lot of headaches for Fuchs."

"The man has scruples Otto." Schiller said.

"He would." Otto hissed.

Chapter Thirty-One
December 10, 1942
18:00 hrs

Twickem-Hallesy
Halton Manor

Sir Peter took the message from the duty sergeant and walked to his chair by the fireplace.

"Something helpful I hope Peter?" Lord Portlander asked. Viscount Portlander was the deputy director of the section. He had been in Washington the last few weeks attending a conference and had just returned.

"Orr has reported to Green that Krieger has been arrested by a Kripo officer from Stuttgart." Austen-Halton said handing him the message.

"I'll be damned." Crawford said pouring himself a drink. "Then the bastard can't run now."

"Good news." Portlander said.

"That should make Edward's job easier." Sir Peter said removing a cigar from the humidor.

"Perhaps not Peter in this case." Portlander said. "The policeman is an unknown."

"What are you worried about?" Crawford quipped. "The arrest means that Colquhoun has done what we expected him to do."

"Not part of the plan General." Portlander said.

"So what if its not part of the plan, sometimes you have to wing it?" Crawford asked. "That cop must have big steel balls to arrest Krieger."

"That is a reasonable assumption." Austen-Halton said. "This policeman has done us a very large favor."

"The trick will be to make Berlin believe Krieger is *Albatross*." Crawford said.

"We have been discreetly dropping hints from Stockholm to Madrid about him." Sir Peter said crisply.

"We better settle on the absolute solution." Portlander said. "It would serve the cause better if Krieger never leaves the town alive."

"Mannerling has not had a change of orders." Sir Peter said curtly. "Tainting Krieger is a bonus."

[2]
18:00 hrs

Gasthof Gruenling
Krieger's room

"Did he believe you?" Ehrlich asked Helmuth as he entered the room.

"No." Helmuth snarled. "He is incredibly stupid or stubborn. I gave him his chance."

"It is our luck to find an honest man." The Countess said coldly.

"Fuchs wants your head as his final trophy so he can retire with glory." Ehrlich hissed sourly.

"No Albrecht." Krieger said. "Fuchs is an idealist."

"That makes him dangerous." The Countess said. "Everything is black and white to him. Do you know what he wants Helmuth?"

"His only interest is the law." Helmuth said.

"We'll have to kill him" Ehrlich said. "And that piss ant Wulff."

The Countess raised her hand to silence Ehrlich. "Klugge, they seem to have no interest in you, keep an eye on Fuchs and Wulff please."

"Yes madam." Klugge said. "You want anything done?"

"Just watch Hauptscharfuhrer." The Countess said.

"Yes madam." Klugge said.

"What in hell was that all about?" Ehrlich asked after Klugge had left the room.

"Klugge is a servant." The Countess said. "He might have to make a sacrifice."

"I can't see Klugge as a sacrifice?" Helmuth hissed.

"He is your enlisted aide." The Countess said coldly. "Not your brother. Klugge has always understood sacrifice."

"Getting him killed senselessly would be a waste." Krieger said sharply.

"Klugge is a hard man to kill Helmuth." The Countess said. "He is a survivor."

Krieger nodded his head. "Okay about Klugge. What about Eidernau, is he still out there?"

"He is not going anywhere." The Countess said. "He knows about the money."

"Being mercenary has its advantages." Krieger said flatly. "He understands what has to be done?"

"No witnesses." Ehrlich said coldly. "You understand that killing over 200 people might produce at least one or two survivors."

"We are getting 100% results in the camps." Krieger said.

"The people here are not Jews." Ehrlich hissed.

"How are you going to explain this?" The Countess asked.

"We could say it was a RAF terror bombing." Krieger answered.

"Who'll believe that?" Ehrlich growled.

"Berlin invented the big lie." Krieger said caustically.

"Berlin will investigate." The Countess said sharply. "Even a Party hack would see instantly that the town wasn't destroyed by bombs." The Countess lit a cigarette. "You should reconsider Helmuth. Only a handful of the people know what is going on. Let's be realistic Helmuth." The Countess said. "Wiping this cesspool off the map would not bother me in the least, but this time overkill might not be the solution."

"Do I hear a plea for moderation from you?" Krieger hissed glaring at his wife.

"She is being pragmatic Helmuth." Ehrlich said. "Kill the direct threat."

"That is understood." Krieger said. "Then what do we do pray?"

"You are the only man qualified to succeed Heydrich." The Countess said in a serious voice. "Himmler will understand that this is a smear."

"He really wants a nonentity." Krieger said. "With the List I had the master prize he couldn't ignore."

"You have an alternative?" The Countess asked.

"Yes." Helmuth said flatly.

"Where is it?" The Countess asked.

"Paraguay." Helmuth said.

"I'm not the peon type." Elsa rasped.

"Hardly the idea I had in mind." Helmuth said. "You have prewar holdings throughout South America. With Colquhoun's money we can live in comfort while we liquefied the holdings." Krieger lit a cigarette. "Albrecht you kill the principles personally."
"Kill Willi too?" Ehrlich asked.
"Kill him anyway." Helmuth said. "He knows too much."

[3]
19:00 hrs

The Cavern

Brother Hugo unfolded the parchment and laid it on the table. "As you can see this whole mountain is honeycomb with tunnels."
"How old is this map?" Carey asked.
"It was drawn in 1756." Hugo said. "They stopped mining a hundred years later. This does not show the private tunnels."
"What about the private tunnels?" Orr asked.
"Almost every house in the villages had a tunnel leading into the main tunnels." Hugo said. "They were all looking for gold; it took them a long time to realize that the gold was never here. Most have been sealed off."
"The tunnel to the Gruenling sealed?" Orr asked.
"No it is not." Hugo said. "The former owner of the hotel was a pragmatic man and did extensive renovations."
"Do your unwelcome guests know about the tunnels?" Browne asked.
"They have knowledge of them." Hugo said flatly.
"You wouldn't have any high explosives lying around Brother Hugo?" Orr asked frankly.
"Will TNT do?" Hugo inquired.
"It will do." Orr said.
"How did you manage to keep that around?" Browne hissed.
"Tree stumps." Hugo said flatly.

[4]
19:20 hrs

The Boathouse

Lang entered the boathouse and found Mannerling waiting for him. Lang placed a bottle of brandy on the table.
"I hope you have good news." Lang asked lighting a cigarette.
"Depends on what you call good news." Mannerling said dryly. "Eidernau has close to a hundred men now."
"Wonderful." Lang grunted. "Is there any chance that Jherling can get something heavier than armored cars?"
"Mountain troops don't normally have heavy tanks." Mannerling said. "However, Jaegerfeld is a training center. He might have Mark IVs, but this weather makes that impossible." Lang sat down at the table. "Regardless Eidernau will come in within the next 30 hours."

"I agree with that." Lang conceded. "Do you have anything else as cheerful?" Lang poured himself a drink. "What are you and your friends going to be doing when he does arrive?"

"The train crew is going to bring the train back to Jaegerfeld." Mannerling said.

"When are they leaving?" Lang asked. "Fuchs can ride back in comfort."

"Neither the train crew nor the station master are going to tell anyone they are leaving." Mannerling said.

"Shouldn't we whisper this to someone?" Lang asked.

"We'll never be allowed on the train." Mannerling answered. "I prefer everyone stays close."

"Returning to Eidernau, what do we intend to do?" Lang asked.

"We'll try to cut down the odds." Mannerling said.

"Fuchs will move him to Berlin eventually." Lang said. "Perhaps during this oncoming confusion there might be a slim chance of rescuing Colquhoun."

"Where do we take him?" Mannerling asked.

"Head for Jaegerfeld." Lang said. "Then make a sharp turn and run like hell to Switzerland."

"We aren't the only ones who'll be heading for him." Mannerling said firmly.

"We will provide the best cover possible." Lang said.

"What about you?" Mannerling asked. "The odds of surviving are slim."

"It takes a lot to kill me." Lang said.

Gerhardt' Room

Klugge turned on the table lamp as Gerhardt entered the room. Gerhardt lowered the P-38 on seeing who it was.

"The judge should invest in new locks." Klugge said wryly.

"Good way to get shot." Gerhardt said. "Anyone see you come in here?"

"No one sees me." Klugge said.

"Get lonely?" Gerhardt asked sitting down.

"Krieger is making travel plans." Klugge said flatly. "They don't include a trip to Berlin."

"That will disappoint Fuchs." Gerhardt said.

"Before he leaves the General plans to rid himself of nuisances." Klugge said lighting a cigarette.

"Meaning us I assume." Gerhardt hissed.

"You are quite correct." Klugge said. "Krieger has no intentions of leaving this shit hole without leaving all of you in a permanent condition of non-communication."

"You are going to help him?" Gerhardt asked plainly.

"Their plans don't include me." Klugge said. "I'm to be sacrificed for the cause. Eidernau is supposed to do all the killing."

"The American will be the prime target?" Gerhardt asked.

"He would be my choice." Klugge said. "Do you plan to get him out?"

"Plans are being made as we speak." Gerhardt said. "When is Krieger planning to leave?"

"Watch the weather." Klugge said.

"What are you going to do?" Gerhardt asked.

"When the shooting starts I will survive." Klugge said. "I've beaten the odds for too long, nothing lasts forever."

[5]
20:30 hrs

Jaegerfeld
Airfield

Major Utlaut paced the floor of the control tower nervously as he waited for the arrival of the JU-52 from Berlin. Utlaut nearly had a shock when he received a telephone call from General Dietermann, the Area commander. The general informed him that a JU-52 was coming with VIPs, to give them the red carpet treatment.

The JU-52 circled the field once and landed. The staff car pulled up to the JU-52 and the passengers disembarked into the staff car. The car brought them to the headquarters' building. Utlaut snapped to attention and saluted as the three general officers entered the office.

"Oberstleutnant Jherling?" Von Tanz asked after returning the salute.

"No Herr General." Utlaut said. "Major Utlaut."

"You are the Adjutant?" Blausen asked.

"Yes sir." Utlaut said.

"We need privacy Major." Von Tanz said.

"You have that sir." Utlaut said. "Berlin did not explain why you are here or who you are sir?"

"Understandable." Von Tanz said. "I am Generalmajor von Tanz, Generalmajor Blausen and Generalmajor Clausborg." Von Tanz said handing Utlaut his written orders. "We expect your full cooperation."

Utlaut read the orders then looked at each man. "Help with what Herr General? The orders are vague."

"They are meant to be." Von Tanz said seeing that Utlaut was the cautious type as well as being intelligent. "Where is Jherling?"

"Is he in the habit of not being here Herr Major?" Clausborg asked tartly.

"The colonel is a dedicated officer sir." Utlaut said bluntly. "He has gone to Adlerberghof."

"Is he on a training exercise Herr Major?" Blausen asked lighting his cigar.

"The Burgermeister requested his help." Utlaut said. "The Mayor is also the Party District Leader."

"What is his name?" Clausborg asked.

"Kurt Schiller." Utlaut answered.

"Did Herr Schiller mention what sort of trouble?" Von Tanz asked.

"No." Utlaut said.

"Are you going to help Herr Major?" Blausen asked.

"I need to know what is going on in order to co-operate Herr General." Utlaut said in a firm voice.

"Need to know." Von Tanz said bluntly. "You don't need to know. This has the highest state security clearance and a brilliant career is at stake."

"What would you do sir?" Utlaut asked.

"I would be skeptical like you." Von Tanz said. "However, in the end I would cooperate with the reality."

"How may I help Herr General?" Utlaut asked.

"You will assemble the battalion." Von Tanz said. "How long will it take?"

"That should take forty-five minutes sir." Utlaut said.

"Faster?" Blausen asked.

"Men are in town sir." Utlaut said. "It will take time for the Provost to round them up."

"I want to be on the road within two hours." Von Tanz said. "I want maximum ammunition for each man."

"Do you want an officers' call?" Utlaut asked.

"No." Von Tanz said.

Blausen lit his cigar after the major left. "The good major will contact Jherling."

"I assumed that he would." Von Tanz said. "I would be worried if he didn't."

"The Major has questions." Clausborg said. "You don't bring in the Alpine Corps for a tea party."

"He won't ask them." Blausen said. "But he is smart enough not to do that just yet."

"Where is the nearest Luftwaffe base?" Von Tanz asked.

"The closest I believe is Fendalhof." Blausen answered. "Why?"

"Back up." Von Tanz said as Major Utlaut entered the room. "Yes Herr Major?"

"I have received a report from the stationmaster that the train that was in Adlerberghof has left." Utlaut said.

"How long before it gets here Utlaut?" Clausborg asked.

"In this weather maybe three or four hours sir." Utlaut said.

"Tell the stationmaster I want enough cars added to bring the rest of the battalion to Adlerberghof." Von Tanz said.

"General Dietermann will have to be informed sir." Utlaut said plainly.

"I'll speak with Dietermann." Von Tanz said. "You get the battalion ready."

[6]
20:00 hrs

Twickem-Hallesy
Halton Manor

Mikhailov walked to the French doors that lead to the main garden and lit the American cigarette. Sir Peter and Crawford had left him in the drawing room to attend to some matter. Mikhailov was amused that they left him alone in the room, a practice never done with the GRU or the NKVD. Sergei knew that once they returned Sir Peter would continue his gentle probe for information of *Boris* and Mikhailov would continue his dance with Sir Peter. Moscow disliked giving any information to anyone especially foreigners. Sergei knew that Sir Peter had more than a professional association with *Albatross*. Mikhailov had the feeling that Austen-Halton might have known him in a former life.

On the other hand, Mikhailov did not have the luxury of knowing *Boris* personally, but he did have his unofficial dossier and other information about him. *Boris'* real name was Maxim Sergeiovich Blenkov. In 1914, Blenkov was a Lieutenant in the intelligence department of the

Tsarist Army. Unknown to the Tsarist military was that Blenkov was a Bolshevik and a friend of Josef Stalin.

During the first three years of the First World War Blenkov served as an agent in Germany. It was not until Lenin made peace with Germany in 1917 that Captain Blenkov returned to St. Petersburg. Blenkov, after a secret meeting with Stalin in St. Petersburg, the Chekka arrested Blenkov. Later Tass later reported that the Chekka shot him in May of 1918. Under extreme secrecy, Blenkov was smuggled across the border; joining the German Army in June 1918.

Blenkov left a wife and infant son in St. Petersburg. As the family of an enemy of the state were arrested then sent to a prison camp in central Russia for six months. Then with no explanation, they were released from prison and moved secretly to Kiev with her son to live with an uncle. In 1923, Anna was allowed to marry a nonparty Army engineer, who adopted the boy.

During the Great Purges when Stalin was settling old scores with real and imagined enemies. In late 1936, the NKVD arrested Anna, her husband and son. They were brought to Moscow and thrown in Lubiyanka prison. Within 24 hours of their arrival, they were released without explanation and transported to a village near the Ural Mountains. Anna's husband was promoted to colonel and placed in charge of building an irrigation system. It was not until Sergei joined the GRU that he learned that the overzealous NKVD officer who had arrested them was shot on Stalin's orders.

Only a few months before the war begun Sergei's mother Anna Blenkov Mikhailov told him the truth about his father. Colonel Khachenovoky, and old family friend, confirmed what his mother told him. For some reason, Stalin wanted Sergei to know the truth. What he could not tell Sir Peter was that *Boris* and Dieter Klugge was the same man once known as Maxim Blenkov.

"It looks as it will be a long Colonel." Sir Peter said moving up next to him.

"It seems like they all are long Sir Peter." Mikhailov said removing a cigarette from the gold cigarette case. "May I ask a personal question Sir Peter?"

"Ask Colonel." Sir Peter said.

"You know *Albatross* personally." Mikhailov said.

"I do." Sir Peter said. "Each year was the hope he could come home; each year he stayed."

"Then you understand my feelings about *Boris*." Mikhailov said stoically.

"There is always hope Colonel." Sir Peter said. "The fire in the living room has been lit and brandy is available."

"Do they have a chance?" Mikhailov asked.

"They have that." Sir Peter said.

[7]

The Monastery

Eidernau lit a cigarette as he stood on the small balcony that over looked the great hall, which the monks used as a communal dining hall. "Get the men ready. I want them clean nothing to identify them."

"Then what Willie?" Hothman asked. "Do you want the uniforms on?"

"No." Eidernau said. "How long will it take the train to get to Jaegerfeld?"

"In this weather I would say three hours." Hothman answered.

"Give them two hours to refuel the train and load up the whole battalion which will give us a six hour window to finish this up." Eidernau said.

"What about them?" Hothman asking motioning towards the monks below them.

"Hinting what? Willi asked

"They know too much Willie." Hothman said. "They can identify us."

"They are Trappist monks, they don't speak." Eidernau said sourly.

"Brother Fritz can speak." Hothman said flatly. "That old bird isn't afraid of much."

"Leave Geiger here with four men." Eidernau said dully. "Tell him to wait an hour before he does anything."

"We better get a big pay off for this work." Hothman grunted. "Not a lousy few thousand marks either. Once we kill them we can't stay here that is for damn sure."

"The Nazis are not very religious." Eidernau hissed.

"The people around here are." Hothman said. "You can't kill thirty unarmed monks without Berlin going crazy."

"We take all the money." Eidernau said. "Krieger can have the glory."

An Honorable Betrayal

Chapter Thirty-Two
December 11, 1942
04:00 hrs

Adlerberghof
Gasthof Gruenling

    Gerhardt entered the lobby of the Gasthof and sat down on the large leather chair by the fireplace. Gerhardt took the cigarette butt and tossed it into the fireplace. He glanced over at Fuchs and Wulff quietly playing chess. Anton had briefly toyed with the idea of telling Fuchs the truth about what was really going on. However, after further thought Anton decided that opening this Pandora's Box would cause questions that could not be answered without placing their necks in a noose.
    Anton lit another cigarette and took a long deep drag slowly exhaling the smoke. Gerhardt was tired, bone-tired of this damn thing. This entire situation was a direct result of trying to stop Krieger's crusade against General von Tanz. Anton had no idea if this *Albatross* really existed or was the creation of someone's fertile imagination, but the simple fact was that Krieger believed he existed and that von Tanz was him.
    Anton could see Von Tanz's activities were bordering on possible treason; a line you did not crossed. Anton had already assumed that von Tanz had Carnaris tacit approval to help the resistance movement. Gerhardt also knew that the Allies viewed the German resistance with uneasiness to outright hostility. Himmler viewed them as a nuisance hardly worth the effort to track them down.
    The Major leaned his head against the back of the chair feeling the weariness surge through his body. He was still a young man but three years of warfare had drained him. Anton glanced over at Fuchs who was over twice his age hardly seemed affected by the strain. This plain ordinary police officer from Stuttgart was the only real hero in this whole mess though Fuchs did not know it. This, however, did not tarnish what Fuchs had unwontedly done. Another person of lesser character might have closed his eyes and walked away. Fuchs had to have an inner reservoir of courage to stand up to a man as dangerous as Krieger.
    Fuchs had most likely achieved his greatest victory, but Anton had the feeling that it could be his last. The powers-that-be in Berlin might outwardly appreciate his zealousness in bringing someone like Krieger down, but they privately would seek away to punish him. They would promote him or give a medal then post him to some remote spot. Anton was quite certain that Fuchs would see what they were doing and retired.
    Gerhardt looked at his watch knowing that with the change in the weather Eidernau would be coming in. Gerhardt knew that telling Fuchs that would hardly change his mind and being too honest had its disadvantages. Fuchs's instinct would be to arrest him immediately and the others, but Anton hoped that Fuchs would be intelligent enough to realize that this was all above his head. His being here was a fluke and not part of the plan. Anton stood up shaking off his weariness and headed towards Fuchs. He was halfway there when a massive explosion hurled him against the front desk.

[2]

"Jherling reports everything quiet and Adlerberghof is a sleep sir." Wulff said somberly sipping his hot chocolate.

"You worry too much Arthur." Fuchs said moving his bishop to check the king. "We'll be in Stuttgart soon enough." Fuchs relit his pipe. "It is your move."

"Why are we heading for Stuttgart, sir?" Wulff quipped moving his knight to block the bishop. "I thought we were going to Berlin directly."

"That was a tactical and necessary deception." Fuchs said. "We have more friends in Stuttgart than Berlin."

"Stuttgart will be paradise." Wulff said icily. "The vultures will be heading to Berlin and we can leave this tomb. How do people stand living here?"

"I was born in a small town like this." Fuchs said picking up his cup of hot chocolate and taking a sip. "I wouldn't mind retiring to someplace like this."

"Really sir, like this place?" Wulff said. "I doubt your wife shares your feelings."

"We could afford a small chalet perhaps." Fuchs quipped.

The younger police officer's face turned serious. "I looked outside sir, the weather is changing. This beautiful snowstorm will no longer protect us. Eidernau will be coming in."

"He has to." Fuchs said dryly. "He has lost men, and the prize is still here. Honor is a funny thing."

"No way of avoiding this is there sir?" Wulff lamented.

"Yes there is." Fuchs said flatly. "Let Krieger go."

"That you will not do sir I know that." Wulff said firmly. "Even if you did, Krieger would never allow this insult to go unchallenged."

"I could give Eidernau the money." Fuchs said. "He loves money."

"Jherling can give us armed escort to Jaegerfeld sir." Wulff said. "We can fly to Stuttgart from there. Eidernau isn't that brave to take on a battalion of regulars in the open."

Fuchs said nothing for a long moment. Wulff reminded him of his youngest son who had been killed when the *Bismarck* sank. Fuchs dutifully displayed his picture with the Iron Cross on his mantel. "Krieger wants to live as much as we do."

"He'll try to send as many of us to Valhalla as he can." Wulff said firmly. "He will start with our friend in the room."

"I do understand that Arthur." Fuchs said. "Kill him if it looks hopeless, that is the most merciful thing I could do for him."

"Yes." Wulff said softly.

Fuchs looked over at Major Gerhardt as he entered the Gasthof lobby and sat down. He wondered what would he be doing now instead of being here if his curiosity about why Schiller's request had gone unanswered. Fuchs felt no pity for the Kriegers or Ehrlich. They lived in the world of Nazi law and they would die by it. The only 'innocent' in this rotten mess was the American Colquhoun.

This damn poor American had been clearly set up by his own people to be some kind of a stalking horse. His superiors in London were hoping that Colquhoun would break and he did what was expected of him. Unfortunately, for Colquhoun, his fate was sealed once he talked. For different reasons, neither side could allow him to live to a ripe old age. London had two choices about Colquhoun, kill him or rescue him. Fuchs tampered his pipe bowl with his finger confident that he had helped Colquhoun a bit by moving him to another room secretly while keeping the illusion that the American was in the manager's room.

Fuchs then looked over at Gerhardt knowing that the young major was involved in this deeply. He had read the reports about the inept Resistance movement, but this time they were getting help. Fuchs relit his pipe being glad that he was not political in any sense of the word. Fuchs saw Gerhardt get up from his chair and move towards him an instant before the lobby exploded into a torrid of flying furniture people and smoke.

[3]

Lang's Room

Lang looked out the window seeing that the wind and snow were lessening which made an attack more likely than not.

"You put that extra uniform away?" Lang asked.

"In the pottery shop across the alley." Franz said. "You have any idea where our English friend is?"

"I saw him wandering around the town." Lang said. "Our friends the policemen keeping up the illusion?"

"Fuchs is a good actor." Franz said lighting a cigarette checking the MP-40 Jherling had given him. "He doesn't suspect we know he moved the American."

"I wished he moved him out of the Gasthof." Lang said pulling back the slide of the P-38 and slowly lowering the hammer of the pistol. "This place is a prime target."

"I rather kill Krieger first." Franz said.

"Our friends want the American saved." Lang said. "A small favor."

Lang had just moved from the window when the explosion rocked the Gasthof. Lang was slammed against the wall; Franz was knocked to the floor. They quickly gathered their senses and dashed out the room as a cloud of dust and smoke bellowed up the staircase filling the hallway. Sporadic gunfire was now sounding outside the Gasthof as they groped their way down the hallway heading towards the American's room.

They found the room door locked and gunfire coming from inside the room. Franz stepped back, sprayed the door lock with his machine pistol, and kicked the door in.

"Don't shoot!" Lang hissed looking at the two bodies laying on the floor and Colquhoun sitting on the bed holding a pistol. "Gerhardt sent us."

"They were inside the room before the explosion." Colquhoun hissed.

"Can you move?" Franz asked.

"Yeah." Colquhoun hissed. "I need boots."

"I'll get them." Franz rasped moving towards the boots when two more of Eidernau's men rushed into the room shooting. Franz fell to the floor with a bullet in his left leg. Lang and Colquhoun cut them down.

"How bad?" Lang growled.

"All right!" Franz snapped struggling to his feet. "Get him the hell out of here now before more company arrives!" Lang grabbed Colquhoun and disappeared into the hallway.

Franz removed his belt and tied it around his left leg to slow down the bleeding. He hobbled over to the room door and closed it bracing a chair against it. He then grabbed one of the dead thugs and tossed him in the bed covering him with a blanket. He blew out the oil lamp sending the room into total darkness. Franz limped over to the bureau and sat in the chair next to it.

Franz did not have to wait long. The door burst open and three more men rushed into room. They fell into twisted heaps as Franz cut them down. Franz tossed the MP to the floor and drew his pistol. Another cluster of men charged into the room shooting. Franz dropped two more before a burst of MP fire caught him in the chest knocking him out of the chair.

As he lay on the floor, Franz saw Ehrlich enter the room with two more men. The colonel stopped by the bed and emptied a full magazine into the figure on the bed. Franz smiled slightly as he saw Ehrlich leave. The smile slowly left Franz's face as death finally came for him after knowing the trick had worked.

Lang carried and dragged Colquhoun down the rear stairs of the Gasthof as hell erupted inside. He dragged him across the alley to the pottery shop. Lang placed the American in a chair.

"Get rid of your identity discs!" Lang said to Colquhoun as he opened the brown paper wrapped bundle on the counter. "Put these on." Lang handed him a set of German ID tags.

"What the hell is going on?" Colquhoun hissed weakly.

"Only a handful of people know what you look like." Lang said briskly. "Bandages around the face and the Luftwaffe uniform should hide you until we get you across the border."

"Christssake." Colquhoun wheezed.

"Damn it, help me." Lang rasped.

The explosions and gunshots echoed all around them as Lang dressed Colquhoun as quickly as possible. Lang was going to bring them to Donner's high meadow barn until this mess died down. As they left the pottery shop and moved up the alley two figures stepped in front of them. Lang lifted up his pistol and fired. One of the figures tumbled to the ground, but the second managed to throw something at them. The hand grenade explosion knocked both of them to the ground.

[5]

Wulff slowly rose from the floor shaking his head trying to clear his head amid the lobby, which was in an eerie semi-darkness filled with smoke from the dozens of small fires spread across it. The taste of warm blood filled his mouth as he crawled over to the motionless Fuchs. Wulff checked the old man's pulse and found him barely breathing but alive.

Wulff leaned back against the wall to collect his thoughts as gunfire exploded in and outside the Gasthof. He heard people coming down the main staircase. Wulff pushed himself up to his feet drawing his pistol.

"HALT!" Wulff shouted firing his pistol. The man standing next to Krieger tumbled down the stairs.

"Don't be stupid Inspector." Krieger rasped. "Bow to overwhelming force."

"Drop your weapons!" Wulff snapped. "You are prisoners!"

"Dead heroes are worth nothing." The Countess said. "Drop your weapon Inspector and live… keep the old man alive."

"Enough talk." Eidernau hissed firing his MP at Wulff. The Inspector collapsed to the floor like a rag doll. "Where is my money?"

"The manager's office." The Countess said coldly.

"Zoeller." Eidernau ordered. "It won't take long for Jherling to get his men reorganized."

"Where are we going?" The Countess hissed.

"I have a rally point." Eidernau said crisply. "The money better be there."
"It will be." Krieger said. "Klugge, finish off Gerhardt and Fuchs and catch up to us."
"Yes sir." Klugge said flatly.

[6]

Mannerling watched the two men with the panzerfausts moved cautiously down the hill towards them. They arrived at a position behind one of the many stonewalls that ran through the woods. He then pushed himself through the snow towards them trying to get into range. Mannerling was still too far away to stop the first rocket from firing. Mannerling saw the first armored car burst into flame followed almost immediately by the second one. Mannerling zeroed in and shot the closest man as he shouldered the panzerfaust for a second shot. The other man turned to fire his panzerfaust at Mannerling when he dropped to the ground with a bullet in his forehead.

All hell broke out in the town below. Mannerling hurried down the hill towards the Gasthof knowing that it would be a prime target. Mannerling took down several of the attackers before reaching the square. He tossed his rifle and picked up one of Jherling's men Mauser 42 semiautomatic rifle and all the extra magazines he could carry.

Mannerling kicked in the front door of the silversmith shop and entered the shop. He was heading to the rear of the shop when three of Eidernau's men entered. They were more interested in looting the shop that they did not notice Mannerling until it was too late. Mannerling fired three quick shots dropping all three. One of them was not quite dead and managed to fire a shot. Mannerling felt the bullet hit his left arm pushing him into the wall; Mannerling emptied the rifle into the man.

Mannerling moved out of the shop, his left arm throbbing despite the bandage. He got only a few yards from the shop. Mannerling heard the shots an instant before he spun around and collapsed to the ground from the bullet that had creased his skull. Mannerling felt the warm blood stream down the side of his face as the blackness engulfed him.

Chapter Thirty-Three
December 11, 1942
06:30 hrs

Adlerberghof

    Mannerling slowly rose from the ground as the sun started to rise; the reddish-orange light shone through the trees. Mannerling touched his forehead feeling the dry blood on it and his left arm throbbed lightly from the gunshot wound, the bullet had creased his arm. In the growing light, he saw the carnage and destruction that had gone on during the night. Bodies were scatted all over the Town Square, but only a few buildings were badly damaged and the smell of burnt wood filled the air. Mannerling picked up a rifle and started to walk towards the Gruenling Gasthof.

    The Gasthof seemed to have survived the night with fire damage. Three of Jherling's men were guarding the front entrance, only lowering their weapons after recognizing him. Mannerling spoke a few words to them and then entered the Gasthof lobby. Once inside he saw Orr, in his German uniform, being helped by a medic. The captain saw the Major and motioned him to sit down.

    "What a bloody mess." Mannerling hissed to Orr after the medic had attended him. "Where is everyone?"

    "Don't know." Orr rasped handing Mannerling a cigarette. "Carey is dead, Browne wounded"

    "What happened?" Mannerling asked.

    "We had a little trouble at the monastery. I'll tell you about it later." Orr said. "I heard someone say that Franz got himself killed too."

    "Great news." Mannerling rasped. "Krieger?"

    "Looks like he made it." Orr said.

    "Damn." Mannerling hissed. "Gerhardt?"

    "I got hit just as I showed up." Boyden said.

    "How the hell did you get here?' Mannerling asked.

    "This place is honeycombed with tunnels." Orr said vaguely. "What in hell do we do now?"

    "Play out the hand." Mannerling said. "Try to slip out quietly before someone decides to look closely at you."

    Mannerling moved into the dinning room and found Colonel Jherling sitting by a wall with his tunic open and a bandage wrapped around his chest.

    "Battalion commanders aren't supposed to get shot sir." Mannerling said.

    "That is a falsehood." Jherling said weakly. "Gerhardt thought you might be dead Lieutenant."

    "I'm hard to kill sir." Mannerling said. "Krieger survived?"

    "Yes." Jherling said flatly. "The bastard slipped out, but I have men on his trail."

    "The cost?" Mannerling asked.

    "28 townspeople, 7 policemen, 8 of Schiller's bodyguard, 17 of my men." Jherling said dryly. "Double that on the wounded."

    "The cops from Stuttgart sir?" Mannerling asked.

    "Wulff is dead." Jherling said hollowly. "Fuchs is barely holding on."

"The Yank sir?" Mannerling asked.
"Haven't found him yet." Jherling said. "That might take days."
"Any good news sir?" Mannerling asked somberly.
"Reinforcements should be here in two hours." Jherling hissed. "Gerhardt is wandering around somewhere."

[2]

Fuchs was sitting propped up in a large leather chair. He was heavily bandage but Fuchs did not have to be told that he was a dying man and moving him to the hospital in Jaegerfeld would be a waste of time.
"Inspector Wulff?" Fuchs hissed.
"He is dead." Schiller said. "He was a good man."
"Damn me to hell." Fuchs hissed weakly. "I got him killed."
"Krieger killed him." Schiller said. "I killed him. If I hadn't brought you into this mess he would still be alive."
"We both made mistakes." Fuchs wheezed.
Schiller looked at Gerhardt then back at Fuchs. "Colonel Jherling could bring your wife here?"
"No." Fuchs said. "I'll be dead before she got here… No need to put her through that."
"I'm sorry." Schiller said.
"No need to be." Fuchs said. "Krieger?"
"He escaped." Gerhardt said bluntly. "Jherling has men tracking him right now."
"You have to catch him." Fuchs hissed.
"The bastard knows how to run." Schiller said. "His party is still heavily armed."
"The American?" Fuchs asked.
"We are searching for him." Gerhardt said.
"Do you want him brought back here?" Schiller asked Fuchs.
"I want him dead." Fuchs coughed. "Stone cold dead."

[3]

"How far is the goddamned chalet?" Teller asked in an exhausted voice.
"Not far." Eidernau huffed.
"Why not the monastery?" Lutzen asked. "We would have been there by now!"
"That's where they would look for us first and I don't want them to find what I left there." Eidernau said raising the field glasses.
"What did you do at the monastery?" The Countess asked tartly.
"I left no witnesses." Eidernau said bluntly.
"An operational necessity." Krieger hissed. "What about our friends?"
"Since we stung them a while back they are following the tracks." Eidernau said. "The damn snow makes it easy."
"Split up." Ehrlich rasped.
"Go to hell." Teller hissed.
"Stop whining." The Countess snapped.

"Sixteen people leave a big trail." Zumwald rasped scratching his beard. "We are no longer a secret."

"I know damnit." Krieger growled. "We keep on going."

Teller looked at Eidernau who said nothing. "Then why in hell are we going to this goddamn chalet instead of heading for the border with the loot."

"I cross the border they'll brand me a traitor." Krieger hissed.

"I think they have that idea already." Schimdt grunted.

"Christ, of all people, you should know you can't deal with Berlin." Zumwald said in a coldly blunt voice. "You have nothing to deal with."

"I'm not holding an empty hand." Krieger said firmly.

"Across the border we will be safe." Teller said sternly. "Who wants to crossover the border and live? Who is with me?"

Teller was met with stony silence and blank faces from his colleagues. He saw that none of them were about to make a move with Willi and his friends were still breathing.

"Are you all fools?" Teller growled. "You all want to be heroes and die?"

"You can go Teller." Willi said icily. "Nobody is stopping you or anyone who wants to go with you."

"My share?" Teller asked.

"You haven't finished the job Teller." Willi said flatly.

"Nothing was said about suicide." Teller barked.

"Move out Teller." Willi ordered lighting a cigarette as he turned his back on Teller.

Teller's right hand moved for his pistol. The sharp crack echoed through the woods and Teller slowly sank to the ground with a bullet in his forehead from the Countess' pistol.

"Any other objections?" Krieger snapped.

"I could have killed him quietly." Willi said putting his throwing knife away. "Now they know where we are."

"Zumwald and Schimdt." Krieger said sharply. "You stay here and decoy our friends away from us. Kill them if you can, but lead them away from us."

"You call that a chance?" Zumwald hissed.

"Better than Teller's." Willi said. "Lead them to the border, but throw away your weapons before you cross over or the Swiss border guards will shoot you."

"How do we get our cut?" Zumwald asked.

"I'll send you a wire." Eidernau said coldly.

[4]

Oberfeldwebel Schnell halted the patrol on seeing the body lying in the snow about 30 meters away.

"This looks too easy." Obergefreiter Theicke hissed lowering the field glasses. "I smell an ambush."

"We have to find out anyway." Schnell said motioning two men to the left and two to the right. "You are next in line for promotion to sergeant aren't you?"

"I prefer to be alive to receive it." Theicke said with a slight smile. "Right up the middle again."

"Hell- of- a- way to get a wound badge." Schnell hissed as Loften, the medic, bandaged his head as he sat down by a tree.

"They weren't trying to kill us." Theicke said lighting his pipe. "Good tactics."

"JA, very good." Schnell said. "Did you get them?"

"One of them." Theicke said handing the sergeant the papers, he found in the man's right boot.

"Adrien Zumwald, Hamburg." Schnell said flatly. "Long way from home."

"Is he a deserter Herr Oberfeldwebel?" Loften asked.

"Invalidated out of Army in 1941, suppose to be a printer." Schnell said. "What about Guipen?"

"You both can walk back to Adlerberghof." Loften said. "A doctor should look at the both of you."

"Check on Peter." Schnell suggested to Loften. "What about the others?"

"One is heading for the border." Theicke said dully.

"One?" Schnell hissed.

"Only one." Theicke said. "Unless the others have developed the ability to fly."

"It's rocky around here." Schnell said.

"They aren't that good all of a sudden." Theicke said seeing Gefreiter Bauer heading towards them. Theicke had sent him out in a wide arc to see if he could cut trail.

"Large party heading southeast." Bauer said. "They are leaving a blood trail."

"That makes no goddamn sense." Schnell rasped. "Switzerland is west."

"There is no sanctuary in Austria or Italy." Theicke said. "They've lost it."

"They are heading towards Keppler's castle." Bauer said.

"Where the hell did this castle come from?" Schnell asked.

"Keppler's built a stone chalet about 12 kilometers from here." Bauer said. "It dominates the countryside from a large hill."

"Why go there for Christssake?" Theicke rasped.

"Bauer." Schnell said. "Take Damlader and Kurtz. Follow our friends to see if they are going to Keppler's place. If they are there send back Damlader. We'll be heading back to Adlerberghof."

[5]

The Monastery

Brother Fritz made the sign of the cross after finishing the last rites and stood facing Donner. "Did you have to kill them all?"

"Seem the best thing to do at the time." Donner said gruffly. "They killed six of your people."

"Killing is never the answer my son." Fritz said. "You could have asked them to surrender."

"These boys aren't the type to surrender." Donner said flatly. "What is done is done Padre."

"We'll bury Carey and tend to Browne until he is well enough for you to smuggle him over the border." The Abbott said.

"That might take awhile." Donner said. "The town caught hell too."

"Krieger made his escape during the hell making." Orr said entering the great hall.

"This seems to have been a waste of people." Donner hissed. "Anyone on our side manage to survive?"

"One of Gerhardt's men died." Orr said tiredly. "It is total chaos down there."

"Do they need our help?" Brother Fritz asked.

"I think they will appreciate it." Orr said.

Donner uncorked a bottle of wine and poured two glasses. "Where the hell is Mannerling?"

"He's still above ground." Orr said. "The whole battalion from Jaegerfeld will be arriving soon."

"Better late than never I suppose." Donner hissed. "What about the American?"

"He disappeared it seems." Orr said. "What is the fastest way to the border?"

"Zimmer Pass or Keppler's." Donner said.

"Which would you take?" Orr asked.

"Either way gets you there." Donner said.

"Get to your wireless and tell London what has happened." Orr said. "Contact Greene and see if he can get his Swiss contacts to increase the border patrols."

"What are you going to?" Donner asked.

"Join holy orders." Orr said.

[6]
07:30 hrs

Adlerberghof
Mayor's Office

Schiller poured the cognac into the coffee cup and handed it to Gerhardt. He then sat down behind his bullet-riddled desk.

"This is no longer a private affair Herr Major." Schiller said sternly. "Krieger must not escape us."

"I already know that." Gerhardt said. "Do you have a point you want to make?"

"It will be better for the both of us if Herr Krieger and his friends become memories." Schiller said in a matter-of-fact voice. "Your intention from the beginning Herr Major was to kill him. Deny it if you want to."

"Hell, I'm too damn tired to argue with you." Gerhardt said. "What do you intend to do about it?"

"Nothing." Schiller said lighting a cigar. "Any reason I had to keep him alive went out the door the moment Fuchs died." The Mayor paused. "You have reasons for wanting him dead besides patriotic ones."

"So what?" Gerhardt said. "Krieger, the sonofabitch, has slipped our grasped Herr Schiller and if I had ulterior motives to see him dead they are gone. I intend to leave your beautiful little town with my people before the shitstorm hits."

"I wouldn't leave just yet Herr Major." Schiller said firmly.

"Why not?" Gerhardt asked. "There's nothing here for me."

Schiller smiled. "I have the American."

"Really." Gerhardt quipped nonchalantly lighting a cigarette. "So what's that to me?"

"We found him and Lang in an alley." Schiller said dryly as he slowly puffed on the cigar. "Seems Colquhoun has joined the Luftwaffe."

"Where are they?" Gerhardt asked flatly in a matter-of-fact voice.

"In a safe place." Schiller answered. "Lang is free now."

"Interesting." Gerhardt said. "What is the point Herr Schiller?"

"I'm not making myself clear." Schiller said leaning back in the chair. "I want to remove this bad taste from my mouth."

"How?" Gerhardt asked.

"I thought that obvious." Schiller said. "Kill Krieger."

"He is gone." Gerhardt said. "It will take time to find him."

"That is one luxury we no longer have." Schiller said flatly.

"Why?" Gerhardt asked.

"Visitors from Jaegerfeld will be arriving soon." Schiller said.

"I wondered how long it would take." Gerhardt hissed.

"The rest of the battalion is coming, so manpower will no longer be a problem" Schiller said. "The battalion is bringing guests from Berlin too."

"Do you know who they are?" Gerhardt asked.

"No idea." Schiller said. "However, we should have the story of what happened here straight."

"The dead make poor witnesses." Gerhardt said.

The door of the office swung open and Jherling entered with the help of one of his sergeants.

"You know about the train?" Schiller asked.

"Major Utlaut radioed me." Jherling said sitting down. "But I have better news, we have the bastards."

"Where?" Schiller asked.

"Keppler's castle." Schnell said.

"Where the hell is that?" Gerhardt asked.

"About 15 kilometers from here." Schiller answered.

"Is it near the border?" Gerhardt asked.

"No really sir." Schnell said. "The border is another 12 kilometers from there."

"Castle?" Gerhardt asked.

"Keppler rebuilt an old watchtower about 100 years ago." Schiller said. "You are certain they are there?"

"I have people watching them sir." Schnell said.

Heinz entered the office with his left arm in a sling. "Good you're all here."

"What is it Otto?" Schiller asked.

"The train is coming now." Heinz said.

"The train damnit." Jherling hissed.

"We better get our stories straight Herr Oberstleutnant before we greet the train. Schiller said in a blunt voice.

"Yes, that would be a good idea." Jherling said. "There are some things that people from Berlin would never grasp."

"We'll settle on the story on the way to the train station." Schiller said plainly as Gerhardt and the others nodded.

[7]
08:50 hrs

German-Swiss Border
Alpendorf

The waiter placed the pot of hot chocolate in the middle of the table and walked away. Major Greene lit his pipe then poured the chocolate into the cups.

"Our people are reporting an unusual lack of wireless traffic to or from the consulates in Zurich or Geneva." Captain Withgate said.

"Good." Greene said. "That means they are keeping quiet."

"The Germans maybe playing clever." Withgate suggested.

"No." Greene said. "They aren't that good of actors to pull that off. What about the Russians?"

"Nothing." Withgate said. "Very quiet."

"The quiet before the storm Thomas." Greene said firmly. "When the storm breaks all hell will come with it when they take the lid off."

"Donner didn't come through very clearly because of the storm." Withgate said.

"Something happened last night." Greene said.

Withgate lit his cigarillo. "We have no idea where along the border they are going to cross over if they crossover."

"We'll have our people do the best they can." Greene said. "London doesn't want us to stir things up here."

"Neutrality is boring." Withgate sighed.

"You'll be back into the fight soon enough Thomas." Greene said. "London wants me to lend a helping hand to the American OSS in setting up shop her."

"Damn, look who just walked in." Withgate said in a surprised voice.

"Colonel Gunnarsohn." Greene mused. "London has been busy it seems."

Gunnarsohn ordered a coffee and lit a cigarette. "Bern has decided that we should increase our border patrols for the next few days."

"I would deem that prudent my dear colonel." Greene said.

"Shall we be expecting a surge of illegal border crossings?" The Colonel asked.

"I can not say." Greene said relighting his pipe. "Are you here to coordinate the process?"

"Busman's holiday Herr Greene." Gunnarsohn said flatly. "The Security police rarely interfere with the Army."

"Army?" Withgate quipped.

"Yes, the Army." Gunnarsohn said. "The High Command has decided to hold military exercises near the borders. They want to impress OKW that we do more than make watches."

"Should make things interesting." Greene said with a quick smile.

Chapter Thirty-Four
December 11, 1942
09:00 hrs

Adlerberghof
Train station

    The mayor and his small delegation met the new arrivals at the train station. The visitors from Berlin were all wearing the uniforms of Wehrmacht Major Generals. The one named von Tanz read his orders to the group inside the train station.
    "Any questions?" Von Tanz asked.
    "Will you evacuate my injured?" Schiller asked.
    "Yes." Von Tanz said. "The train will be returning to Jaegerfeld this evening. We'll also transport anyone wishing to leave at that time."
    "Have you declared martial law Herr General?" Kohlberger asked.
    "Civilian authority remains intact." General Clausborg said dully. "For the moment."
    "We have to be flexible." Blausen said. "Circumstances change during these kinds of operations."
    "Why are you here?" Schiller asked bluntly.
    "We have been ordered to conduct an investigation." Von Tanz said looking around. "People seem to be missing."
    "Direktor Fuchs and Inspektor Wulff are missing because they are dead Herr General." Schiller said in a cold voice. "Along with their sergeant. Major Gerhardt is helping the wounded Colonel Jherling. My town has been viciously attack, my people killed"
    "Who attack you?" Blausen asked nonchalantly as he lit his cigar.
    "A gang of mercenaries working for Krieger." Schiller said caustically.
    "Wild allegations are not helpful." Clausborg said sharply. "Obergruppenfuhrer Krieger is a respected officer in the SS."
    "I do not make wild allegations." Schiller hissed.
    "Proof." Clausborg said bluntly. "We need witnesses, live witnesses."
    "We have a whole town full of witnesses." Heinz said coldly.
    "Eye witnesses often make the worse witnesses." Blausen quipped.
    "This means you are here to bury the truth." Schiller said.
    "If we were going to do that Herr Schiller." Blausen said stoically. "We brought too many witnesses with us." Blausen relit a cigar. "We would have arrived at a totally destroyed town with smoldering ruins."
    "The central reason we are here." Clausborg hissed. "Where are Kriegers?"
    "That is a major problem Herr General." Schiller answered. "They seemingly escaped during the attack."
    "I suggest that we move to town hall." Von Tanz said. "Major Utlaut will report to Colonel Jherling and the town can be made secure."
    "Make certain that Major Gerhardt understands that we want to speak with him." Clausborg said bluntly.

[2]

Twickem-Hallesy
Halton Manor

"Our British friends won't disturb us sir?" Colonel Franklin asked.
"No." Crawford said. "What brings you from the comforts of London?"
"Headquarters is wondering how you are going to handle the Colquhoun problem?" Franklin asked flatly. Franklin was from the Adjutant General's office of the OSS and was in charge of the OSS' endless supply of classified paperwork. Franklin was recruited from regular army and disliked reserve officers with a passion.
"At the moment he is listed as missing-in-action." Crawford said. "The Germans read casualty lists in the newspapers in Dublin and to protect our Ally's asset we'll change it to killed-in-action."
"Unfortunately United States Senators read the newspapers too." Franklin said. "Has his name been submitted to the Theater GHQ?"
"No." Crawford said. "Eventually it will be."
"Once that is done the War Department will notify the next-of-kin." Franklin said in a dull lifeless voice. "Then the Senator finds out his son is missing or dead officially."
"No special treatment?" Crawford grunted.
"The Director wants this made low keyed as possible." Franklin said. "Any casualty report that his organization is the Rangers."
"Lewis, you are full of shit as always." Crawford said. "That is special treatment, the krauts know we exist and so does the American public."
"Then you understand the problem Henry." Franklin said. "Headquarters wants you to understand that completely Henry. They feel that you must have had similar experiences with the police."
"I didn't work that way." Crawford said. "No fear or favor."
"The Senator is a very influential man on the Hill Henry." Franklin said. "He is not well known but has a large chest of IOUs."
"He was an isolationist before the war." Crawford said. "Hell, he voted to cut your pay in the 1920's."
"I know the Senator." Franklin said. "He drove MacArthur crazy when he was Chief of Staff. He will assume that the War Department will lie to him. Therefore, he would by-pass the chain-of-command without a second thought. He will go directly to Marshall and Stimson."
"This is top secret." Crawford said. "He'll hit a stone wall."
"He'll go to Roosevelt then." Franklin said. "FDR needs the windbag on the Hill to keep the war effort going."
Crawford lit one of Austen- Halton's cigars seeing why Headquarters keep Franklin around. "I see what you mean Lewis. You have a solution no doubt?"
"Only a suggestion sir." Franklin said.
"What is it?" Crawford said. "You don't have to convince just me."
"List Colquhoun as killed-in-action now." Franklin said matter-of-factly. "If he turns up alive at a latter date, mistakes do happen. Give Colquhoun a medal which will make his old daddy happy."
"I'm glad you are on my side." Crawford said chillingly.

"Just doing my job Henry." Franklin said. "I've been in the Army for thirty-two years and I'll be in the Army after this war is over."

"Understood Lewis." Crawford said. "I'll list Colquhoun as killed-in-action as of 13:00 hours. I'll write out the recommendation for the Distinguish Service Cross and start the ball rolling."

"Very good Henry." Franklin said. "It is to no one's advantage to have a U.S. Senator throwing his weight around upsetting things."

"You are beginning to become almost likable Lewis." Crawford said wryly.

[3]

Adlerberghof
Town Hall

"Evidence?" Von Tanz asked. "You do have evidence."

"We have a sworn affidavit from an American OSS officer stating that Krieger is the allied ghost *Albatross*." Schiller said icily. "Also an attaché case filled with money, American currency."

"You at least have the American in custody?" Clausborg asked somberly.

"He is missing too." Schiller said.

"He is gravely wounded." Clausborg rasped. "Or have we been misled."

"Heinz's men are looking for him now." Schiller said. "He can't get far."

"You seem to have bungled this Herr Schiller." Blausen said. "This will be hardly a gold mark on your record. Have you done anything right Herr Schiller?"

"I did what I thought was right." Schiller said.

"We'll talk further Herr Schiller." Von Tanz said. "Hauptman Linden bring in Colonel Jherling and Major Gerhardt."

"Why didn't they head for Switzerland?" Von Tanz asked after Jherling finished his briefing.

"No idea sir." Jherling said.

"Colonel Jherling." Von Tanz said lighting a cigarette. "Surround this castle and keep them contained."

"I can very easily take the place sir." Jherling said firmly.

"Under no circumstances are you to attack." Von Tanz said bluntly seeing the confusion on Jherling's face. "You have questions?"

"No Sir." Jherling answered.

"You do have an opinion Major Gerhardt?" Blausen asked.

"No sir." Gerhardt replied. "Do I join the Colonel?"

"We prefer that you find this American." General Clausborg said. "That is your kind of work isn't Major?"

"Yes sir." Gerhardt said. "He could be long gone by now Herr General."

"Colonel Jherling's Chief Medical Officer tells us he couldn't get far without help." Blausen said. "It should be relatively easy to find him shouldn't it?"

"Yes sir." Gerhardt said.

"You have your orders Herr Major." Von Tanz said bluntly.

"I'm getting the feeling that you are not taking this seriously." Kohlberger said sourly. "You have overwhelming force, but you refuse to attack, why?"

"We have orders." Von Tanz said.

"Krieger is a common criminal now." The Judge said. "Attack and end this immediately."

"We are not here to be his executioners." Blausen said.

"They are mass murderers." Schiller rasped.

"State Security takes precedence." Clausborg said bluntly.

"I smell whitewash." Kohlberger rasped. "You bastards are going to let them live and get away with this."

"Hardly." Von Tanz said. "Berlin can not allow this to continue now."

"Then finish it now." Schiller said grimly. "Don't allow him the chance to talk."

"Berlin wants a complete thorough investigation of this incident." Clausborg said sharply. "You can't question the dead."

"Why question them at all?" Heinz asked.

"Where there is one traitor there are usually more." Blausen said.

"I'll hold you all personally responsible for the out come." Schiller said. "I still have friends in Berlin."

"Threats are not necessary Herr Schiller." Von Tanz said. "Krieger also has friends in Berlin. Your people need you Herr Schiller, now."

Blausen lit a fresh cigar. "Kohlberger is right damnit, why are you hesitating?"

"We are not dealing with amateurs." Von Tanz said. "Krieger should have crossed the border not sitting on his ass in a damn castle."

"Who cares?" Clausborg asked. "Attack and kill them. Jherling will take a few more casualties, but they will be dead." Clausborg paused. "Do you have objections to that?

"Not personally." Von Tanz said.

"What is the problem then?" Blausen asked.

"We have an unforeseen problem." Clausborg said cynically. "So would you mind sharing with us your doubts?"

"Berlin is dealing from the bottom of the deck now." Von Tanz said handing Clausborg the telegram; he had received before leaving Jaegerfeld. Clausborg read the paper then handed it to Blausen.

"It's very clear now why the bastard is sitting in that castle." Blausen growled clinching the cigar butt tightly between his teeth. "So much for a free hand."

"Vochner." Clausborg hissed. "I didn't Krieger was smart enough to know a man like him."

"Not him." Von Tanz rasped. "Her, she is the intelligent one. The Countess has made it almost impossible to kill them."

"Vochner is that powerful?" Blausen grunted.

"Vochner was the fixer." Von Tanz said grimly. "By hinting very loudly that this whole affair is part of a greater conspiracy. If you don't know by now Berlin is paranoid about conspiracies real or imaged."

"You said was the fixer." Blausen hissed. "What the hell is going on?"

"Vochner is dead." Von Tanz said frankly.

"Vochner always played both sides against the middle." Clausborg said. "He finally got caught. When did this happen?"

"The night before we left." Von Tanz said.
"How was it done?" Blausen asked.
"Accidentally shot him self cleaning his pistol." Von Tanz replied cynically. "Danzig had paid him a visit a few hours before,"
"Himmler is cleaning up the lose ends if this goes sour." Clausborg said honestly. "That's why we need them alive."
"Keeping them alive will not go over to well with the townspeople." Blausen said. "They did a good job on the town."
"We have to find out what exactly Krieger has." Von Tanz said. "They know they have crossed the line and they are seeking survival."
"That means a parley of sorts." Clausborg said.
"Exactly." Von Tanz said.
"When?" Blausen asked.
"Let them stew." Von Tanz said coldly. "We have time on our side."
"Then what?" Blausen asked.
"Order caskets." Von Tanz said.

[4]

Keppler's Castle

Eidernau relit the cigar stub as he glared out the window. "Didn't take them long to lock us in tight."
"It was expected." Krieger said. "This place is well fortified."
"Jherling does have the ability to bring up artillery." Hothman said flatly.
"Takes time in the winter to bring it up." Krieger said.
"A squadron of Stukas will make short work of this place." Hothman said.
"The Luftwaffe marches to a different drummer." The Countess said. "They will not interfere."
"What in hell do you expect to get from them?" Eidernau asked bluntly.
"Our freedom." The Countess said.
"The destruction of my enemy." Krieger said bluntly.
"That is fine in an ideal world." Eidernau hissed. "We just shot up a town, a German town killing a lot of fellow citizens, massacred a bunch of monks. I don't know of anyone who will forgive that."
"I do not beg forgiveness." Krieger said. "They live in the real world as do I."
"Do we look that stupid to you?" Hothman said bluntly. "I've heard a lot about this Schiller. You try shoving this mess up his ass and he'll kill us."
"Schiller wants to return in Berlin in glory." The Countess said. "We are his ticket back to the circle of power and he'll take us back as long as if we don't make him look like a complete idiot."
"Forget this pipe dream." Eidernau rasped. "What if your little plan farts out? How the hell do WE get out of here or are you that interested in finding out about Valhalla?"
"I always have an alternate plan Willi." Krieger said. "I'm not interested in dying just yet."
"We are 13.6 kilometers from the border." Hothman said. "But, we are surrounded."

"Keppler built this tower during the Thirty Years War." The Countess said. "He made a tunnel to connect to a natural cavern system that extends to the Swiss border. This section is as honeycombed as the town."

"Good alternative." Eidernau said. "We have a chance now if your fancy parlor game fails Helmuth."

[5]

Adlerberghof

Gerhardt and Mannerling followed one of Heinz's men to a warehouse at the far side of the town. Waiting for them inside the warehouse office was Heinz. The Chief had not been his jovial self since the attack.

"What is going on Heinz?" Gerhardt asked crisply noticing the sawhorses with planks on them and the vague human forms outlined by the white sheets. "My people are accounted for Chief."

"Schiller thought this would be the safest place for him." Heinz said flatly.

"Who?" Mannerling asked.

"Klugge." Heinz said signaling his man. "He is a little roughed up but alive."

"Interesting." Gerhardt said.

Klugge entered the office with his left arm in a sling and his head bandaged, but the SS pride was still there despite the ruined uniform.

"Schiller says he is your problem." Heinz said flatly. "Keep him under wraps for his own health. The townspeople know how to use a rope."

"Tell Schiller thank you." Gerhardt said dourly.

"This is his deal, not mine." Heinz said. "I would rather put a bullet in his brain than let him walk out of here."

Klugge sat down. "Which one of you has a cigarette?"

"It is embarrassing." Mannerling said handing Klugge a cigarette. "Of course this was planned."

"Unfortunately this was not planned." Klugge said dourly. "Who are the red stripes?"

"Berlin." Gerhardt said. "We assumed you were with Krieger."

"Best laid plans." Klugge said. "Why is Berlin here?"

"Officially to find out what is going on?" Gerhardt said blandly. "Unofficially to kill Krieger and his close circle of friends, this by the way includes you."

"They hardly kill enlisted men." Klugge said.

"This time they might make an exception." Mannerling said. "You are walking the tightrope without a net over a mine field."

Klugge took a long drag on his cigarette. "What I understand this whole mess was designed to protect a British agent. Moscow would be very unhappy if I died in the process."

"Your best defense would get you hanging by a wire on a meat hook." Gerhardt said.

"I could just disappear." Klugge suggested.

"That won't work either." Gerhardt said. "You understand that your usefulness as a Soviet agent is gone. Moscow could easily turn you in to the Gestapo."

"I just want to survive." Klugge said. "I do have a conscience."

"You do." Mannerling said. "However, you'll talk to buy a few more minutes of life."

"Unfortunately that is true." Klugge said unflinchingly. "Survival is the name of the game."

Gerhardt lit a cigarette. "You have to convince three general officers that you are not connected to the Krieger's body and soul."

"I've been his enlisted orderly for almost twenty-years." Klugge said. "I know how to work officers.

"Then you are a nonentity." Mannerling said. "Never seen or heard."

"But always there." Klugge said.

"As a counterintelligence agent you would be." Gerhardt said. "You can't be shot for doing your duty."

"You don't know Himmler very well do you." Klugge said. "I would be considered a traitor to the SS."

"Hardly that if you were ordered to spy on the Kriegers." Gerhardt said.

"By whom?" Klugge asked.

"Heydrich." Gerhardt said flatly.

Klugge stared at Gerhardt for a few minutes before nodding his head. "Brilliant Herr Major."

"How?" Mannerling asked.

"Himmler would never question that." Klugge said. "The Reichsfuhrer SS was afraid of him if the truth be known."

"It would make sense even to those red-stripes." Gerhardt said. "Keep your explanations simple and uncomplicated."

"What do you know about Keppler's Castle?" Mannerling asked.

"The Countess' family secretly owns it." Klugge said. "Keppler belong to the cadet branch of the family."

"Why go there?" Gerhardt asked.

"Tunnel lead to a cavern system that goes to the Swiss border." Klugge said. "Keppler had the path marked out with luminous rock."

"Keep that our secret." Gerhardt said. "We better get you clean up."

"While you are doing that I'll snoop about." Mannerling said looking at Klugge. "You are a lucky bastard but you know that."

"Always have been." Klugge said.

"You might get the Iron Cross and the Order of Lenin." Gerhardt hissed.

"Anything is possible Major." Klugge said.

Chapter Thirty-Five
December 11, 1942
13:30 hrs

Keppler's Castle

"Has Broekelman returned?" The Countess asked anxiously.
"It takes time to travel the cavern." Ehrlich said. "He should be back within the hour."
"Do we have the time?" The Countess asked.
"Yes." Krieger said. "Jherling and Schiller are no longer in command."
"How the hell do you know that?" The Countess asked sharply.
"It has been two hours and we are still alive." Krieger said lighting a cigar. "You know Schiller Elsa. We wrecked his town, killed his people and nothing would stand in his way of vengeance except someone more powerful than him stopped him."
"Berlin." Ehrlich said.
"Yes." Krieger said. "Someone at Prinz Albrechtstrasse woke up."
"Perhaps so Helmuth." The Countess said dryly. "We still have the problem of getting out alive."
"Himmler dislikes loose ends." Helmuth said. "He would give his eyeteeth to bring *Albatross* to a gallows."
"Bormann might not want to know." The Countess said.
"We'll be safe once we are in Berlin." Krieger said.
"Himmler can not ignore someone like Schiller." The Countess said firmly. "Someone will have to pay for what happened."
"Eidernau." Ehrlich said coldly.
"Willi?" The Countess sighed.
"Someone has to pay." Krieger said. "Willi has outlived his usefulness."
"It is all moot unless we make contact." The Countess said. "I doubt even Willi could get a volunteer to go out under a flag of truce."
"They'll make contact." Krieger said.

[2]

Adlerberghof
Town Hall

"Does it sound right to you?" Clausborg asked his colleagues after hearing Klugge's story.
"It sounds plausible." Blausen said puffing on his cigar.
"Major Gerhardt." Von Tanz said. "Do you believe Klugge?"
"He gains nothing by lying sir." Gerhardt said. "You could check his story with Berlin. There has to be a written order."
"Not necessarily." Clausborg said grimly. "We are running out of daylight to take action."
"I feel that we have no choice but to contact Berlin about this." Von Tanz said in a firm voice. "Rash or premature action might make matters worse."
"Mistakes can be forgiven." Blausen said.
"You might not like Berlin's forgiveness." Clausborg hissed. "The Eastern Front is full of people who made mistakes."

"Major Gerhardt." Von Tanz said. "Inform Colonel Jherling of the situation. He is to ask a volunteer to take a flag of truce to Krieger. Tomorrow morning 08:00 hours."

"Yes sir." Gerhardt said saluting. "Klugge sir?"

"Place him on the first train to Jaegerfeld under guard." Von Tanz said.

"Major." Blausen said. "That train leaves with the civilian casualties tomorrow morning."

"Understood sir." Gerhardt said. "I'll keep Klugge under close arrest."

[3]

Donner's Farm

"Another cave?" Orr said in a grim voice. "Do I look like a tunnel rat to you?"

"Not my idea." Mannerling said. "Did the Abbot have anything helpful?"

"They have kept everything since the 12th century." Donner said. "Rittmeister Keppler donated volumes of books and papers. He was very proud of what he done at the watchtower."

"Do you have it or not?" Mannerling asked.

"This." Donner said handing Mannerling a scroll. "It is in Latin."

"I read Latin." Orr said matter-of-factly. "The benefit of an old fashion education and my father wanted me to be a priest."

"If I find this place." Orr said glancing through the scroll. "What do you want me to do?"

"C-4?" Mannerling asked Donner.

"The monks have TNT, enough to do some serious damage." Donner said dryly.

"Blow up the cavern." Mannerling said. "Cut off the escape route."

"Okay." Orr said unfolding the scroll and placing his finger on a spot. "Do you know this place?"

"Yeah." Donner grunted.

"Wreck it as best you can." Mannerling said wryly. "Nothing heroic."

"You Edward?" Orr asked.

"One way or the other they have to come out of Keppler's." Mannerling said flatly lighting a cigarette. "He'll go no further."

"I'll do my part as quickly as possible and get back to help." Orr said. "Krieger will not be your only problem out there."

"You have white sheeting Donner?" Mannerling asked.

"Yes." Donner said. "There is an old logging trail that will bring you near Keppler's depending how much space Jherling will give them."

"Fine." Mannerling said. "You better get started."

[4]

Adlerberghof
School House

"How are you doing?" Gerhardt asked Colquhoun as he sat down next to him in the schoolhouse that had been converted into a temporary hospital.

"I'm alive." Colquhoun said in a low voice. "Better than many around here."

"Your name is Rudolf Bekker." Gerhardt said. "Captain in the Luftwaffe, can you remember that?"

"Bekker" Colquhoun murmured. "Luftwaffe."

"You have papers in your kit and Luftwaffe ID discs." Gerhardt said. "Lang will get you off the train in Jaegerfeld."

"Then what?" Colquhoun asked. "Some idiot might call the Luftwaffe."

"Lang will take you to a private hospital in Kirstenberg. The trail should grow cold rather quickly. " Gerhardt said. " We'll wait for a few weeks then move you across the border to Switzerland when everything dies down."

"What about London?" Colquhoun asked.

"You'll be reported as killed-in-action." Gerhardt said. "Our signal intelligence will pick this up from Switzerland. We'll use a signal that Sigint can read."

"How will London know that I'm not?" Colquhoun asked.

"They won't know until Lang turns you over to your people in Switzerland." Gerhardt said.

"Krieger?" Colquhoun asked in a painful voice. "Is he alive?"

"Unfortunately he escaped but he'll be taken care of." Gerhardt said. "He is no longer your concern."

"I got my whole team killed." Colquhoun lamented. "All to make him a goddamn hero."

"Browne is alive." Gerhardt said. "You did almost what you ordered to do."

"Was this all worth it?" Colquhoun hissed. "Such a waste."

"I don't know." Gerhardt said. "This isn't finished yet."

[5]
16:00 hrs

Keppler's Castle

"Do you expect surrender?" Ehrlich asked Major Utlaut in a sharp voice as they stood in the open field.

"Not my reason for being here Standartenfuhrer." Utlaut said glumly.

"You don't like this Major." Ehrlich said.

"If I had my way Colonel your refuge would have been a smoldering ruin by now." Utlaut said. "Fortunately for you I'm not in command."

"Your superiors asked for this truce." Ehrlich said. "What are your conditions?"

"They want a parley." Utlaut said flatly. "08:00 hours here tomorrow."

"Who are you talking about?" Ehrlich asked.

"Three general officers from Berlin." Utlaut said. "You, the Countess and the General."

Ehrlich smiled slightly as he lit the cigarette. "Generals who?"

"Generalmajor Clausborg, Blausen and von Tanz." Utlaut said flatly.

"Low level." Ehrlich hissed not indicating that he knew von Tanz.

"Berlin dislikes scandal." Utlaut said. "Even with a controlled press and radio this kind of scandal will become public."

"How much time do we have to agree?" Ehrlich asked.

"You have one hour." Utlaut rasped.

"Impossible." Ehrlich growled.

"One hour." Utlaut snapped. "No middle ground."

"Guarantees?" Ehrlich asked.

"No offensive action during the night." Utlaut said. "If you accept hang the truce flag out the window?"

"Yes." Ehrlich said.

"You are slipping Albrecht." The Countess said after one of Eidernau's men hung out the truce flag. "You allowed a major to browbeat you into submission."

"We are not dealing with a rational opponent." Ehrlich said. "We killed Jherling's men and Major Utlaut would gladly burn this place down with us in it."

"Can't you see old Max at work Elsa?" Krieger asked.

"Where do you see that?" Elsa rasped.

"Berlin has given me von Tanz." Helmuth said. "My salvation has been delivered."

"Von Tanz." Elsa said sourly. "He is that pain-in-the-ass Abwehr officer? Why in hell are you happy about that?"

"Von Tanz is *Albatross*." Helmuth said.

"Are you mad?" Elsa snarled. "You have begun to believe your own myth-making."

"You don't understand *Albatross* is not a myth." Krieger said. "I can make von Tanz or anyone be *Albatross*." Krieger lit a cigar. "However, von Tanz is *Albatross*."

[6]

Mannerling crawled through the snow using the smoke from the campfires that surrounded the castle as guides to a small gully about 800 yards from where the men were talking. Mannerling raised his field glasses and recognized the two men talking- Ehrlich and Utlaut.

Mannerling using a long pole probed the snow trying to find the pillbox built hunting stand Keppler had built a hundred years ago. If he failed to find he would have to burrow into the snow like the Indians use to do in Canada when they went hunting during the dead of winter.

Mannerling found the hunting stand and found the door less than four meters of snow. Mannerling quickly cleared the snow in front of the stand giving him a field of fire. Mannerling started the potbellied stove; the smoke would be channeled to an out pipe 200 meters away. Mannerling laid the rifle on the ledge, he had wrapped his rifle with the bed sheet to break up the outline of the weapon. Mannerling was not worried about hitting stationary targets at 600 meters distance. He once had a much more difficult shot in the past, running target at over 1000 yards a few years back.

When was all said and done this was the reason he was here. All the rest of this was just window dressing to protect one man from a possible threat. They could not just kill Krieger outright because the Nazis would want to why. This production was solely designed to get all the players in one place for Mannerling to kill them. Mannerling doubted that Gerhardt knew the real why. Once he started to shoot, hell would break loose and survival would become his sole objective after killing his targets.

An Honorable Betrayal

Chapter Thirty-Six
December 12, 1942
02:00 hrs

Great Danby
RAF Airdrome

    Group-Captain Witcombe lit his pipe and pointed to the map on the wall with his swagger stick "Gentleman, this is a straightforward mission. The target will be the rail line running from Jaegerfeld and Adlerberghof. You should be over the target between 08:00-09:00 hrs."
    "Are the tracks the target sir?" Flight Lieutenant George of the Royal Australian Air Force asked.
    "Anything on the tracks is a target." Witcombe said.
    "What about the Luftwaffe?" Pilot Officer Mackey asked.
    "Minimal interference is expected." Witcombe said. "You'll be coming behind a bomber command raid. The German radar should not be able to pick you up." Witcombe paused for a moment. "Good luck, dismissed."
    "How many are you putting up Roger?" Sir Peter asked.
    "10 crates." Witcombe answered. "Mosquitos are the fastest planes we have."
    "Losses?" Austen-Halton asked.
    "On a mission of this type you'll have to expect one maybe two." Witcombe said. "Most likely from mechanical problems." Witcombe relit his pipe. "Since this is one of your missions Air/Sea will not be alerted."
    "You've been with us long enough not to have illusions." Sir Peter said dully.
    "Twenty men." Witcombe said tersely. "You don't have to write the letters sir."
    "They are all volunteers Roger." Sir Peter said grimly.
    "Do the Americans know you plan to blow the shit out of the train carrying their man?" Roger asked coldly.
    "It has not been discussed in detail." Sir Peter said. "Take a long holiday after this is over Roger, come back in January."
    "No need sir." Witcombe said flatly. "I get cranky at times sir."
    "Keep me informed Roger." Austen-Halton said.

[2]
06:00 hrs

Hotel Fairmonte
Washington DC

    "I hope this time of day is not an inconvenience Admiral." Senator Colquhoun's second son John said pouring the coffee.
    "I've been up since 5 AM." Coffin said. 'There is a reason for this meeting?"
    "It is a simple reason." John said. "I intercepted the telegram from the War Office."
    "Your father has the right to know about your brother." Coffin said firmly.
    "My father is not a well man Admiral." John said. "The news of Jeff's will cause him great harm."

"He does not leave that impression." Coffin said. "You have to talk to the War Department about that. Normally the War Department frowns on pissing senators off."

"Your agency could help." John said with a broad smile. "A change of status from KIA to WIA would be helpful."

"Helpful for whom Mr. Colquhoun?" Coffin asked.

"My brother's campaign for the senate." John said crisply.

"Your father's term doesn't end for another three years." Coffin said.

"My father plans to resign in late January." John said. "The Governor, instead of appointing someone to fill out the rest of his term, will have a special election nominating Jefferson Davis Colquhoun."

"How can a dead man run for office?" Coffin asked cynically.

"Jeff will handily win the special election." Colquhoun said. "Before we can get his discharge from the Army we shall learn of his tragic death in combat."

"The Governor will reluctantly appoint you to fill out the vacancy." Coffin said.

"You get the picture quickly." John said. "May I count on your help?"

"I'll pass the word along." Coffin said dryly.

[3]

Berlin
RSHA

The Reichsfuhrer was standing by the window when Danzig entered the office. "You handled the others in an excellent manner."

"Thank you Reichsfuhrer." Danzig said.

"Clausborg has informed me that the identity of *Albatross* has been confirmed." Himmler said in a low voice.

"That is good news sir." Danzig said cautiously.

"The evidence proves beyond a doubt *Albatross* is Krieger." Himmler said turning from the window.

"I find that hard to believe sir." Danzig said firmly.

"I can not afford not to believe it." Himmler said bluntly. "I know you can be discreet Standartenfuhrer."

"Sir I'm at your disposal." Danzig said bluntly.

"I need you to go to Krieger's estate and search it thoroughly." Himmler said. "Detain anyone there for questioning, move them to Flossenberg." Himmler paused. "Any one resists they are to be shot then and there."

"How many men do I take to Krieger's sir?" Danzig asked.

"I have a SIPO company waiting for you." Himmler said. "Remove every scrap of paper you find and bring them here."

"When do I go to Adlerberghof sir?" Danzig asked.

"You don't Standartenfuhrer." Himmler said moving to his desk picking up a paper. "This is your commission as a Standartenfuhrer." Himmler handed the paper to Danzig. "I want you to go to Linz after Krieger's and escort Kaltenbrunner to Berlin."

"Yes sir." Danzig said saluting.

London
Soviet Embassy

"Colonel Mikhailov is still at Twickem-Hallesy General Sergeyev?" Kandinsky asked somberly. Lieutenant Colonel Kandinsky was one of the NKVD officers assigned to the embassy. Sergeyev looked up from his morning cup of coffee. The security office always got extreme nervous when someone left the controlled environment of the embassy

"That is where he should be Comrade Kandinsky." Sergeyev said tersely. "He is of no use if he was here."

"He is becoming too familiar with the English and Americans." Kandinsky said flatly. "Too much time alone with them."

"That is his job." Sergeyev said. "Our friends wouldn't talk with you as his constant shadow."

"He is acting like the Spanish." Kandinsky rasped. "Too much foreign contact."

Sergeyev remained silent knowing that having an intellect was not a requirement of the NKVD. He also knew what happened to the Party volunteers who served in Spain on the Republican side. They brought the gold reserve out of Spain and most of the heroes got a bullet to the back of the head after they got home.

"I would refrain from setting my eyes on Mikhailov." Sergeyev warned.

"I'm not afraid of him." Kandinsky said sternly.

"The point is Comrade is that Mikhailov isn't afraid of you." The General said plainly. "Our cooperation with our Allies will return to normal once this operation is over."

"He is sending the wrong message." Kandinsky hissed.

"Read Lenin for once." Sergeyev said dully. "The capitalists will sell us the rope that we'll hang them with, but we have to give them the chance."

Chapter Thirty-Seven
December 12, 1942
07:00 hrs

The Cavern

Brosch stopped at the rope bridges that lead to the tunnel that lead to the surface in Switzerland. "No more lanterns Hothman."

"Good." Hothman said. "All the lanterns were filled with new wicks."

"Spooky." Brosch said dourly. "The rope on the bridge is new too."

"It is called careful planning Manfred." Hothman said. "We still have to rig the charges and set the timer."

"Fifteen minutes is not enough time." Brosch said. "Not everyone will get out Rolf."

"What do you care?" Hothman said. "As long as you get out."

"Poor bastards." Brosch hissed. "We better set things up."

Hothman and Brosch moved back through the cavern heading back to the castle when they stopped on seeing that a section of the path was now in darkness. Instinctively Hothman and Brosch drew their pistols, which became the last act of their lives. Half a dozen gunshots rang out and they tumbled to the ground in lifeless heaps. Donner and Orr stepped out of the darkness.

Donner looked at the rope bridge. "Cutting the rope bridge will be a lot quieter."

"They are industrious people." Orr said. "They could easily rebuild the bridge. We need to bring the roof down."

"Good idea." Donner said. "Make it a small explosion in the right place and the ceiling will come down."

"Even small explosions will more than likely bring everything down." Orr said. "We'll have to be across the bridge when we blowup this place which means we are out of this Donner."

"It can't be helped." Donner said.

"We better hurry they might decide to miss our friends." Orr said flatly.

"They might just conclude they got smart" Donner said.

[2]
07:00 hrs

Keppler's Castle

Schiller's black Mercedes slowed to a stop a few yards from the command tent. Schiller emerged from the car dressed in his NSDAP uniform followed by Heinz and Kohlberger. They walked slowly towards the command tent in a slow deliberate pace. Major Utlaut called off the guards moving towards them to stop them. Von Tanz and the others emerged from the tent.

"You were instructed to stay in town." Von Tanz grumbled on seeing them.

"You have no authority over me." Schiller said firmly. "I'm still the Party District Leader and Chief of Civil Defense."

"Martial Law trumps that." Blausen said curtly. "Go home Herr Schiller."

"Go to hell." Kohlberger snarled. "Only General officer commanding can declare martial law in his district."

"This doesn't concern you." Clausborg said plainly. "Berlin has no interest in you at the moment."

"I'm here to stop you from making any deals with that bastard." Schiller said icily.

"That is a dangerous stand to take." Von Tanz said.

"You have not lost people to this madman." Schiller said bluntly. "I order you to stop."

"Nothing you say or do will change our minds." Von Tanz said plainly.

"Then you are ignoring my direct order?" Schiller asked.

"Yes." Von Tanz said sensing what Schiller was doing. The mayor was clearing himself of all responsibility if this meeting failed for any reason. "Your protest will be noted for the official record."

"I will observe." Schiller said. "That shouldn't interfer too much."

"Of course." Blausen said lighting his cigar. "Colonel Jherling will provide you with accommodations."

"Yes sir." Jherling said.

"Have you found the American?" Clausborg asked.

"He could have been in the Gruenling when it burnt down." Schiller said. "He was too badly injured to go far."

"Have you sifted through the wreckage" Blausen asked.

"That has not been a priority Herr General." Heinz said. "The hotel is still smoldering."

"Colonel Jherling will find you place to observe." Von Tanz said.

"Schiller is going to be a problem von Tanz." Clausborg said bluntly watching Schiller head towards Jherling's tent. "Especially, if we get a deal with Krieger."

"Any arrangement with him will require his safety." Blausen said. "Schiller isn't the type to sit on his hands as Krieger waltzes away."

"That could work to our advantage." Clausborg said. "If Schiller assassinates Krieger they can not blame us."

"Berlin wouldn't honor any bargain to begin with." Von Tanz said. "Krieger knows that and he's not about to stay in Germany."

"He has to leave the castle to get to Switzerland." Clausborg said. "It is an option."

"Major Gerhardt." Von Tanz said as the major entered the tent with Colonel Jherling. "You will carry the truce flag."

"It will be my honor sir." Gerhardt said.

"Colonel Jherling." Von Tanz said firmly. "At any sign of treachery you will open fire with the heavy mortars and kill everyone in that castle."

"Yes sir my pleasure." Jherling said.

"Try not to kill us during the process?" Clausborg suggested.

[3]

Keppler's Castle

"Schiller has made is grand entrance." Eidernau said lowering his binoculars. "He brings with him the judge and the fat cop."

"They are here only to witness my fall." Krieger said. "Schiller was always a showman."

"This is not what we expected." Eidernau said. "We can escape now, Hothman and Brosch will be back soon. They'll mull it over for at least an hour before they rush the place."

"No." Krieger said. "We meet with them and discuss points of interest, lull them into thinking they are winning." Krieger paused. "I'll force another meeting for two hours later."

"Why delay the goddamn escape?" Eidernau growled.

"Illusion my dear Willi." The Countess said. "They won't suspect a thing when we fail to march out to the field."

"We'll need a few to keep them busy once they find out we are not coming out as scheduled." Ehrlich said.

"Volunteers?" Willi hissed.

"A smaller party travels faster." The Countess said. "We don't want to overburden our Swiss host."

"Understood." Willi said. "I'll hand pick them."

"Excellent, you understand at last." The Countess said looking at her wristwatch. "We have time for coffee before we venture out into the cold."

[4]
07:30 hrs

Adlerberghof
Train Station

"The train should be ready by 9:30 at the latest Herr Leutnant." Hronska the stationmaster said in a clipped voice. Hronska had been brought out of retirement after seven years. "They plan to keep the line open for now."

"That is good Herr Hronska." Lang said.

"No non injured civilian passengers." Hronska said.

"Thank you." Lang said leaving the office.

Lang went to town hall where the passengers were being assembled for the journey back to Jaegerfeld. Browne, in the uniform of a corporal was sitting at a desk eating a sandwich. They had smuggled Browne down from the monastery during the night

"The train leaves about 9:30." Lang said sitting down next to Browne.

"Not that long time to wait." Browne said seriously. "This is being held together by a thread."

"I'm not keeping you here." Lang said. "Try to get out by yourself."

"The odds are bad here." Browne rasped. "Worse on my own. What if they don't come back?"

"Stay to the plan." Lang said. "Don't panic now and throw everything away. Once we get to Jaegerfeld you fade into the woodwork."

"Sounds like a plan." Browne said. "You better grab a sandwich, it will a long day."

"Longer than you think." Lang said.

"I don't have to think about that Leutnant." Browne said. "I want this all to end with me coming out of this god damn thing alive in one piece. Is that too much to ask for?"

"No." Lang said in a faraway voice.

An Honorable Betrayal

Chapter Thirty-Eight
December 12, 1942
08:00 hrs

Keppler's Castle

    The four men in feldgrau uniforms of the Wehrmacht waded through the waist deep snow towards the imaginary line that divided the slope in half. Gerhardt was first carrying the flag of truce. Von Tanz followed him about three meters behind. Behind him was Clausborg at the same distance with Blausen taking up the rear. Unlike most truce, parties they were all armed.
    As they moved up the hill, Krieger and his party moved down the hill in a slow deliberate.
Eidernau was carrying the truce flag. Following him was Ehrlich and the Krieger; no uniforms, but were armed.
    The two parties stopped about two meters from each other. They silently checked each other out.
    "Hardly what I call a show of good faith Herbert." Krieger said icily.
    "I knew who I would be dealing with." Von Tanz replied tartly.
    "You two know each other?" Blausen asked frankly as he lit the cigar stub.
    "We have met before." Krieger answered.
    "Why wasn't that relayed to us?" Clausborg asked sternly. "You have an unwarranted advantage on us."
    "Berlin needed someone who knew how his mind worked." Von Tanz said unapologetically.
    "I thought that we would meet alone?" Krieger asked.
    "Only a fool meets you alone." Von Tanz said. "I'm not a fool."
    "Are you afraid, Herr General?" The Ehrlich taunted.
    "Always when dealing with vermin Colonel." Von Tanz answered.
    "Gentlemen." Krieger said. "I need to speak with General von Tanz, one on one. He has nothing to hide."
    "That is unacceptable." Clausborg rasped. "This is not a private affair."
    "The longer you delay the harder it is for Goebbels to contain this." Krieger said. "Rumor is far worse than the truth."
    "We are not here to bargain with a traitor," Clausborg hissed.
    "Then there is no sense in us being here." Krieger said bluntly.
    "What the hell you two talk." Blausen said in a matter-of-fact voice. "I'm certain that von Tanz will tell us everything."

[2]

    "It has been a long time Herbert." Krieger said lowering his right hand on seeing that von Tanz was not going to take it. "You didn't have to bring your friends."
    "Berlin insisted that I bring them." Von Tanz said.
    "They at least sent one friend." Krieger hissed cynically.
    "You have only one friend here Helmuth." Krieger said. "Has she told you what to say?"

"You shouldn't believe rumors." Helmuth said opening up a gold cigarette case. "Elsa is just ambitious for me."

"You have something you want to say?" Von Tanz hissed getting his own cigarette and lighting it. "Say it."

"I thought it would be obvious to you." Krieger said.

"I'm stupid." Von Tanz rasped. "Enlighten me."

"*Albatross*." Krieger said grimly.

"Really, that old chestnut is still out there?" Von Tanz said. "Who is your candidate?"

"He has become famous or more to the point infamous. I know he is here." Krieger said. "I lured him here."

"Lured who?" Von Tanz asked. "I thought he was supposed to be smart."

Helmuth smiled before his face turned deadly serious. "You were at the top of list. In fact Herr General you are the only one on the list."

"Interesting." Von Tanz hissed. "You of course have proof or have you gone delusional?"

"Once the American is found the list will be found." Helmuth said. "You got sloppy in your old age Herbert."

"I'm not *Albatross*." Von Tanz said grimly. "We were using him to relay false information to London since before the war."

The light of victory drained slowly from von Krieger's face after absorbing what von Tanz said. "You are *Albatross* damnit, I have proof."

"There was an *Albatross* during the First War." Von Tanz said. "He died of a massive heart attack in 1929."

"We've been chasing him for years." Krieger said tartly. "Information has been leaking out beyond 1929."

"*Albatross* isn't one man." Von Tanz said. "He is a network of agents unknown to each other. We find one and another arm grows. The last we caught was a clerk in the telephone section of the post office."

"You spin a good tale." Krieger hissed. "What you say is impossible, we know nothing of this."

"Heydrich knew." Von Tanz said. "Perhaps Himmler does."

"Albatross exists." Krieger said. "I know he does."

"Who then?" Von Tanz asked.

"You." Krieger said. "Everything points to you."

"Prove it." Von Tanz challenged.

Krieger tossed down his cigarette. "You are arrogant enough to believe you are invincible." Helmuth lit another cigarette. "You haven't asked why I'm here in this shit hole."

"I really don't care." Von Tanz said icily. "All you seem to have accomplished is the mass murder of innocent citizens of the Reich."

"Arrogance." Helmuth hissed. "That will be your down fall Herbert."

"Proof." Von Tanz rasped. "You have to have it."

"Viktor Skasch stole a list of allied agents operating in Occupied Europe and Germany." Helmuth said. "He contacted Jung and I agreed to buy this list from Skasch."

"Who has seen this list?" Von Tanz asked.

"Jung." Helmuth said. "Skasch."

"Both are conveniently dead." Von Tanz said. "Hardly good witnesses and the American Skasch is missing too."

"Berlin might find it interesting that your name was on the top of the list." Helmuth said coldly.

"Not because of an imaginary list." Von Tanz hissed. "If I was *Albatross* you are a dead man."

"Your friends might not be that supportive if they knew the truth." Krieger said.

"Tell them." Von Tanz said bluntly. "Let the chips fall as they may."

"You are pushing your luck." Krieger said.

"I have a clear conscience." Von Tanz hissed.

Chapter Thirty-Nine
December 12, 1942
09:00 hrs

Adlerberghof

They saw the smoke billowing from the direction of the train station as they raced towards the town. They had gotten word of the air attack as the truce party was returning from the parley. Schiller and his party immediately left with von Tanz and Blausen following them.

The train station was fully engulfed in flame as they arrived resisting the efforts of the fire brigade to put it out. The train engine was a twisted wreck blown off the track about 500 meters away. The train driver had tried to get the train into the tunnel, but failed by 2500 meters. Most of the passenger cars were destroyed and smoldering on the track.

Helder, the chief of the volunteer fire brigade walked up to Schiller with a half daze look on his blackened face.

"Christssakes what happened Emil?" Schiller asked.

"They came out of the sun." Helder said. "Three of four of them strafed the station first then the bombs started to fall. The train driver head for the tunnel but they blew the hell out him and rained hell on the place."

"Was the town hit?" Von Tanz asked.

"They just attacked the station." Helder said. "We moved the casualties to the church."

"What kind of aircraft?" Blausen asked.

"They looked like ME110s." Helder said. "They were English."

"How many dead?" Schiller asked.

"28 dead and 64 wounded." Helder said tiredly. "Hronska was loading the train when they hit, he didn't make it."

Von Tanz leaned against the car and lit his cigarette. "This was no accident."

"Sounds like Mosquitos." Blausen said. "The vaguely look like a ME110."

"They were sent to destroy someone." Utlaut said. "We might have hit one or two of them, all we had were machineguns and rifles."

"How long will it take to get a crane up here and a new train?" Von Tanz asked.

"Maybe two days or more sirs." Utlaut said. "The crane has to come from Munich and we won't have priority."

"We'll get the priority." Blausen said as Schiller approached.

The mayor had been to the church and talked to the wounded and the rewounded. From the expression on his face and his gait Schiller was not in a good mood.

"Are you bastards responsible for this?" Schiller roared.

"No." Von Tanz fired back. "The planes were English."

"Why think it was us?" Blausen hissed. "What the hell would we gain?"

"My town has been attacked twice." Schiller snapped.

"This attack was well executed, but uncoordinated." Von Tanz said coldly. "This raid was to be a diversion so *Albatross* could escape. The RAF would have no idea he wasn't in the town."

"You're saying that bastard Krieger." Schiller rasped.

"I'm saying nothing." Von Tanz said. "You have a town to take care of Herr Burgermeister; we'll handle this other problem."

[2]

Keppler's Castle

Eidernau emerged from the cellar with a grim look on his face. He went to the room where Krieger and the Countess where staying straight to the table with the wine bottles on it and poured a glass of wine.

"What in hell is going?" Krieger asked.

"The escape route is blocked." Eidernau hissed.

"Have your men clear it." Krieger said bluntly. "We have to get out while they are distracted."

"You don't understand." Eidernau said. "The whole roof caved in, it would take a full regiment of engineers to clear it."

"Is that what happened to Hothman and Brosch?" The Countess asked.

"No." Eidernau rasped. "I detected a trace of cordite in the air."

"It was brought down deliberately." Krieger hissed.

"Your friends are smarter than you think." Willi said. "You'll need a new plan."

"I'm working on it." Krieger hissed. "Keep an eye on our friends."

The Countess lit a cigarette as she glanced over at her husband. "You should have cultivated von Tanz as a friend Helmuth; his hardness would have made him an excellent ally." The Countess glanced out the window. "It will be a pity to kill him."

"Von Tanz is a stuck-up Prussian aristocrat." Helmuth hissed. "Damn Junker."

"He isn't Prussian." Ehrlich said dryly. "Swabian by birth. He went to the War Academy before 1914 but dropped out."

"He will die, but not here." Helmuth said. "We have to get to Berlin by any means."

"How?" Ehrlich asked. "We are trapped in this relic."

"Give them what they want." Krieger said. "Clausborg will insist that we be brought to Berlin."

"They don't want all of us." Ehrlich said bluntly.

"I don't think that's what Helmuth has in mind." The Countess said coldly. "Thus sacrifices have to be made."

"Willi and his gang of cutthroats have outlived theirs usefulness." Helmuth said flatly.

"He is a tough man to kill." Ehrlich said. "He isn't stupid either. He will see what you are doing and he will move to save his own skin. Eidernau knows too many secrets about the both of you."

"Secrets die when you are dead." The Countess said. "You have to be strong in dealing with them Helmuth. Does it right and the fools will take us to Berlin."

"Survival." Krieger said. "At any cost."

[3]

Outside the castle

"The planes were English?" Clausborg asked on von Tanz and Blausen on their return from the town.

"Jherling's men identified the planes as English Mosquitos." Von Tanz said

"This shithill has no military value." Clausborg hissed. "I wouldn't waste a Blenheim on it let alone a squadron of Mosquitos."

"The train was the target." Blausen said. "The English confined the attack to the train station and the train."

"That makes no sense." Clausborg quipped.

"It does if they wanted to prevent their man from being captured." Von Tanz said coldly.

"Did it work?" Clausborg asked.

"No." Von Tanz said bluntly. "I'll tell you why."

"The bastard has a vivid imagination." Blausen snorted as he chomped down hard on his cigar stub. "A list of allied agents is a crock of horse shit."

"Still such a list might exist." Clausborg said. "It could be a fountain head of power for the possessor."

"The Allies are many things, but being stupid isn't one of them." Von Tanz said. "We don't have a master list of agents on paper anywhere. It would be sheer madness to do so."

"Skasch would not sell something like that sir." Gerhardt said. "Not for the piddling amount of money Schiller found."

"It could have been a down payment." Blausen said.

"Sorry sir." Gerhardt said dryly. "Skasch never dealt in paper currency only gold or silver."

"You seemed to be well aquatinted with Skasch Major." Clausborg said. "Why didn't you detect the impostor?"

"I was not in Adlerberghof when the American Skasch arrived on the scene sir." Gerhardt said. "Unfortunately for us we did not know that the real Skasch was liquidated by the NKVD before the events here transpired."

"Why were you sent here Herr Major?" Von Tanz asked.

"Jung was under investigation for being a war-profiteer and possibly a double-agent." Gerhardt answered.

"You speak English Herr Major?" Blausen asked.

"Then speak it." Blausen said.

"Who was Jung working for?" Clausborg asked.

"We believe the French." Von Tanz said. "He lived in Paris for six years and acquired a French mistress, who was a French agent."

"Who owns *Albatross*?" Clausborg asked.

"The general opinion is he is controlled by the British." Gerhardt said.

"Anything else you might want to share with us?" Blausen asked somberly.

"From the quality of our intercepts over the years *Albatross* is not a file clerk." Gerhardt said firmly.

"Could he a general officer?" Clausborg asked.

"Anything is possible sir." Gerhardt said.

"Krieger's accusation could be true then?" Clausborg quipped.

"He is a desperate man throwing out everything hoping something sticks." Von Tanz said.

"Every lie has a grain of truth." Blausen said brusquely.

"Eventually every liar will trip himself up." Von Tanz said.

"Allow him to continue." Clausborg rasped. "He will supply the rope that will hang him."

[4]

Adlerberghof
St. Elizabeth Church

      Lang pulled up a stool next to the cot where Hauptman Bekker lay. The Medical Officer told him that Bekker was extremely lucky this time too. The fragment from the 20mm cannon round had struck him in the shoulder.
      "I'm getting tired of getting shot." Colquhoun hissed through his fake face bandages.
      "It was our idea." Lang said. "You're luckier than Browne."
      "Dead?" Colquhoun asked.
      "Took a 20 mm in the head." Lang said dryly. "He'll be buried as Corporal Heinrich Kirstenthal."
      "Nothing has gone right with this goddamn mission." Colquhoun said wryly. "Some body is going to ship me over to the Luftwaffe."
      "They are sending another train in a day or two." Lang said. "This will be an express to Munich, where you can get lost."
      "Why not get Donner to smuggle me over the border?" Colquhoun asked.
      "We'll do that if we have to." Lang said.
      "Just try not to get me shot again." Colquhoun said.

[5]
09:15 hrs

Keppler's Castle

      The two parties converged at the imaginary line with the same people.
      "What have you decided?" Krieger asked dourly.
      "You have only two choices." Von Tanz said coldly. "Surrender this list or die here and now."
      "That isn't a choice." The Ehrlich growled.
      "It is the best we can do." Clausborg said firmly. "This list will save your life."
      "Threats produce nothing." Krieger said. "There is a list."
      "Then simply produce it." Blausen challenged. "The request shouldn't be out of your grasp."
      "You are being manipulated by *Albatross*." Krieger growled. "Von Tanz is behind this scheme."
      "We reject that idea." Blausen said sharply. "He could just as easily be you."
      "You are blind fools." Krieger rasped. "This has been an elaborate attempt by the Allies to discredit me and protect the names on the list as well as his neck. Everything that has happened is a setup."
      "Why would the Allies bother with you?" Clausborg asked caustically. "Who the hell are you?"
      "Krieger will be the new Chief of the RSHA." Ehrlich said icily.   "Doubtful." Clausborg said.

"That is why Himmler sent me here." Krieger said. "He wants *Albatross* destroyed."
"You have 30 minutes to make your decision to surrender or die." Blausen said bluntly.

Chapter Forty
December 12, 1942
09:38 hrs

Keppler's Castle

"What the hell are you going to do?" Eidernau asked smashing the wine bottle against the wall. "They will take this place on the first charge."
"Surrender might be the only option." The Countess said sternly.
"It might be for you." Willi hissed. "They want to take you to Berlin. All me and my men get is the goddamn wall."
"Cut off the head." Krieger said bluntly.
"How?" Willi rasped.
"Von Tanz, Blausen and Clausborg will be there to take our surrender." The Countess said. "You cut them down at my signal. In the confusion you can make your escape."
"Escape where?" Lutzen asked.
"Switzerland isn't that far away." Ehrlich said. "Use the sally port at the rear will take them by surprise."
"We'll talk a bit to give them a sense of victory before you kill them." Krieger said.
"What about you?" Eidernau hissed.
"Surrender is a viable option for us." Krieger said. "Take the attaché cases with the money."
"You have a deal." Willi hissed.

[2]

Von Tanz lit a cigarette as he glanced up at the castle. "Krieger has only one option left and that is to kill the three of us Colonel."
"Don't go back up there sir." Jherling said. "I can take castle."
"You don't have artillery to soften up the target." Von Tanz said. "The casualties will be too high; they are not worth it."
"Why give him the chance sir?" Jherling asked.
"It is part of the job." Von Tanz said. "The objective is to cause confusion in order for them to escape."
"They'll never make it." Jherling said.
Major Gerhardt entered the tent carrying a vest-like object and placed it on the chair.
"Very strange thing you brought in Major." Von Tanz said.
"It's called a bullet proof vest sir." Gerhardt said.
"Bullet-proof?" Von Tanz quipped.
"I don't trust Krieger sir." Gerhardt said. "He's apt to put a bullet in you before he rides off to Valhalla."
"That vest of yours won't stop a bullet to the head." Von Tanz said cynically.
"Krieger will instinctively aim for the chest as he has been trained to do." Gerhardt said. "You can wear under your great coat sir."

"I'll think about Major." Von Tanz said. "Is the package alright?"
"Slightly damaged sir" Gerhardt said. "Lang is watching it."
"Any other packages?" Von Tanz asked.
"Only one package sir." Gerhardt said.
"Is he out there?" Von Tanz asked dourly.
"He is." Gerhardt said. "Another reason to wear the vest sir."

[3]

"All the comforts of home." Donner grunted as he entered the stand. Mannerling lowered the P-38. "You forgot to lock the back door."
"You did cover your tracks?" Mannerling asked.
"Of course." Donner said.
"What are you doing here in the first place old man?" Mannerling asked.
"I can keep the others off your neck." Donner said. "You'll start to draw fire once they start to tumble."
"I felt some shakes." Mannerling said grimly.
"The RAF paid us a visit." Donner said flatly. "Blew the hell out of the train station and the train."
"Colquhoun?" Mannerling asked.
"He made it." Donner said. "Looks like you two will be the only ones going home."
"I'm not surprised" Mannerling hissed.
"Do you wonder whose side your bosses are on?" Donner rasped.
"I stopped wondering about that many years ago." Mannerling said removing the sight covers.

[4]

They assembled on the hillside with about six meters separating them. Krieger and his wife stepped out of the pack at the same time as the three generals.
"You've had time to radio Berlin." Krieger said. "Does this stupidity stop now?"
"You have been too isolated while you have been here Krieger." Blausen grunted with a thin damning smile. "Himmler has already made his selection."
"Then you know who you are dealing with." Krieger hissed with a touch of arrogance in his voice. "Arrest von Tanz now."
"What gives you the idea that Himmler selected you?" Clausborg asked.
"He's the only choice possible." Ehrlich snapped.
"Sorry you didn't make the cut." Blausen said.
"Who did he select?" The Countess asked bitterly knowing that this had become a disparate fight for survival.
"Himmler selected someone from Vienna Gruppenfuhrer Ernst Kaltenbrunner." Blausen said.
"That ape?" Krieger gasped.
"Impossible!" The Countess snarled disbelievingly.

"Helmuth Krieger." Von Tanz said icily. "You are under arrest for treason and murder. The rest of you are arrested for conspiracy."

"No!" Helmuth growled. "Impossible! Impossible!"

"Kill them!" The Countess shouted. "Kill all of them!"

The gunshot shattered the silence after Von Tanz tumbled backwards with blood gushing from his right shoulder. Krieger turned from where the gunshot came from an instant before all hell broke lose. Krieger collapsed into the snow after being hit by the same shooter. The Countess was drawing her pistol when a bullet smashed into her forehead. She fell on top of her husband in a lifeless heap.

Gerhardt felt the sledgehammer hit him dropping him to the snow. Blausen collapsed face first into the snow with a gapping hole in his chest. Clausborg fell backward screaming loudly as he hit the snow. Eidernau and Ehrlich fell to the snow a moment later. The maelstrom of gunfire shifted to the fleeing men running towards the castle.

Gerhardt turned on his side groping in the crimson snow for his pistol as Jherling's men concentrated on the fleeing men. As he did, he saw Krieger pushed his wife's body off him and get to his knees. Gerhardt after finding his pistol pushed himself up to shoot, but three shots cracked from Ehrlich's pistol hitting Gerhardt twice.

Gerhardt saw Ehrlich crawling towards him. The grim-faced Ehrlich got close enough so he could not miss and raised his pistol. Ehrlich's head suddenly explodes splattering brains and blood all over the snow. Gerhardt slipped slowly into blackness as Krieger came to life.

Krieger started to fire at the gun flashes coming from the gully in a vain attempt to hit the man shooting at him. Realizing that it was futile Krieger tossed his pistol away and stood raising his arms as he moved towards Jherling. Krieger took two steps before he fell to the snow with a hole in his chest where his heart once was.

[5]
13:00 hrs

Adlerberghof
St Elizabeth's Church

Jherling lit a cigarette as he watched the wounded being carried into the church. It had taken most of the morning to take Keppler's castle. Eidernau's men had nothing to lose by fighting to the bitter end. It was not until nearly the end of the bitter fighting that Jherling managed to get a corpsman to the truce party without getting them killed.

"Stop looking so glum Jherling." Schiller said joining the pensive colonel on the front door. "Your worries are over."

"Easy for you to say." Jherling said sternly. "You don't have a dead SS general and his wife, another dead general along with two wounded ones." Jherling threw down his cigarette to the ground. "Throw in two dead policemen and a missing American spy. My worries have just begun. The Eastern Front would be a vacation once they roll me through the wringer."

"This never happen Jherling." Schiller said.

"What the hell are you talking about?" Jherling hissed.

"The Party controls the news." Schiller said. "Officially nothing has happened."

"The destruction and deaths?" Jherling grumbled.

"Allied bombing raid." Schiller said.

"You have too many goddamn witnesses." Jherling said.

"My people have learned the trick of not hearing or seeing." Schiller said. "I think you'll find that your battalion will be transferred to Southern France or Italy."

Jherling lit another cigarette. "What about this damn American and *Albatross*?"

"*Albatross* never existed." Schiller said. "Krieger died a hero, which is what Berlin will say. As for the American he is most likely dead and if he managed to survive he is none of your concern."

"All of this will be swept under the rug." Jherling said dully.

"Southern France or Italy is better than Russia." Schiller said. "Stop being the idealist and you'll live a lot longer."

"What about the dead at the castle?" Jherling asked.

"Burn them." Schiller said. "Shattered the ashes."

"Sounds good." Jherling said tiredly. "The crane will be arriving tomorrow morning with the train."

Donner's Farm

Donner placed a brandy bottle on the kitchen table followed by three glasses. "My last bottle."

"Appreciate this." Mannerling said pouring the brandy into his glass.

"We better have one then leave." Orr said. "The border is a long way."

"Are they all dead?" Mannerling asked somberly. After killing, Krieger Mannerling and Donner made their escape in the confusion.

"From what I saw none of them survived." Orr said. "They fought to the last man in the chalet."

"Don't bother me again." Donner snarled. "If I see either of you again I'll kill you."

"I'm never coming back." Mannerling said.

"Nor I friend Donner." Orr said. "We'll change into civilian clothes and leave."

"No." Donner grumbled. "I'll fix something to eat, drink and get some sleep. You can leave in the morning."

"Fine." Mannerling said.

Chapter Forty-One
January 15, 1943

Bonn
St. Maria's Hospital

The two orderlies helped Gerhardt into the chair by the window in his room. One of the draped a new uniform tunic over his shoulders with the shoulder straps of a full colonel. His doctor lectured him about overdoing anything that would fatigue him. The doctor also told him that he informed his visitor not to overtax him.

"Have they been treating you well Anton?" Von Tanz asked as he limped into the room with the aid of a cane. The General sat down in the chair opposite him.

"Very well sir." Anton said. "May I ask why a civilian hospital sir?"

"The Admiral has connections." Von Tanz said firmly. "Some patients in military hospitals have a habit of dying."

"You have returned to duty sir?" Gerhardt asked.

"Still official convalescing." Von Tanz said. "When you are ready a big shot from OKW will present you with a Knight's Cross."

"Full grade promotion and the Knights Cross." Gerhardt said dourly. "Am I being bought too cheaply sir?"

The General smiled slightly. "Take everything they give you my young friend. The doctors inform me that you will be able to leave this place in a few days. After a month medical leave at home you'll be returned to duty."

"Where sir?" Gerhardt asked.

"France most likely." The General said.

"Paris?" Gerhardt asked.

"Sorry no." Von Tanz said. "St. Lorient."

"That sounds unexciting Herr General." Gerhardt said disappointedly.

"You are being returned to the regular Army." Von Tanz said. "Lang is being reassigned to the U-boat operations/naval intelligence."

"Why?" Gerhardt asked.

"The Admiral feels that your career would last longer if you were removed from the Abwehr." The General said. "You'll be assigned to the military police."

"Is that because of Adlerberghof sir?" Gerhardt rasped.

"They want to forget Adlerberghof." Von Tanz said. "No one really wants to know what happened let alone why."

"Is everyone is dead?" Gerhardt asked.

"No survivors." Von Tanz said. "Officially the Kriegers died in a tragic car accident."

"I don't remember much after getting hit sir." Gerhardt said. "Who was killed on our side?"

"Blausen was killed." Von Tanz said drably. "Clausborg has been invalidated out of the service."

"What about our friends?" Gerhardt asked.

"Heard nothing." Von Tanz said. "If they survived London isn't broadcasting it."

"Colquhoun?" Gerhardt asked.

"His fate is unknown." Von Tanz said seriously.

"They didn't come for him?" Gerhardt hissed bitterly.

"The second train to Jaegerfeld was bombed and strafed too" Von Tanz said. "Some how five Mosquitoes got through and blew the hell out of the train. Many bodies were burnt beyond recognition."

"What about Klugge?" Gerhardt asked.

"The Sergeant-Major is a master of survival." Von Tanz said. "He is at the military hospital in Wurzburg; he will be assigned administrative duties with the Waffen SS."

"I see." Gerhardt said in a faraway voice. "Was this worth it sir?"

"An unqualified yes Anton." Von Tanz said. "We stopped a very dangerous man. Kaltenbrunner is not Heydrich in any sense of the word. He is a dullard at best and just plain brutish at worse."

"Adlerberghof?" Gerhardt asked.

"Those five Mosquitoes gave Berlin the excuse to blame the destruction on the British." Von Tanz said. "The government is paying for all the damages."

"So it is finished." Gerhardt said with a sad voice.

"I would say so." Von Tanz said.

[2]

Twickem-Hallesy
Halton Manor

Colonel Tremayne escorted Mannerling into the private study on the second floor. The second and third floors were off-limits to most of the personnel working at the manor house. Sir Peter and Lord Crosland occupied these floors as their private residence; meeting with Sir Peter upstairs was tantamount to an invitation to the Palace.

Mannerling stood as Sir Peter entered the room. Austen-Halton sat down at his desk motioning Mannerling to sit down.

"Do you wish a drink Major?" Sir Peter asked politely.

"Too early for me sir." Mannerling answered.

"Very well, perhaps later." Sir Peter said.

"Any information sir?" Mannerling asked. "Boyden and I have been isolated in Northern Scotland since we returned sir."

"I understand that Keithton is very relaxing Edward." Sir Peter said.

"It is sir." Mannerling said. "The inn has no pub. Information sir?"

"It is not good Major." Sir Peter said.

"Nothing connected with that mission has been good sir." Mannerling said sternly.

Sir Peter lit a cigar. "The Free French in a moment of magnificence have informed us that they have regained contact with Donner then presented us a bill for his services."

"Bloody frogs." Mannerling quipped. "What did you give the Swiss not to raise the alarm sir?"

"That was handled by the Foreign Office." Sir Peter said tartly. "Something to do with Swiss bank accounts."

"Was the raid part of the plan sir?" Mannerling asked deftly.

"It presented itself." Sir Peter said. "The Air Ministry approved it."

Mannerling lit a cigarette. "Colquhoun?"

"Nothing." Sir Peter said.

"Are the Americans accepting that sir?" Mannerling asked.

"The cars carrying the wounded caught fire." Sir Peter said. "Many of the wounded were killed."

"Still no confirmation sir." Mannerling said. "I could be ready to return to Adlerberghof in 24 hours sir."

"For what?" Sir Peter asked.

"Rescue mission sir." Mannerling said. "Orr is still in Scotland and he can start preparations immediately."

"We have no intentions of mounting any rescue mission." Sir Peter said. "Nor will the Americans."

"He could still be alive, sir." Mannerling said.

"The matter is closed Major." Sir Peter said. "You are being posted to the Middle East Command. Your transportation will be ready at 18:00 hours."

"We are abandoning him sir?" Mannerling asked seriously.

"The mission has ended." Sir Peter said. "The war continues."

[3]
21:00 hrs

Bonn
Military Hospital

Captain Dr. Androsky adjusted his glasses then looked at his visitor; the hospital was not large enough for someone from Berlin to visit.

"I'm very curious sir." Dr. Androsky said. "Why are you here sir? This hospital is hardly on the grand tour Herr General."

"I understand that you are one of the best hospitals in the Reich." Von Tanz said.

"I will not deny that sir." Androsky said. "How may I help you?"

"I'm only interested in one patient Herr Doctor." Von Tanz said. "Leutnant Rudolf Bekker."

"The Luftwaffe officer." Androsky said.

"Yes." Von Tanz said. "What is his condition?"

"That information is for the Luftwaffe sir." Androsky said firmly.

"This should change your mind Doctor." Von Tanz said showing him his Abwehr identification.

"He is still listed as critical." Androsky said. "He was very badly burned in the fire. Dr. Hassle feels that massive reconstructive surgery will be needed."

"His chances of survival?" Von Tanz asked.

"50/50." Androsky said. "Our staff pyscharitrist feels that his wounds are much deeper."

"That branch of medicine is officially discouraged Captain." Von Tanz said in an icy tone.

"The lieutenant has suffered a deep emotional trauma." Androsky said. "Politics make bad medicine Herr General. Without therapy, his condition will not improve. Bekker is capable of verbal communication, but he refuses to speak."

Von Tanz lit a cigarette. "You will keep Bekker incommunicado; his identity is to be concealed from the rest of the hospital staff. His name will not appear on any patient lists."

"The Luftwaffe will come for him eventually sir." Androsky said. "He belongs to them."

"He is not here Captain." Von Tanz said wryly. "Only you and I know that he is."

"I can't do that sir." Androsky said. "It is against Army regulations."

"The Reich Security Law gives me the authority to order this." Von Tanz said. "That supersedes Army regulations."

"I'll need something in writing sir." Androsky said. "If you get killed where does that leave me sir?"

"If Bekker is found out for any reason Herr Androsky you'll be on the first transport to the Eastern Front as a member of a penal company." Von Tanz said coldly. "You'll be under surveillance."

"You have no right to do this." Androsky snapped.

"List him as unknown." Von Tanz said.

"Tell me why sir?" Androsky asked. "Who the hell is he?"

"We owe him a debt." Von Tanz said firmly. "I intend to see that we pay it. When he is well enough to travel you'll be transferred to the hospital at Jaegerfeld."

THE END

An Honorable Betrayal

www.ingramcontent.com/pod-product-compliance
Lightning Source LLC
Chambersburg PA
CBHW031139160426
43193CB00008B/187